Sister
in the
Band of
Brothers

Sister
in the
Band of
Brothers

Embedded with the
101st Airborne in Iraq

Katherine M. Skiba

 UNIVERSITY PRESS OF KANSAS

© 2005 by the University Press of Kansas

Published by the University Press of Kansas (Lawrence, Kansas 66049), which was organized by the Kansas Board of Regents and is operated and funded by Emporia State University, Fort Hays State University, Kansas State University, Pittsburg State University, the University of Kansas, and Wichita State University

Library of Congress
Cataloging-in-Publication Data

Skiba, Katherine M.
   Sister in the band of brothers : embedded with the 101st Airborne in Iraq / Katherine M. Skiba
      p. cm. — (Modern war studies)
   Includes index.
   ISBN 0-7006-1382-X (cloth : alk. paper)
   1. Skiba, Katherine M. 2. Iraq War, 2003—Journalists—Biography. 3. Iraq War, 2003—Personal narratives, American. 4. United States. Army. Airborne Division, 101st.
I. Title. II Series.
   DS79.76.S58 2005
   956.7044'342—dc22
                                        2004026475

British Library Cataloguing-in-Publication Data is available.

Printed in the United States of America

10 9 8 7 6 5 4 3 2 1

The paper used in this publication meets the minimum requirements of the American National Standard for Permanence of Paper for Printed Library Materials Z39.48-1984.

For my late grandmothers,
Katherine V. Skiba and Marie G. Urban,
my parents,
Chesterine T. and Michael J. Skiba,
and my darling,
Thomas E. Vanden Brook

Contents

Prologue

"It will be dangerous. If it comes to conflict, we could very well see journalists killed in action."

My husband, Tom, was negotiating the traffic of northern Virginia on a bleak late-winter morning. Spring, that day, was too sleepy-eyed to play hide-and-seek. My spouse was listening to Diane Rehm's call-in radio show on WAMU—half listening, actually. Rehm's guest was Bryan Whitman, the architect of the Pentagon's program to "embed" hundreds of journalists with the U.S. Armed Forces, and Tom felt he knew all the details of the historic undertaking to place journalists on the front lines. He'd heard it all before, straight from the horse's mouth—from me (not that the equine reference should suggest I'm a nag, since I'm not).

Hearing Whitman's blunt prediction, Tom turned up the volume. "Hey, that's new," he thought. "They said the battlefield was dangerous, but now they're acknowledging journalists could be killed. Shit."

It was March 13, 2003, six days before the war; I was 6,598 miles away from my husband and our Labrador retriever and our ranch home in a leafy enclave of Arlington. I was smack in the middle of Kuwait, a tiny, oil-rich emirate that outlaws alcohol and bans women from so much as voting. I was trying my best to adjust to the United States Army, to a sometimes malevolent environment, and to my new tent city, the hastily improvised, hopefully named Camp Victory, home to the 159th Aviation Brigade, a helicopter unit within the storied 101st Airborne Division. As the crow flies, the sun-bleached installation was forty miles south of "Bad Guy Land," the slang even some officers favored in place of the four-letter word "Iraq."

For ten days I'd been living with 2,300 Army troops at Victory, whose amenities a professional observer such as I could fit on five lines of a spiral-bound notebook. We had portable latrines, canvas tents with wooden floors, cots, prepackaged MREs (short for "meals ready to eat"), and bottled water with the brand name Al-Rawdatain. From Day One, the soldiers I accompanied asked me to report on the absence of electricity and showers as well as on the scarcity of toilet paper and baby wipes. These items hardly seemed extravagances, so I mentioned them in my first story from Kuwait, the twelfth foreign country from which I'd collected a byline.

The early days of my crash course, "Introduction into the Middle East"—an elective, let's remember—saw me by turns jet-lagged, sleep-deprived, and sun-scorched; fleeing a tent as it collapsed under sixty-mile-an-hour gusts; calling it a night in soaking wet socks; plucking beetles from my head (maybe it was the hair spray); and spurning a proposition from a helicopter pilot (maybe it was the soap—by then showers had been trucked in). If it wasn't one thing, it was another. Because of my insistence on wearing contacts in this sand-swept no-man's-land, my lenses felt like manhole covers and my eyeballs stung so badly they might have been jabbed with pinking shears. Eventually a private with a generous heart gave me a pair of sturdy goggles.

If Tom was concerned about me dying, he had thousands of kindred spirits across the United States worried about their own loved ones. But these families were virtually unknown to him, just images on TV and in the newspapers, like his own, *USA Today.* An estimated 320,000 troops—and roughly 600 embedded journalists—were massing in the Middle East for the showdown with Saddam Hussein, leaving legions of spouses brushing tears from their cheeks, ripped from their partner's embrace and relegated to an edgy, bizarre half-life.

My life was bizarre, too, but I had plenty of company in the Kuwaiti sandbox; and so I soldiered on, filing stories about the troops so that people at home would have a sense of what, and how, these husbands and wives, sons and daughters and brothers and sisters were doing.

Some of the troops were eager to speak to a reporter, others weren't, but I'd catch their names embroidered on their desert-camouflage uniforms, realizing before long that I was in *Encyclopedia Americana,* traveling with Allen, Ballard, Beierlein, Butaro, Camejo, Carter, Covert, Cruz, Denham, Dixson, Driggers, Ferrell, Fink, Fish, Forrester, Gilbert, Goetzke, Goveo, Gregg, Haberzettl, Jacobs, Jenkins, Jones, Kamann, Kitch, Lynskey, Marmuziewicz, Maxson, McDurmon, Mertes, Moore, Napier, Nowaczyk, Null, Oates, Oviatt, Patton, Peeler, Rambo, Rodriguez, Rzasowski, Scenie, Shenk, Smalley, Tengel, Toeller, Trigg, Valencia, Wood, and Zeman, plus my first real friend, Ruiz.

The 159th Brigade flies air-assault missions in Black Hawk and Chinook helicopters, dumping infantrymen and supplies—ammo, fuel, food, water, and heavy-duty vehicles—into the fight. The brigade, known as a helicopter lift element, is home to fliers who can drop 4,000 soldiers into combat more than ninety miles away in six hours, thundering over enemy lines, minefields, and blown-up bridges just as the traditional "front lines" of warfare are increasingly blurred. My companions, in addition to the pilots, were machine-gunners, air-traffic controllers, and mechanics; operations planners, intelligence officers, and signal operators; physicians and medics; truck drivers, chaplains, and cooks.

My assignment was open-ended, but the others were here for the duration, amid threats ranging from Scud missiles to the snakes prone to seek shade in the freshly dug foxholes, or survival trenches, that fringed our tents. I was canny enough to keep up a game face in front of the Army, styling myself a woman with more moxie than the National Arctic Wildlife Refuge has crude oil or caribou, depending on your side of the debate. My sixth sense told me to keep up this front, since despite endless predeployment briefings—on weapons, aircraft, laws of armed conflict, and exotic diseases such as the tick-borne Crimean-Congo hemorrhagic fever—nobody had prepared me for what only now is a fun fact to know and tell: I was the only female civilian at Victory. Believe it or not, it took me a full week to figure that out. I had so much else to learn, like whether "Kevlar" meant my helmet or my flak jacket and why in the world the Army was insisting on "Navy showers."

My husband is the night rewrite man for America's widest-circulation newspaper, while I am a Washington correspondent for Wisconsin's largest, the *Milwaukee Journal Sentinel*. His paper, with 2 million plus readers, was founded in 1982. My paper's roots date 145 years earlier, to 1837, when Solomon Juneau, a fur trader, land speculator, and the city's first mayor, founded the *Milwaukee Sentinel*. Our Sunday readership is 435,000, dipping to 258,000 on weekdays.

My paper had leased for me a phone, the size of a laptop, which relied on Inmarsat satellites 22,000 miles above the equator. A foreign correspondent's lifeline, my phone worked during roughly four out of five tries; calls cost $2 a minute when they reached the States. No doubt Tom got an earful about the subsistence-level conditions and the sandstorms and the suspicion with which some in the military greeted me, an alien in their midst. "Your stories are great," he'd say enthusiastically after I'd sound off. "I feel like I'm there."

After we'd hang up, I'd resort to my latest mantra to carry me through the experience I had so aggressively sought. I'd been so eager to be airborne rather than chair-bound in Washington. "I can handle this," I'd assure myself, staring onto the soft, undulating blond sand and conjuring up the majestic dunes rising along Lake Michigan's shoreline, a favorite place to play in my youth. I was fond of the name "Victory," since I'd been a cheerleader in junior high and remembered spelling out V-I-C-T-O-R-Y while performing the flying splits. I may have prided myself on being an objective reporter, but the last place on earth that I ever wanted to call it a night cocooned under canvas with sour-smelling feet and snoring and farting was a place named V-A-N-Q-U-I-S-H-E-D or D-E-F-E-A-T or R-O-U-T.

I'd traveled a lot as a reporter, always with a proper roof over my head, if only an Econo Lodge without functioning showers and toilets, as was the case during the flood and fire in downtown Grand Forks, North Dakota, in 1997, when water-treatment woes shuttered restaurants and the mayor, for some reason, banned the sale of alcoholic beverages. Shades of Kuwait; but in Grand Forks, at least, I had a good book, Katharine Graham's autobiography, and a big, comfy bed, which was more than the flood's 50,000 evacuees could claim.

Tom would have jumped at the chance to cover a war. Being a fitness demon and outdoorsman, he probably would have taken the hardships in stride. He was making his daily trip to the gym, in fact, on that stubbornly gray morning when Bryan Whitman sounded to him like the Grim Reaper.

Only after I'd been back from the war for two months did Tom point out that he and I had never actually sat down and discussed whether I should go; it seemed to him a foregone conclusion, given the cyclone he had wed. I winced when he reminded me that I hadn't taken the trouble to clear my plans with him. I imagined myself a news junkie so hell-bent on getting a fix at what one Army public affairs boss called the "Big Party" that mine was a heart of stone. But I suspect there were various reasons that Tom and I didn't speak at length about my going, one being denial. For many months we, like plenty of Americans, thought that diplomacy might force Iraq to cooperate with the United Nations weapons inspectors and disarm. Even at my ersatz Econo Lodge in Kuwait, where military-operations planning spilled into the wee hours, there was talk that with Uncle Sam flexing his incomparable military muscle just across the border, the Iraqi dictator might yet capitulate. "Persuasive in peace, invincible in war"—that's how our Armed Forces were described when I went to "media boot camp." A final reason I avoided a sit-down with Tom was my cockeyed optimism—a blessing and a curse: I had swallowed the predictions from those Washington pundits forecasting a "short, triumphal war," which was hogwash.

I didn't really jump at the chance to cover a war, not least because I'd had "Thou shalt not kill" drummed into me during seventeen years in Catholic schools. And I didn't relish the chance to eyeball enemy corpses, much less friendly ones, as U.S. troops marched north toward Baghdad. My editors did not point a gun at my head to make me go. Nor was I an accidental tourist.

In a series of meetings beginning in the fall of 2002, the Pentagon disclosed its plans to embed journalists in unsurpassed numbers, prompting me to set up a string of conference calls with my editors, who left the decision on whether to go for it up to me. The possibility of my going to the war independent of the military wasn't a reasonable option, since ours is a medium-sized, regional paper without a single foreign bureau. In the calls to my paper's headquarters, I betrayed not a whit of fear, although indeed I had fears. I simply fought my demons like a woman with a broom ridding cobwebs from the attic. Meanwhile I turned to a "war council" of advisers whom I consulted on matters ranging from the prospect of Iraqi nuclear weapons to whether I really needed to roll up my sleeve for an anthrax vaccination.

Some critics of embedding began raising questions about the arrangement even before it began, with the key question being: How can journalists maintain their objectivity if they're living side by side with the subjects of their story?

Perhaps a bit of the clamor resulted from the unfortunate choice of the word "embedded," since it triggered the charge that the journalists would be "in bed" with the government—a criticism I thought was facile, uninformed, and too clever by half. Of course it was a departure from the ordinary to be in close and constant contact with the people one wrote about, but war isn't an ordinary story. And I had to wonder why the issue of professional detachment rarely arises with respect to the reporters assigned to trail professional sports teams or presidential campaigns for months on end.

The fact is, the military wasn't planning to keep the embeds on a short leash, feed them pabulum, and censor their stories for good measure. It's unlikely that experienced journalists would have bought into a program like that—and unthinkable that they would have stuck with such an arrangement had it turned out that way.

As I made my calculations about such ethical matters, there were concerns about health and safety to confront as well.

A colleague from another major daily paper tried to warn me off the story, saying a friend of his who covered the first Gulf War came home with permanent lung troubles after the retreating Iraqi forces torched more than 700 oil wells in Kuwait.

I worried about weapons of mass destruction, imagining myself blasted with a nerve agent and morphing into some kind of freak. "I might come back with two heads," I told close friends. Sometimes I imagined losing a limb—or worse. Other times a vision emerged of a gray, stoop-shouldered woman drooling on herself in a nursing home, unwanted, unloved, and ignored except for an infrequent murmur: "She hasn't been the same since the war in Iraq. She was a reporter then."

In the end, I identified several reasons to go, including the obvious, which was to tell America about the men and women who had "come to the colors" and were prepared to make the ultimate sacrifice. I'd been in tight spots before, from the violence-charged Gaza Strip to the crumbling Soviet Union to the uneasy streets of postwar Kosovo. I'd sat out Gulf War I while on something akin to a sabbatical; I was a Nieman Fellow at Harvard University during the 1990–1991 academic year, and I envied the two men my newspaper dispatched to Desert Storm. Over the years I'd written about the military, ramping up my coverage after the 9-11 terror attack at the Pentagon, which happened in my own backyard. I'd gotten to know people who worked for the Department of Defense as a result of the Kosovo trip, which was sponsored by the DOD in 1999 to shine some light on the U.S. soldiers who took part in peacekeeping operations after the NATO-led bombardment of Serbia.

Women had covered wars long before my time: Mary Roberts Rinehart, Margaret Bourke-White, and Martha Gellhorn, to name a few. In 1988 a book about their exploits was published—Julia Edwards's *Women of the World: The Great Foreign Correspondents.* I gobbled it up, thinking these forebears so fearless, so adventuresome, and so daring, especially in an age when many female reporters were relegated to "soft" stories—food, fashion, and furniture, that sort of thing.

Rinehart might have been speaking for me in 1914 when she told her editors at the *Saturday Evening Post* after the start of World War I, "I do not intend to let the biggest thing in my life go by without having been part of it." She beat most U.S. correspondents to the front lines and scored many exclusives, I learned as I read the book. But I never really thought that my day would come.

Still, I'd earned a few reportorial stripes with the military. I'd been to France for the fiftieth anniversary of the D-Day invasion; to Norfolk, Virginia, for the final journey of the USS *Wisconsin;* to Arlington National Cemetery for military burials; and to Washington's Mall for the groundbreaking of the National World War II Memorial. So I wasn't a neophyte standing before the Department of Defense pleading for some colonel to sign my permission slip.

Try to keep me from this war, and I just might go nuclear. When one superior suggested I stay in Washington, I simply rattled off the aforementioned stories until he shut up.

I'd started reporting for the *Milwaukee Journal Sentinel* back in 1977, when I was a senior at Marquette University. Except for a stint writing for the *Minneapolis Star,* I've worked for the *Journal Sentinel* ever since. I rose to become national correspondent for a five-year period ending in 2000, when I was promoted to the Washington bureau.

To spend five years on an odyssey across America as a national reporter was a great gift. I appreciate why national political candidates tolerate the brutal, coast-to-coast travel; maybe for them, as for me, it was gratifying to see the country's unmatched mosaic, to meet people of all backgrounds, faiths, regions, and walks of life, and to take a gander at the nation's many treasures. I had covered some tough stories, like the Oklahoma City bombing and the Jonesboro, Arkansas, school shootings, but I had other experiences as compensation: photographing moose swimming in the shadow of Mount Katahdin in Maine, watching the fog steal past the Golden Gate Bridge, and returning to Yellowstone National Park to capture the park's rebirth, ten years after I'd chased the wildfires that roared through it.

Having the whole country for a beat at times made me feel like Miss America, though I suspect that she, like any road warrior, comes to regard frequent flier miles as insufficient payback for missing hearth and home. Another downside was feeling like a marionette every time CNN broke in with another big one.

So I went for the job in Washington with Tom's blessing, and though he had to give up his reporting job at the *Journal Sentinel,* soon he found a new home at *USA Today.*

We sensed that the nation's capital was a nine-ring circus, but the onslaught of news after our arrival had even old hands shaking their heads: the contested presidential election of 2000, the 9-11 attacks, the anthrax-tainted letters on Capitol Hill, the war in Afghanistan, the congressional debate over war in Iraq, and finally, the Washington-area snipers.

Any story in D.C. is fair game for me, though my focus is government and politics. Tom is a true generalist, working as a rewrite man from five in the afternoon to one in the morning and pursuing the top news of the day. The job has him reporting, taking feeds from outlying correspondents, and writing or shaping the final story. It might be a missing intern, a kidnapped kid, or an endangered species; it might be a White House leak or an overseas trip by a State Department bigwig. If it's midnight in Washington, it's rush hour the next morning in Jerusalem; such time differences mean that overseas developments are often on his radar screen.

Tom and I met covering a story: we were assigned to secretly trail the Wisconsin treasurer in 1989 to document his neglect of the office. The war in Iraq was a rare instance in which we were on the same story, more or less. We were in different places—one-third of the world apart—with different vantage points. He was in a newsroom in McLean, Virginia, poring over information from the White House and the Pentagon and U.S. Central Command in Qatar, from reporters in the field, from the wire services, and from broadcast outlets. I was in the Persian Gulf with a satellite phone and short-wave radio, getting a "keyhole" view of the war—richer, deeper, three-dimensional, and colorful, but infinitely narrower, never much beyond the activities of the 2,300-strong 159th Brigade.

Like the soldiers around me and their loved ones back home, Tom couldn't see my life and I couldn't see his. He couldn't watch me bumming one Marlboro Light after another, worrying that I would collapse from heat prostration in a gas mask and bulky overgarments during a prewar chemical-attack drill, recycling the same dirty joke ("Why does it suck to be an egg?"), having heart-to-hearts with the chaplains if not speaking directly to God, leaving my gear in disarray just to annoy a female lieutenant whom I belittled with the nickname "Tinker Bell," or reenacting the orgasm scene from *When Harry Met Sally* when I spied the sweet-looking Sergeant Jason Ashworth on his knees in the sand in front of a plastic bucket, washing his fatigues by hand.

Tom couldn't see this woman, nor did he know her. Neither did I.

1 *War Games*

I'd marched with infantrymen for practically five miles on the soft, rust-colored clay soils of Fort Benning, a vast Army base in west central Georgia, just across the Chattahoochee River from Alabama. My back was groaning from toting a rucksack that the military said weighed twenty-five pounds but had to be heavier than that. The end of the line was in sight when nature called, telephoning on speed dial, in fact. I needed to pee, so I fell out of line, shed the cumbersome pack, spied a large oak, and let the others go their merry way.

No doubt I should have done my business at the march's halfway point, when all of us—Benning's young soldiers, its stout-voiced drill sergeants, and the sixty journalists suffering through media boot camp—had the chance. I couldn't do it then, though, not with a small army of men relieving themselves in every direction I looked and creating such a torrent I thought only of a childhood visit to the Budweiser Clydesdale stables in St. Louis, Missouri.

When I arrived at Benning, which bills itself as the world's premier training ground for infantry, I'd been presented with an "Initial-Entry Training Soldier's Handbook," 365 pages of do's and don'ts governing the average grunt. The pocket-sized book on page 73 predicted my plight: "In the field, female soldiers may drink too little and hold their urine due to lack of privacy."

But I was no soldier. I was a newswoman, huffing and puffing through the lower Piedmont region during a weeklong course on battlefield survival, preparing for what looked to be a war against Iraq. When I fastened my pants, hoisted the ruck over my shoulders, and rejoined my unit, bloody casualties were littering the ground, injuries that I knew meant I needed to spring into action, since fortunately the Army had given me a heads-up. I was told that I would be leading a team of first responders, meaning that my peers and I would administer first aid to one of the injured and rush him onto a Black Hawk, which would take him to the rear.

"Radio man, medevac!" I shouted, alarmed at my own voice, which sounded like a drill instructor's and was nearly as loud. My order was directed to a soldier with a field radio to summon the helicopter for the medical evacuation.

The "casualty" was Neil King, Jr., a lanky, dark-haired reporter for the *Wall Street Journal,* whose left hand looked like road kill and whose lower leg suggested a compound fracture, injuries enhanced by Hollywood-style special effects. With real Army medics watching our every move, I and the others tended to King. We stanched the bleeding with field dressings, rigged a tourniquet on his arm, got his leg into a splint, and ferried him on a nylon stretcher to the waiting aircraft.

Once King was hoisted onto the "bird," and, according to the plot line, prepared to be flown to a mobile Army surgical hospital (MASH), my adrenaline stopped pumping and I was able to exhale. Then I felt tears coming on, since I wasn't Florence Nightingale—not yet, anyway—and every time we practiced combat first aid during boot camp it seemed so horribly real to me, as if a soldier's life hung in the balance, with my novice hands spelling the difference between life and death. Some sort of explosive had taken out a few of King's fingers, for God's sake, and a newsman needs fingers, if for no other reason than scribbling in a notebook and banging at a keyboard.

I bit my lower lip to beat back the tears as my media colleagues began slapping me on the back, mouthing things like "Good work" and extolling my talent for barking orders. Now I was beaming, pleased to have done something right with challenges being thrown at us rat-a-tat-tat. My self-satisfaction was short-lived, however, because a sergeant got in my face, reprimanding me, berating me, castigating me even, in a manner I hadn't known in many years.

"You shoulda worked faster," he bellowed, nostrils flaring and rivulets of sweat spilling down his suntanned brow. "You kept that bird waiting nine minutes."

I looked him in the eyes and said nothing, then glanced to my left to see a lieutenant colonel stomping in my direction, preparing to finish lowering the guillotine on my ego.

"You were the team leader!" he reminded me. "You should have gotten things rolling and gotten out of the way. You should have led. You should have delegated."

I had no impulse to cry now. I was livid. I had not been briefed on the need for speed; I had not been instructed to delegate. I presumed that it would be best to be a hands-on leader, and now I wanted nothing more than to give these two scolds a piece of my mind, saying something along the lines of "How dare you speak to me that way? Don't you people believe in positive reinforcement? My *colleagues* thought I did a good job."

Instead, I bit my tongue. I'd lobbied hard to get into media boot camp—after all, there were more than 800 applications for 240 training slots—and I wasn't about to lose my cool. I'd been told how to behave. Lane Van de Steeg, a friend of mine who is an Army colonel in Washington, had spelled it out for me: "Be up for anything. Be on time for everything. Don't moan, groan, bitch, whine, or complain—not in public, anyway. And if the going gets too tough, tell your handlers."

Heeding Lane's advice, I'd even taken the trouble of getting up early and ironing my khaki pants before our first full day of training, which began at 6:30 a.m., Monday, December 16, 2002. I figured I'd wear spit, polish, and perfectly creased pants in case they were meting out extra credit; but what a waste of time and electricity pressing my khakis turned out to be. Later that day another officer, gesturing at my mud-stained pants, implied that it was stupid to wear off-white trousers if you're tramping on red clay.

Later I forgave the sergeant and the lieutenant colonel; maybe I even forgave the guy who ribbed me about my pants. I absolved them after hearing from Sergeant 1st Class David Estabrooks, a thirty-one-year-old Army Ranger who addressed our class. "You learn from your mistakes," he said plainly. "If you don't, you're dumb."

Only later, when I interviewed Estabrooks, did I find out that he had lost six friends during the tragic hours of October 3–4, 1993, that were depicted in the book *Black Hawk Down,* when eighteen soldiers taking part in a United Nations peacekeeping operation perished in Mogadishu, Somalia. That incident represented the deadliest twenty-four hours, up until then, that the U.S. military had endured since Vietnam.

So as Estabrooks counseled, I would indeed learn from my errors. His no-nonsense formula was underscored by a quote framed in the mess hall of Benning's Ranger Training Brigade. It was from legendary four-star general George S. Patton, Jr., who helped bring the Nazis to their knees during World War II. The framed quote from "Old Blood and Guts" advised: "Correct even your most loyal subordinates. Dead men have no egos."

My father had been a sergeant in Patton's Third Army headquarters company in postwar Germany. I thought that the quote helped explain, years after the fact, why, when I'd brought home a report card during my junior year of high school with A's in English, history, chemistry, and religion, but a C in trigonometry, I had hell to pay with Dad.

Just as Patton wanted to keep his troops alive, so, too, did the U.S. Department of Defense want reporters who would cover the potential hostilities in Iraq to come back in one piece. Hence during boot camp we inhaled tear gas, responded to simulated enemy fire, and tried on the so-called NBC gear, heavy overgarments worn to protect against nuclear, biological, or chemical attack, clothing that always seemed to me like a get-up more appropriate for deer hunting.

We practiced giving ourselves injections of atropine and pralidoxime chloride, which counteract nerve agents. We sat through PowerPoint presentations displaying deadly snakes and spiders. We skittered through forests lush with longleaf pines, flew in a Black Hawk over the treetops and, during one training exercise, beat a path out of harm's way traveling backwards on our bellies on rolling grassland as a "bad guy" with an M-240B machine gun and two more with M-16 rifles, all hidden within a grove of trees, played laser tag with us. They didn't nail me, prompting me to recall what Winston Churchill once said: "Nothing in life is so exhilarating as to be shot at without result."

We traipsed through heavy brush and we forded creeks, counting our paces and keeping an eye on our compasses. We even learned what it means to "own the night," hiking in the woods late one evening wearing night-vision goggles, which paint the world a surreal, blurry green. That was cool.

One morning we left our Spartan officers' quarters—$27-a-night single rooms in Olson Hall—to train all day long and then camp in heated tents overnight. The schedule called for us to rise at five o'clock, but I was one of the first to be up and at 'em in my all-women tent. So from my cot, I quietly sketched out the start of a Sunday story I was planning to write about the training. After crafting a workable lead, I gathered a towel and soap, toothbrush and toothpaste, wearing my eyeglasses but not a lick of make-up. As I pulled back the tent flaps, I found myself face-to-face with a video camera. The ten women in the class were experiencing what was regarded alternatively as a mark of distinction or a pain in the ass: we were being trailed by a film crew sent at the direction of Barbara Kopple, an Academy Award–winning documentarian. The field producer and cameramen hadn't shown the courtesy of letting us know in advance about their predawn visit to our bivouac. I tried to take the oversight in stride, probably because I myself have been known to make unannounced, Mike Wallace–style visits in the pursuit of a story, if I felt the situation warranted it. So even though this documentary wasn't investigative journalism, I felt I had no business complaining.

Still, I felt trapped like a deer in headlights with no idea of what to say— chiefly because I'm "pencil press," which is to say, a newspaper reporter; sound bites are not my strong suit. On top of that, it felt weird going on camera with morning mouth. Not knowing what else to do, I bellowed, "Good morning, Georgia!" ripping off Robin Williams when he portrayed a hyper-kinetic disc jockey in Vietnam. Then I gave my inquisitors my impressions of the training, minimizing how hard it was, how long the days seemed to stretch, and how I screwed up my face when the PowerPoint presentation showed the snakes in mid-slither.

As I walked off to the portable sinks set up near the tents, I found the cinema vérité kept up. I answered questions in between washing my face and working over my teeth with an Oral B. Next I stepped over to the honey wagons. The videographers continued their pursuit. Finally I reached for the doorknob, stared into the lens, and announced, "Now we're going off the record." Geez, Louise, even Washington reporters have better manners, which, ordinarily speaking, is not saying much.

It puzzled me that they found women correspondents training for war so fascinating; I didn't think I was special. I'd been in some hot spots around the world, but so had many others in the class. The focus on the women trainees made me feel sorry for the men in our group: they were being slighted, just as all of us were being pushed and prodded through boot camp.

After I'd given the interview, I finished freshening up, as dictated by our written schedule: "0500 hours, personal hygiene." The line made me laugh whenever I saw it, since as a grown woman I was hardly in need of typed instructions to cleanse at the dawn of a new day. "Personal hygiene" completed, I found myself having to cover my ears, lest I go deaf, as I rolled my eyes in front of Staff Sergeant Robert Weber, a twenty-something cutie who was one of our escorts. Bone-rattling booms, blasts, bangs, and shrill whistles were going off in the distance, unmistakable sounds of war. Benning's literal and figurative wake-up call prompted the reporters to gauge each other's reactions as our minders grinned broadly, no doubt regarding us as a bunch of wimps.

I noticed that Weber's eyes were slits and his voice was raspy. He told me he'd had to stay up all night on fire-guard duty to make sure none of the tents went up in smoke. Part of me thought that was valiant of him; the other part wondered why the Army was so callous, treating this nice young man like a puppet on a string and forcing him to work day, night, and into the next day, with Christmas just days away. It seemed inhumane.

But this was the famous Fort Benning, former stomping grounds of Patton and other celebrated generals such as Omar Bradley, Dwight D. Eisenhower, and Colin Powell. Four times between 1994 and 1999, President Bill Clinton gave Benning the commander-in-chief's award as the "Best Army Installation in the World," so I concluded early on that this was a tough, take-no-prisoners kind of place.

As the "Home of the Infantry," Fort Benning, located near the city of

Columbus, about ninety minutes south of Atlanta, reaches across 182,000 acres. The base traces its beginnings to 1918, when it was just a small tent camp on Macon Road called Camp Benning, after a Columbus native, Major General Henry Lewis Benning, a distinguished Confederate general, attorney, and Georgia Supreme Court justice. The base grew in fits and starts until its construction boom was triggered in the 1930s by Depression-era federal works projects.

Today Benning trains five kinds of infantry soldiers: mechanized, light, airborne, air assault, and Rangers. "Mechanized" warfare involves armored vehicles, such as tanks. "Light" means that the soldiers are carrying relatively small armaments, such as rifles or machine guns. "Airborne" means they enter combat by parachuting from the skies. "Air assault" means they join the fight from helicopters. And the Rangers are some of the fittest troops the Army has, steeled for combat after sixty-one excruciating days of training in mountains, woodlands, and swamps where they are driven mentally and physically to the point of exhaustion.

Benning has sixty-three training sites, some designated for the use of "live fire," or real ammunition, plus landing zones (for aircraft) and drop zones (for troops, equipment, and supplies) and rolling terrain where Bradley Fighting Vehicles rumble in rehearsal. On an average day, 20,000 troops are in Benning's forests and fields training for combat duty; an adage has it that every drop of sweat in training means one less drop of blood in battle.

When soldiers at Benning salute a higher-up, many say, "Love of Country," and the superior officer returns the salute, answering, "Patriots." That impressed me. I liked that exchange more than what seemed like the base's verbal tic, "Hooah!" It's slang favored by airborne soldiers and Rangers, a term said to have sixteen meanings, none of them "No." "Hooah," for example, may mean "Roger" or "Yes" or "Thank you" or "I don't know what you just said, but I am too embarrassed to ask for clarification."

We were told that "Hooah" also means "Heads up, asshole," but I was picking up lots of stuff like that—profanities and dirty jokes and smart-ass comebacks. Imagine a twelve-year-old from a good family who falls in with the wrong crowd, takes a car on a joy ride, and gets tossed into Juvenile Hall, where the advanced-level courses in thuggery commence. That's a fair approximation of how I felt at Benning. I was surrounded by young men in fatigues in units named "Predators," "Executioners," "Gladiators," and "Bushmasters." I was examining weapons, and while handling these instruments of death, albeit unloaded, posing for souvenir snapshots affecting a "tough gal" stance. I had on a black fleece beret with a little doodad at its crown, just different enough from the Army-issue berets to draw curiosity.

The packing list we'd been e-mailed specified a black knit cap, but I didn't like the $2 watch caps at Wal-Mart, so instead I found myself a jaunty tam-o'-shanter at Hecht's.

By now, perhaps you can tell I was enjoying my walk on the wild side. I was like a runaway, happy to be gone from home instead of wrapping things up before the holidays back in Washington, a place awash in black, navy, and gray suits just as it is invariably lashed by political tempests. If I liked suits, I never would have left; I would have just hung back at the U.S. Capitol with a tape recorder, notebook, and Cross pen.

Benning was drenched in testosterone, saturated with machismo, and crowded with men of action in crew cuts and combat boots, the home of 33,423 active-duty personnel, 6,639 reservists, and 11,940 military retirees. It was Boy Land, to be sure. A butchered version of a song about the place begins "Far across the Chattahoochee, to the Upatoi, stands a little outhouse, the Benning School for Boys."

The reporters arrived in haircuts from pricey salons, wearing high-tech anoraks; I already had rough-weather gear from the old days when I covered tornados and floods and other disasters. There were some genuine media stars in my class—including John Roberts, the CBS White House correspondent; Michael Gordon, military writer for the *New York Times;* and Martha Brant, a *Newsweek* columnist—along with up-and-comers like Chris Cuomo, a producer for ABC News (and Mario Cuomo's son). We learned the concept of "battle buddy," somebody who would be there for encouragement when the going got rough or when you simply needed help, like lifting a rucksack onto your back or pulling rubber galoshes, part of the NBC gear, over your regular boots. Among my best friends were Gordon, the writer from the *Times;* Rosiland Jordan from NBC-TV, who also covers the White House; Deborah Block, a broadcaster for Voice of America; and Rob Schlesinger, a Washington reporter for the *Boston Globe.*

Our group was welcomed by Benning's top boss, Paul Eaton, a two-star general and 1972 graduate of West Point. The fifty-two-year-old commandant doesn't wear this on his sleeve, but he's the son of a Marine Corps fighter pilot killed in Vietnam. Eaton impressed me as a hands-on leader, often turning up at an early hour to observe our class in the field.

He told the media that Benning's staff was "absolutely delighted" to have us, since the Vietnam-era distrust that splintered the military and the press "has got to get out of here, just has to go away." He said that he regretted that few reporters were embedded with military units during the war in Afghanistan, saying it was crucial for America to see what its "sons and daughters" in uniform were doing. He judged that Benning's boot camp would make all of us "a little bit safer" when we deployed to dangerous territory and began writing stories for the folks back home.

One of Eaton's subordinates, Lieutenant Colonel Don Sando, who was running the boot camp, didn't mince words when he explained why the military wanted the story of the U.S. soldier in combat told. "It's so sad," he said, "to have someone die in your arms with nobody knowing what he did to die."

Eaton, hinting at what was to come, said three things were crucial to the preparation of soldiers: physical fitness, psychological hardening, and equipment. Those of us in the press would get a taste of all of them, though if it came to war, we wouldn't be carrying around an infantryman's M-16A4 rifle, since we would remain noncombatants.

In between breaking into a sweat during physical training, we got to take a load off every so often for lectures like the one from Eaton. We learned about the Geneva Conventions, the laws of warfare, and the rules of engagement; about the distinctions between combatants, noncombatants, and belligerents; and about how to stay healthy in the field. In this last talk, we were introduced to the "Five F's": food, fluid, flies, fingers, and feces—as in, eat food, drink fluids, watch out for disease-toting flies, keep your fingers and nails clean, and wash your hands after hitting the latrine.

We also heard from Bryan Whitman, the architect of the Pentagon's program to embed journalists in never-before-seen numbers and himself an ex–Special Forces commander. Whitman is a soft-spoken man, forty-four years old, perpetually pale, and favoring dark suits. Suits are de rigueur if you are a Washington bureaucrat; a pale face is a tip-off that you never see sunshine—you toil day and night, show up at the office six days a week, and can't remember your last vacation. Whitman is a senior Defense Department spokesman, a job that places him in the fortress-like Pentagon—where he's worked for eight years—overseeing information released to both national and international audiences.

Whitman measures his words carefully, and nothing about his exterior suggests his past life. For fifteen years he was active duty, commanding combat units in trouble spots around the world. His last posting was in Somalia, where as a major he oversaw the final withdrawal of United Nations forces.

As he spoke to our class, he didn't brag that he'd been there, done that. Instead, he revealed the latest from the Pentagon drawing board on plans to embed journalists. Embedding is not a new concept; reporters in this country have reported from battlefields as far back as the Civil War, perhaps even longer ago than that. Much has been written about journalists' accounts of the War Between the States, such as when a self-described "Bohemian Brigade" of reporters, using unreliable telegraph wires to file, incurred the wrath of Union general William Tecumseh Sherman, among others, who thought them enemy spies.

Whitman told us that today's boot camps—ours was the second of four separate sessions—were intended to make us "safer on the battlefield for the job you have to do on behalf of the United States." He said embedding was taking place because newsroom bosses and television honchos—not to mention reporters in the field—had been clamoring to cover combat close up. Journalists long had been frustrated with the crumbs meted out at press conferences and from "pool" reports, in which a select few reporters accompany soldiers, then return to the rear and share their information with those stuck behind.

As Whitman spoke, it was by no means certain that the United States was going to war; he talked antiseptically about "the situation emerging in Iraq." But in an allusion to Saddam Hussein, Whitman said that when one's adversary was a "practiced liar" there was no better way to combat "disinformation" than to place reporters in close contact with U.S. military units, as the press would judge independently what was happening and send the news home.

Noting that defense chiefs at the highest levels were committed to embedding journalists, Whitman set out the "ground rules." Reporters would be forbidden from leaking battle plans and from behaving in a way that would jeopardize the security of a military operation or put a unit or an individual soldier in harm's way. Unit commanders had to agree to have a reporter tagging along; our boot camp, in fact, was taking place in part to show commanders that those of us in the media would not be liabilities and, moreover, that we could hack it. "We want you to be safe," Whitman said. "We want you not to compromise military operations. And we don't want you to be injured."

Boot camp, he quipped, wasn't meant to kill us. The training was neither a prerequisite to nor a guarantee of landing an embed spot, he added. Whitman tried to persuade us that we would not be graded ("I'm not keeping a list of who's been naughty and who's been nice"), but being a professional skeptic, I had to wonder.

Finally, Whitman emphasized that embedding was not going to be a come-one, come-all proposition, since there was a limit on how many journalists could be accommodated. Planners were trying to reach "the correct balance between operational risk and the need to provide access to our great men and women in the armed forces." The goal, he said, was to let journalists "see the professionalism and dedication of the Armed Forces preserving our way of life."

We also heard from a former commander who has walked the walk, retired Lieutenant General Harold G. Moore, who in 1965 during Vietnam led

450 troops from the Seventh Cavalry into a landing zone surrounded by 2,000 North Vietnamese troops. Moore had with him what could be called an "embedded reporter," a man in his early twenties from United Press International, Joe Galloway. The against-all-odds fight in the Ia Drang Valley led Moore and Galloway to coauthor a book, *We Were Soldiers Once . . . and Young.* The book eventually became an acclaimed movie, with Mel Gibson portraying Moore and Barry Pepper as Galloway. Some scenes from the movie were filmed at Fort Benning.

Moore, now a gray-haired eighty-year-old, said that he gave Galloway a few pieces of guidance in Vietnam: go anywhere, but do not interfere with operations and do not disclose my plans. The combat commander counseled his troops this way: if you want to talk to the media, go ahead, but talk only from your level. Moore might as well have used the military cliché "Stay in your lane," which means don't talk about matters that are beyond the realm of your rank.

Today Moore refers to Vietnam as "that tragic war," but admitted that he loved seeing his men appear in the newspapers and remained a "great believer" in press freedom. He said that during the hostilities he wanted the public to "get the truth about what was happening—not the five o'clock follies." The latter was a reference to U.S. military press conferences in Saigon, where there was a huge disconnect between what was happening on the battlefield and what the brass divulged in official statements.

He concluded his opening remarks with these suggestions: "Join a unit. And stay with them for a while and be under fire with them."

Moore, fielding a few questions, took one from a reporter who asked about the antiwar sentiment that shook the nation during Vietnam. He replied that people in America have freedoms, including the freedom to protest, and emphasized that he had fought wars to maintain those liberties.

I got in the very last question: "Is there any special advice, Sir, that you have for women reporters covering combat?"

"Know the troops you're covering," he answered. "You're a member of the media, and it's irrelevant that you're female. And report to the best of your ability."

Afterward several young officers lined up to have Moore sign a copy of his book and have a few words with this old gray warrior out of West Point—a former aviator and master parachutist who led troops not only in Vietnam, but earlier, in Korea. I regretted that no copies of his book were for sale, since I was impressed with him. Gentlemanly and articulate, the retired three-star general was so respectful of the Bill of Rights that he seemed to have no quarrel with the people who protested the very same war he fought. I'd never met anyone like him before.

His talk, moreover, was a welcome respite from pounding the ground and being screamed at or laughed at—though I much preferred to amuse the drill sergeants than to incur their wrath. Once during a "survival-level navigation" class in a thick forest, I decided to run, not walk, so a sergeant ran right alongside me. After several minutes, my chest was heaving, so I slowed down to catch my breath. The sergeant then christened me "B. P. Amoco," nothing more than a rest stop, and went into hysterics over his own joke. It cracked me up, too. I found it infinitely more original than my other nicknames during boot camp, including "Army of One" and "Trouble." I'm not exactly sure how I earned those, but it may have been because I have an independent streak and can give as good as I get—both traits, I'm sure, listed in the voluminous "Soldier's Manual" as verboten.

All told, and despite the two-man dressing-down I got after medevac training, I relished the week at boot camp. I enjoyed the Peach State and peoples' slow-as-molasses drawls, the early-winter sunshine, and the tall, fragrant pines; I enjoyed pushing myself and seeing how much I could take; and I enjoyed breaking into a sweat with my media brethren.

Everybody in the press wore blue jeans, even me, after my khakis got up close and personal with Benning's red clay on Day One. Everybody groused about how hard the training was. Hardly anybody pulled rank based on the size of his or her fame or paycheck or news organization; it only mattered how well you performed, especially during training drills.

All of us endured what the Army termed "physical readiness training" early one day ("Assemble at 0445 hours"). Naïvely I assumed the calisthenics would take place in a well-lit, well-equipped gymnasium. Instead, by 5:32 a.m., I was out in the cold, studying a navy blue, star-studded sky, eyeballing the Big Dipper and asking no one in particular how I happened to be plopped outdoors with hundreds of twenty-somethings in gray sweats who'd been training for the infantry for ten full weeks. To me, each of the young men might have been an all-state linebacker for his high school back in Massachusetts or Texas or Minnesota or Colorado.

"Trained to kill, and kill we will," the young soldiers chanted as they ran with us on a quarter-mile track. I believe that I speak for most of the press when I say that our jaws dropped, but knowing a good quote, we committed it to memory for our stories on boot camp.

As my friend Van de Steeg, the colonel in Washington, had warned me, I wasn't able to do it all, but I don't remember seeing any journalist succeed at shimmying up a twenty-foot rope the way the young soldiers did.

The journalists trained alongside the troops for a few reasons, not least the cost savings involved in slotting us into ongoing military exercises. The bonus was that we could talk to the soldiers, and they could talk to us. It was a win-win situation. We needed to know about their lives, their motivations for joining the Army, and their thoughts about the prospect of going off to war in Iraq. They stood to gain from the encounter, too—if nothing else, they could meet a reporter and learn how we operate. Some of the soldiers were still teenagers battling acne; most had never met a member of the press. Finally, there was what I perceived to be the military's subliminal message to the media: "Our soldiers are so young they think they're immortal and so well-trained they think they're invincible. Try keeping up with them when the war breaks out."

Most humbling to me were the soldiers at Benning, some of them eighteen or nineteen years old, who told me they joined the military after 9-11, because of 9-11. It made me feel as though everything I had done in my entire life was trivial by comparison.

* * *

On October 30, 2002, the Pentagon made official its plans to hold boot camps for reporters. My bureau chief, Craig Gilbert, gave me this news one afternoon in the suite we share in the National Press Building at Fourteenth and F Streets, NW, a few blocks from the White House. At the time, both of us were focused on the upcoming midterm congressional elections, so the idea didn't register with me at first.

Only with the announcement of the initial class of media trainees—who were off to learn first from the Navy in Norfolk, Virginia, and later from the Marine Corps in Quantico, Virginia—did I sit up and take stock of the situation. When I got around to phoning the Pentagon, I learned that places in the remaining three boot camps were highly sought after; no one could guarantee that someone from an organization the size of mine would merit a spot. That tidbit of information got my competitive juices flowing, so I polished my résumé and launched a full-scale lobbying campaign. I contacted practically everyone in uniform I knew along the military-rich corridor running from Washington to Virginia Beach.

I reminded the Department of Defense that I was in its National Media Pool, a rotating group of correspondents who are on stand-by for three months at a time; when your number comes up, you're to have your gear packed, be prepared to reach Andrews Air Force Base in Washington within four hours, and be willing to be flown anywhere the armed services are conducting a major operation. In truth the pool is kind of a dinosaur that hasn't been activated in ages, but I had the distinction of being on call during the 9-11 attacks, though my stint lapsed at the end of September 2001, just days before the war in Afghanistan.

I hauled out every military story I'd written, from one on the fiftieth anniversary of "Operation Overlord," as D-Day was formally known, to my coverage of "Operation Noble Eagle," the mission that had F-15 fighter planes patrolling the skies after 9-11.

In the midst of my bid to get into boot camp, I remembered somebody I'd met once before: General Richard B. Myers, four-star Air Force general and chairman of the Joint Chiefs of Staff, who, as such, is the principal military adviser to President George W. Bush and Defense Secretary Donald Rumsfeld.

Several weeks before the Pentagon unveiled plans for the media boot camps, Myers had been my tablemate at a National Press Club luncheon during the emotion-charged week when the nation bowed its head to remember those lost in the 9-11 attacks a year earlier. On the actual anniversary, Myers was at the Pentagon's memorial, and I was reporting about the tribute in Shanksville, Pennsylvania, held in memory of the thirty-three passengers and seven crew members aboard United Flight 93 who had staged a revolt and died trying to thwart the hijackers. In the words of Homeland Security chief Tom Ridge at the Shanksville commemoration, these brave souls kept "hundreds, if not thousands" of people alive in Washington, since the al-Qaida terrorists had intended to attack another Washington landmark, such as the U.S. Capitol.

Myers addressed the press club on September 13, 2002, a year during which I was cochair of the club's speaker's committee. That role had me seated next to him during the thirty-minute lunch that precedes the speeches, which are carried by National Public Radio and C-SPAN as well as numerous other media outlets. Over lunch, I asked Myers how the Pentagon's commemoration had gone two days earlier; I was curious, not least since I'd reported from the Pentagon on the day of the attack and for several days afterward. He, in turn, inquired about Shanksville, so I said that I would tell him, but warned him that I'd probably cry.

Here's what I wrote from the once anonymous Pennsylvania backwater:

They were saluted as citizen-soldiers in the first battle in the war on terror, heralded as the first patriots of the 21st century, and remembered as mothers and fathers, sons and daughters, brothers and sisters: ordinary people with extraordinary courage.

A year after United Airlines Flight 93 careened into an abandoned strip mine, people turned out from this tiny community and beyond Wednesday to remember the passengers who recited the Lord's Prayer and coined a two-word battle cry, "Let's roll."

Later I mentioned to Myers that my father had served under Patton in the Army, as an eighteen-year-old sergeant with the occupation forces in Germany in the months just after victory in Europe was declared. Michael J. Skiba was a translator, courier, and postal clerk in Patton's headquarters. Myers seemed respectful even though Dad was a lowly enlisted man; the general shared some Patton lore and whetted my appetite to pick up a biography about the bold, sure-footed general.

The time I spent with Myers, who later spoke and took questions, passed pleasantly. Later, as I was trying to elbow my way into boot camp, I had doubts about writing to such a big gun. My first impulse was that that would be presumptuous, something only an asshole would do. My second impulse was to think, "What are they going to do, throw me into Asshole Jail?" So I wrote a letter on November 21: "Dear General Myers: Your appearance at the National Press Club last September 13 was a great success. . . . Today I am writing because I am very interested in taking part in the next Joint Military Training for Media Members course and hope that you might consider recommending me."

Myers replied on December 4:

Your interest in attending . . . is commendable. Your package has been forwarded to the Office of the Assistant Secretary of Defense for Public Affairs for consideration of your participation in the next training class.

Thanks for your support—through your writing—of America and our military during this Global War on Terrorism.

In his own hand was a postscript: "I hope this works out for you."

Even after this written exchange, I was only offered a spot on the waiting list for the second boot camp, which was already full. Still, it was a minor breakthrough, so I enthusiastically agreed to be on stand-by. On Monday, December 10, as I was sitting in a meeting room in the Capital Hilton at Sixteenth and K Streets, waiting for the start of a press conference featuring a dozen newly elected Democratic governors, including Wisconsin's Jim Doyle, my mobile phone rang. It was Lieutenant Colonel Gary Keck in the Pentagon press office, the officer tasked with slotting reporters into boot camp. He offered me a spot at Benning.

"I'm there!" I told him. "But I'm going to have to call you back when this press conference is over."

Thus I had five days to rearrange the travel plans my husband Tom and I had made to visit family in Wisconsin and Illinois for the holidays, assemble my gear, confront my fears, and stay afloat despite a tidal wave of Army paperwork surging my way.

My fears focused on two things: I imagined austere barracks with metal bunk beds straight out of *Gomer Pyle, USMC;* and I worried that at the drop of a hat, I could be ordered to "Drop forty" while some sadistic guy in fatigues stood there guffawing, laughing as hard as he ever had laughed in his entire life, steadying himself only by raising a hand to a cinder block wall.

Which brings me to the paperwork. All of a sudden the United States of America wanted to know my Social Security number, nation of citizenship, date of birth, next of kin, shoe size, glove size, T-shirt size, blood type, allergies, height—and weight.

Now, having lied to the government about my weight in all the places where I've had a driver's license, this would seem a no-brainer. But I had two stark choices: Either I could mislead the government about how many pounds I was packing and forget about being able to fit into the NBC gear; or I could tell the truth to Uncle Sam, who would quickly ascertain from a review of my paperwork that I was overweight, middle-aged, incapable of dropping five—let alone forty—and unfit for duty.

So I lied about my weight—just a little. Not a whopper, more like a white lie—maybe "gray" would be more accurate—but not so grand a prevarication that when Armageddon arrived unexpectedly in the form of a nuclear bomb, I would risk splitting a seam in the rear of my too-tight pants as I sprinted away from the mushroom cloud. Nothing like that.

Immediately afterward I signed up for a membership at *USA Today*'s health club (which happens to be my husband's second home). There, as a new arrival, I was put through my paces, pinched with calipers to determine my body-fat ratio, placed on a scale, and directed to stretch and strain in front of a woman with a stopwatch. Later, as I examined six humiliating pages of computer-generated findings, a single, glaring truth emerged: *I was overweight, middle-aged, incapable of dropping five, and unfit for duty.*

*　*　*

The military's eagle eyes were upon the journalists from the moment we landed at the small airport in Columbus, Georgia. A welcoming party had come out in full dress uniform (something we'd never see again during that down-and-dirty week). I could feel their penetrating stares as I strode toward a baggage carousel with Deborah Block, the woman from Voice of America. I imagined them looking at me as they ran through a mental checklist: Is she fit? Is she fleet? Is her gear in trim? Is she able to carry all her bags without assistance?

Block, I, and the other newcomers then boarded two white Ford Econoline vans for the trip to the base. During the ride David Willis, a reporter for the British Broadcasting Corporation, had us chortling with his dead-on imitation of Austin Powers. "Do you think I'm sexy, baby?" he'd ask, just as he'd do during the days that followed, when our faces were streaked in forest-green and olive paint, when our clothing was spattered in red dirt, and when we resembled nothing but the Michelin Man, bloated from the NBC gear.

Willis's antics suggested the possibility of frivolity during *Fear Factor: Benning*—and I was all for that.

Early on, Michael Gordon and I seized on the idea of thanking our trainers by parodying ourselves. Gordon remembered a bawdy, no-holds-barred comedy sketch he'd witnessed during a visit to a Navy ship; he said it contained the filthiest material he'd ever seen or heard. And I remembered so many funny moments from my Kosovo trip with the military that I took it up later with my father. Question: "Dad, why are soldiers always telling jokes?" Answer: "You have to stay loose for battle."

At dinner the first night I'd gotten to know Sando, the forty-three-year-old leader of the boot camp, who was the highest-ranking officer at my table. I'd thrown "softball" questions at the lieutenant colonel and dutifully copied down his answers, trying to put my best foot forward. The next day, in a clearing in the forest, when Sando saw me in the black beret, he called out, "What are you doing, trying out for the circus?" I kept on walking, crisply sounding out, "I'm already in the circus, Sir." We were friends from then on.

A few days later, during a session on "military operations in urban terrain," I told Sando about our entertainment idea and got his tentative approval to present it before the farewell dinner, though first he'd have to clear it with a higher-up. But he was game, agreeing to have a few microphones set up for us, and, to my delight, even springing me from class for an hour so I could buy an outfit at the post exchange. Reporters had temporary privileges there, but, given the rigorous schedule, I had never set foot in the place. Sando even commandeered a van to take me there and back and ordered a seargent to do the driving. I was in hog heaven, since I had brought along nothing but outdoor clothing and the prices at the exchange—akin to your average department store—were lower than retail and tax-free.

When I returned to the group, I sat in the back of the bus and furtively displayed my bargains to Rosiland Jordan from NBC-TV; I didn't want anyone else in the class to know I'd played hooky. She betrayed not an iota of jealousy, saying to me, "There's enough good going around in this world for all of us." I thought that showed class, and we remain friends.

Besides Jordan and me, only two women were willing to sing in front of an audience: Block, from Voice of America, and Ann Tyson from the *Christian Science Monitor*.

Gordon and I set up guidelines for the performance: We would make fun of ourselves a lot, and the Army only a little. The dinner and revue were held at Benning's Officers Club. In attendance were Eaton, the commanding general; Sando, the boot camp leader; other officers; our drill sergeants; plus spouses and other guests.

An officer from Benning took the microphone, announcing "Katherine and the Not Ready for Prime Time Players." Gordon, a devastatingly droll emcee, doubled as the director. He introduced John Roberts, from CBS, who posed as the "prototypical male TV reporter covering combat," equipped with a Mont Blanc pen, leather-bound notebook, a make-up compact, and what was dubbed H.I.S., the "hair-immobilization system" (hair spray). A newspaperman played the archetypal print guy, off to war with only a notebook, a Bic pen, and a Trojan.

John Burnett from National Public Radio, his face camouflaged and his helmet festooned with olive-colored burlap, led a group of male reporters who were escorting the female singers into the ballroom. "Okay maggots, move out!" Burnett shouted, with all of us marching in as clumsily as we could.

Our female quartet, borrowing from infantry's nickname, The Queen of Battle, fashioned itself "The Battle Queens." Using the melody from "On the Street Where You Live" from *My Fair Lady,* Gordon and I penned the song performed by the Battle Queens:

> People stop and stare;
> they don't bother me,
> 'cause I trained at Benning, Georgia;
> I'm a wannabee.
>
> I am battle's queen,
> and there's a war ageen.
> And this time I intend to embed.
>
> String up a poncho hooch;
> no pup tent for me,
> 'cause those dogs of war wish only to
> embed with me.
>
> Just the facts for me:
> print, radio, or TV.
> Rummy says A-OK to embed.
>
> And oh, what a wonderful feeling
> just to know a Pulitzer's near.
> And oh, what a beautiful feeling
> that after Benning I'm a gal
> without a fear.

(Aside) As long as my battle buddy's near.
And I've got my snivel gear.*

Meantime I'm a star;
just you watch for me.
There are cameras filming everything I do
but pee.

Move over Amanpour,
this is my damn war!
Saddam takes his stand?
Battle's queens on hand.
'cause this time I intend to embed.

*Snivel gear is slang for cold-weather clothing.

We drew howls of laughter, and the kudos kept coming even in the powder room, where some officers' wives congratulated me. I read the wives' approval two ways: what an amusing spoof—and what a relief that you do not covet my husband.

That night, Gordon and I netted an exclusive invitation—one I finagled, to be honest. General Eaton and his wife, P.J., had us over for a tour of their sprawling home, Riverside, a two-story mansion that was once the residence of the plantation owner whose land was sold to the federal government at Benning's birth. There we sipped cognac, traded views on the Middle East, and made a trip upstairs to the wide verandas that wrap around three sides of this stately house. The place was dolled up for Christmas in the lush, floral, beribboned way only Southerners seem to achieve. Tiny plastic paratroopers, spray-painted gold, hung from one of several Christmas trees decking the halls. They reminded me of a time years ago, when my brothers would line the entire living room floor with "Army guys," two-inch plastic figures that were picked off, one by one, with marbles, until the bitter end. I played that game with them, too, but not too often; probably because of my DNA, I preferred to stage happier scenarios in my Barbie Dream House.

On the veranda of Riverside, we soaked up the December night, balmy by the standards of the Midwest, the place I'd spent every Christmas of my entire life, and I thought of my husband, my family up North, and my holiday plans. Baghdad did not cross my mind, not once.

So as not to overstay our welcome, Gordon and I left after one drink; Eaton and his wife were so solicitous they even drove us back to Olson Hall. Later, I heard on the grapevine that after the dinner, almost everybody had hit the Officers Club bar, except for the younger members of the class, who went back to Olson Hall to throw back beers, becoming so raucous that ultimately came a knock on the door and a warning from the military police.

Friday, the final day of boot camp, saw us watching 119 Rangers graduate after their arduous training program. They put on quite a show for us: dropping out of a helicopter and into a lake while clinging to a cable, from a height of about fifteen feet; using a rope to climb a thirty-foot wall and rappelling down; going mano a mano with their bare fists; and even sneaking up from behind another Ranger and simulating how to strangle him with a garrote, and finish him off with a bullet.

The demonstrations found my new friend Lieutenant Colonel Sando and I sitting side by side in the bleachers, where he kept badgering me about where I had disappeared to the night before. But my lips were sealed, until I judged it was too delicious a morsel, and confessed.

"I had cognac at Riverside with General and Mrs. Eaton," I said smugly.

He rolled his eyes. "You did not."

"I did, really. Me and Gordon."

"You didn't."

"I did."

There was only one way to end this Mexican standoff. I pulled the reporter's notebook out of my jacket pocket and sketched out Riverside's floor plan, drawing three tiny figures to represent the Eaton family dogs, one of which, I informed Sando, had only three legs. Aha! He knew then that I had clasped Benning's Holy Grail.

Meantime the Rangers kept up their he-man show, with a guy palming C-4, the plastic explosive. He extolled its potency, shaped it into a baseball-sized wad, and casually tossed it into the bleachers precisely when a blast thundered in a remote location. What I saw and heard had me jump out of my skin. The one-two punch of the special effects suggested a real strike against the people in the stands.

Terrified, I reflexively grabbed Sando's upper arm—until I realized that the audience had been hoodwinked. "Jesus Christ, enough already!" I said to Sando. He was buckling in laughter, explaining that if C-4 wasn't detonated, as with a blasting cap, it was harmless.

And so Sando had settled the score. I'd sipped cognac with a two-star, but he had had the last laugh. He could only smirk, knowing that in the waning moments of his crash course, he'd given his protégée precisely what the Pentagon planners and the Benning brass and the boys who would be infantrymen wanted: one more battle scar.

2
Back to the Heartland

Once boot camp was over the press left Fort Benning in a stampede. Christmas was around the corner: it was Friday, December 20. No more 0400 hour wake-up calls, no more sixteen-hour days, no more boom-boom-booms—each reason enough to celebrate.

I said my good-byes to classmates and trainers, mouthed some final thoughts in front of the documentarians (who, to my relief, had not been invited to the farewell dinner), and sought out Sando. There he was, in a knot of people in the lobby of Olson Hall, seeing his mission to its conclusion by making sure everybody took their leave, even taking the trouble to map out directions to Atlanta's Hartsfield Airport. I flashed a smile, gave him a bear hug, and slipped a little something in his palm. It was a tiny thing I'd picked up in a post exchange for next to nothing. When he opened his firm, bronzed hand, he gave me a sour look, as if I'd handed him a nine-millimeter Glock and invited him to play Russian roulette with his career. My parting gift was a general's star. I meant it as a compliment, to tell him I was sure he was going places; but his reaction made me feel ridiculous. As a lieutenant colonel, he was just two rungs—but let's face it, two continents—away from collecting the real thing. And, it appeared, this West Pointer didn't want something like my "present" to jinx his chances.

Our class of sixty had had its ups and downs—some people fell ill, one I heard with pneumonia—but most of us were high from the weeklong endorphin rush. Now the two species, the media and the military, were going their separate ways. It was like the foreign-exchange student from France leaving your high school or your hometown. You forget the early culture shock—her upturned nose at hot dogs sizzling on the grill, and her insisting that her host parents buy her a unicycle to compensate for her homesickness; you find yourself remembering the good times, wondering if your paths will ever cross again and realizing, with some regret, that it's a long shot.

I hitched a ride to the airport with my husband's colleague, Dave Moniz, who covers the Pentagon for *USA Today*. Dave, bespectacled, with curly, salt-and-pepper hair, is as smart as he is nice. Washington is full of Mensa hopefuls, but people like Moniz are few and far between. He wouldn't even take gas money.

As we sped up Interstate 85, we traded minor gossip about our classmates and the people at *USA Today*. My husband is a lot like Dave: bright, soft-spoken, and kind-hearted. Dave pronounced Tom "a good soul," which I knew to be gospel. Both of them are introverts—something I've never been called. So I was feeling a little sheepish about having been such a ham at the dinner the night before, though I knew I couldn't do a thing about it now. "Caught in the act of being myself," I thought. Dave did not strike me as a blabbermouth, and even if my antics made the rounds in Washington, I'd heard worse about other reporters—a lot worse.

During the ninety-mile trip, I was dead tired. But there was only one "dead" thing that mattered now: my deadline. All I had to do was rearrange the twenty-six letters of the alphabet in such a way that a reader could envision what I'd just endured, and why. I knew the story would get done, but I was in a dither, worried about disappointing Tom and showing up late for my family's Christmas gathering in Illinois.

Foolishly, I'd thought I might even finish my story for Sunday before leaving Benning, but that game plan, in retrospect, was a complete fantasy. Usually after a day of training I'd stagger like a zombie into Olson Hall, yank the gel pack I'd brought along out of my room's mini-freezer and ice my upper back until it was numb, then muster enough strength to set the alarm and turn off the lights. (When I discovered my nondescript accommodations had a freezer, all else was forgiven: the paper-thin walls, the broken thermostat, and the shower stall in place of a bathtub.)

OK, so I wasn't flat on my back every single night. I did skip out to the base's brew pub for Karaoke Night on Wednesday—an "optional" activity on our schedule—since I just couldn't resist letting loose. It was a royal disappointment, chiefly because the lady who ran the place monopolized the microphone as if we were gathered in her very own knotty pine basement. And when I cajoled classmate Bob Woodruff of ABC News into a duet, "Fly Me to the Moon," the tempo was so downbeat it's astonishing that someone didn't bang a gong.

Now I was paying the piper; actually, I was emptying my emotional wallet to the partridge, turtle doves, French hens—the whole kit and caboodle. Dave had his eyes on the road, but I was madly sorting through three brown accordion files, whose contents—reporter's notebooks, handouts, a wall-sized topographical map of Fort Benning, and my new Bible, the "Soldiers Handbook"—cascaded from my lap onto the floor.

We arrived at the airport with plenty of time before our flights, and Dave asked if I wanted to get a quick lunch. There was no way I had the time to join him, even though I owed him for the lift. Once I checked my bags, I made a beeline to a Delta President's Club and paid $50 for a day rate to snare a cubicle, bag of pretzels, and bottomless glass of sparkling water—and began writing.

By the time I boarded my flight to Milwaukee, I'd made some progress, but not much. So I worked off the tray table until my brain felt like stir-fried Szechwan beef. I'd left behind the chaos of the world's busiest airport on the Friday before Christmas and soon after takeoff, the flight attendants, in Santa caps and jingle-bell earrings, dimmed the cabin lights. Before long the sound of the aircraft swooshing through the night skies seemed like only a lullaby. I drifted into sleep.

Some people—my husband, Tom, for example—are natural writers. They sit down in front of a computer and play the keyboard like a concert pianist bringing to life a nineteenth-century Steinway. Not me. I'm from Red Smith's camp, he being the sportswriter who famously said, "Writing is easy: you just sit down at the typewriter, open a vein, and bleed it out, drop by drop." For me it goes like this: Time permitting, I, in anal retentive mode, first number the pages of my notebooks and pore over every page of scribbles, marking important facts with a checkmark and good quotes with a "q," smearing all these gems with highlighter, and copying key elements onto an 8½-by-11-inch lined pad in handwriting that another human actually might have a crack at deciphering. I try to style a catchy lead. I throw in a "nut graph," which gives readers the story's greater significance; sometimes it's called the "WHOGAS" paragraph (for "Who gives a shit?"). Finally I attempt to finish with a flourish.

Tom was waiting for me at the gate at Milwaukee's Mitchell International Airport. I was in trouble, since I wasn't halfway finished with my story.

"Hey, soldier!" he greeted me. I felt I'd done something wrong; maybe it was just guilt about what I was about to disclose: "Honey, I haven't finished my story yet." His appellation was a nod to my black beret, my Army look-alike, but I didn't know that, and I was sweating bullets. Going to Georgia meant I'd already screwed up Christmas, since I was showing up in the Midwest two days after Tom arrived, and we'd had to bow out of previously planned revelry with our *Journal Sentinel* friends. These people have come to count on me. It's newsroom legend that as a newlywed in 1994, while dancing with Tom at the office Christmas party, I broke my left ankle but, thinking it merely a sprain, hobbled off to another night spot for some bois-terous rounds of caroling.

Since moving to D.C., Tom and I don't have a lot of quality time. He works evenings, Sunday through Thursday, and I work days, Monday through Friday, leaving the weekends for bills, laundry, Home Depot runs, and what may or may not pass as wedded bliss. Come late Friday afternoon, I'm often staring a Sunday deadline in the face, so I've derailed our TGIF plans before—and I knew now that once again I was on a trajectory for a train wreck.

We checked into the downtown Hilton in Milwaukee and dropped off several suitcases. I had my Army clothes; Tom brought my party clothes and our Christmas presents. We grabbed a sandwich in a hotel pub, where my former home—a place I'd lived for twenty years before leaving for Wash-ington—came into focus. The pace was slower, the people were friendlier, and the power suits far fewer. The other patrons were sucking Marlboro Reds and downing Miller on tap; these weren't proper Washingtonians, they were rough-hewn people, the sort who made their living with their hands and backs.

Traffic along Wisconsin Avenue was sparse, and people seemed to be driv-ing slowly and carefully, nothing like what occurs on the Beltway, where everyone seems a distinguished alumnus of the Me, Me, Me School of Driv-ing. The hotel was across from the city's new, handsome convention center; but with no pre-Christmas meetings, the downtown seemed dead. I had a sinking you-can't-go-home-again feeling in my belly.

Amid this melancholy, I entertained, momentarily, a desperate thought. Remembering that Tom is a rewrite man, I considered asking him to write my story. But no sooner had I mentally rehearsed my pleading, "Tom, I'll tell you what happened and you write my story," than I realized that was a mistake.

We returned to our corner room on one of the hotel's upper floors, where we could make out Lake Michigan, inky black in the distance, and the vast Hoan Bridge marrying the city's north side with the south side, and the Allen-Bradley industrial plant, home to "the largest four-sided clock in the world." The illuminated timepiece is nicknamed the "Polish moon," since it towers over what's known in the vernacular as "dah Sout Side," that part of the city that was settled by people who share my heritage.

So while we were ostensibly home for the holidays, I was still on the clock, hunched over my laptop in the same pinched-for-time place I've been a thousand times. Tom, oblivious to my tremulous search for a beginning, middle, and end, nestled under the covers of the king-sized bed and crashed. He retreats when he's angry, which only frustrates a "Let's talk it out" type like me. But I had no time or inclination to try to reason with him. I wrote until after midnight, set the alarm for six o'clock, woke up before it even rang, and resumed my labor. Finally the end was in sight. I wrapped the story up by eight and sent it electronically to my newspaper, just a few blocks away. As a reward I collapsed into a bubble bath, examining the Benning-inflicted bruises on my body and wondering whether Tom, still dozing, would dress me down—again—for being too absorbed by my work.

Soon we were bound for my sister's home in Clare, Illinois, a two-hour trip from Milwaukee. The sun was shining, the roads had only a dusting of snow, and we programmed the rental car's radio to the all-Chistmas stations. By the time "Jingle Bell Rock" was playing for the second or third time, I was done relaying last-minute fixes to my editors ("Make it a twenty-foot rope they wanted us to climb, not a thirty-foot rope") and put away my cell phone. Only then did Tom resume polite conversation with me. Both of our moods lifted as we breezed past the familiar, comforting sights of Wisconsin's wintery countryside: the black-and-white Holsteins against drab pastures, the weathered red barns with faded ads for chewing tobacco, the billboards for our old haunts, like The Elegant Farmer, a roadside market. Sailing down Interstate 43, Tom and I resumed an old tradition inaugurated with my sister's four children—whom I think of as my own—and began rating people's outdoor holiday decorations on a scale of one to ten. For the rare home and lawn worthy of a made-for-TV movie, we'd announce, "Eleven!" and burst out laughing. The only stop Tom and I made en route to the Mangans was at a Pick 'n Save grocery store, where we felt guilty about buying store-bought stollen and choosing from among picked-over poinsettias, and as penance dropped a good chunk of change on bottled cheer.

This must be understood about Nancy Mangan: while I love my only sister madly, we grew up into very different women. She's a soccer mom living far west of Chicago with her husband and their two girls and two boys. The family homestead is what real estate agents call a "farmette," which means that what had been a working farm was subdivided, with the house, barn, silo, Morgan building, tool shed, and five acres going to the farmettians and the surrounding land left to corn and soybean growers.

Nancy, who is seven years younger than I am, works for two veterinarians and keeps a small menagerie at home: six cats, two dogs, two donkeys, one goat, and a love bird. It's as if she can't have enough beating hearts around. It was actually only some months earlier that the Mangans had begun living episodes of *Green Acres* on the farmette, and this was the first trip Tom and I were making to Clare, population 48. Among my surprises was that livestock weren't lawn ornaments; one actually has to rise early, put on heavy-duty duds by Carhartt, slog through the malodorous stalls, and feed the animals. My own morning ritual is to walk our Labrador retriever, Princess, toss back two cups of coffee, devour three newspapers, down a bowl of Mueslix, and rush to the subway.

Differences aside, Nancy is a delight, having never been shackled by the duties attendant to being the oldest daughter in the family. She is more spontaneous than I am—imagine that—and having had kids at a young age, matured fast but never lost her childhood devilish streak. Once, when her children were younger and we were weekending at her in-laws' summer home near Whitewater, Wisconsin, she stopped her minivan at a boat shop so she could buy an ear-shattering air horn. She wanted the device to shag her kids to dinner back in the Chicago suburbs, where the family lived then, but in the meantime, for laughs she kept blasting it out the car window on Whitewater's somnolent streets. This story summarizes how she lives: loud and large.

I came to frivolity later in life, since as the oldest girl I was the mother hen, saddled with babysitting my youngest siblings and helping out in the family-style tavern and restaurant that my grandparents had started just after Prohibition. When school let out for the summer, my friends ditched their books, hit the beach, smeared their bodies with Johnson's Baby Oil, and studied guys. Often I was in the restaurant waiting tables, if not changing diapers at home.

Nancy married young and had children in short order while I was off chasing the news and seeing the world. But she is one tough cookie, and I suspected that she'd support my fledgling notion of going off to war, even if it meant staring down weapons of mass destruction.

The Mangan kids? They were delighted that "Aunt Koo Koo"—that's what Molly called me once, and it stuck—had toughed out boot camp. I handed each one of them an Army Ranger T-shirt, regaled them with stories, and demonstrated how to use camouflage paint, which comes in a metal tube and has a consistency somewhere between lipstick and candle wax.

Here's a page out of Camouflage 101: "Paint shiny areas of your face—forehead, cheekbones, nose, ears, and chin—with dark green. Cover the shadowy areas—around the eyes, under the nose, under the chin—with light green."

The Army could have made it plainer, telling soldiers to render their faces into split-leaf philodendrons.

My nieces and nephews listened intently during my show-and-tell. I detected in them a "United we stand" patriotism and pride, suspecting it came from having their innocence shattered at 9-11. To them, everything Army was "awesome." Though I welcomed their interest, their exuberance stopped me in my tracks. It was a far cry from how I felt coming of age during Vietnam, when my entire family anxiously watched the televised lottery for the draft in the early 1970s, since young men were going to be called—or spared—depending on a lottery number, keyed to the day their birthdays fell. In our household hosannas went up when my oldest brother, Tom, drew a high number, meaning he would miss the fight and could finish the University of Notre Dame.

Now a partner in an accounting firm, Tom and his wife and kids were on hand for the holiday get-together in Clare, and Tom gave me the impression that he thought it was prudent that I'd undergone combat-survival training, just in case.

John, the family's youngest, a suburban Chicago policeman, made the trip to the Mangans with his wife and their sons. John had taken to boasting to anyone who would listen that his big sister was fearless. He seemed proud that we shared the same DNA, behaving as if courage can be contagious, which of course it can; and after the holidays he put me in contact with the sergeant in his department most familiar with the ins and outs of bulletproof vests.

Mom and Dad didn't make the trip that year, in part because fifteen years in the Sunshine State means they're no longer inoculated against Chicago's often fierce winters. My father's absence at the holiday table likely was a blessing in disguise, since there was no way the former soldier would give his imprimatur to his daughter's reporting from a war zone. Years back he'd even thought newspapering itself too rough-and-tumble for me, although he came around once my career took off. As for my mother, it took a forty-minute phone call some weeks later, but she came to see it my way and half-heartedly signed off on my plans.

With respect to my covering a war, my parents could have been booked as battling guests on *Crossfire,* except for one thing: of the two, only Dad's a screamer.

Mom, by contrast, rarely loses her cool. She practically drowned us in love when we were growing up. An only child, she'd sometimes pretended that her dolls were brothers and sisters. Once she'd grown up and had five children—practically textbook for a traditional Catholic woman in the 1950s—she regarded us as trophies. After high school, she'd completed a degree at the Chicago Academy of Fine Arts, gone to some chi-chi baking school, become a capable seamstress, and unleashed all of her energies into creating a happy home.

Mom had never punched a clock in her life, working only at the restaurant, which she and Dad eventually took over. When she was a young woman, her Polish-born father thought it would reflect poorly on him if she took a job someplace else, suggesting to outsiders that he couldn't provide for her. She told me that while in art school, she whiled away her lunch hours comparing china patterns at Marshall Field's, her only aspiration, it seems, to get married. My teenage years were far different: by then the women's movement was unleashed, and I saw no reason that I couldn't have it all: career, marriage, and kids. (Hah.)

That my siblings were unified in their support for my latest venture improved my standing with Mom. By the time I had a sense of just where I was heading, my brother Steve, a financial whiz in Denver, spoke to her on the phone and made it sound as though I was heading off on a routine business trip. "I'd like to go to Kuwait, too, Mom," he told her, as if he might have to check on oil derivatives there.

Old habits die hard, so Nancy's Christmas spread could have fed twice the number of family members assembled. Right after dinner and gifts, my husband left for Wisconsin to be in place for his own holiday ritual, a Green Bay Packers game. He left me to sleep in rural peace for the next two days, stirring only for occasional forays to the malls.

Once Tom retrieved me in Clare we moved on to his hometown, Madison, Wisconsin. He's from a family of seven kids, reared in the shadow of the sprawling university, and Christmas Eve at the Vanden Brooks meant more food, more gifts, more bottled cheer, and more nieces and nephews on sugar highs. Tom's family seemed warier about my stories from Fort Benning and what might follow—probably because, as with my father, war was not an abstract concept to them. During World War II my father-in-law, Bill, served in the Army Air Corps as a navigator in a bomber over the Pacific while my mother-in-law, Mimi, and a sister were real-life Rosie the Riveters, working in a vast munitions factory in Baraboo, Wisconsin. They'd done their part, to be sure, but never seemed to shake their grief over the many friends and neighbors who didn't make it back from combat.

On Christmas morning, as the two-state, three-city, five-day merry-go-round ride wound down, my heart was heavy. Tom and I boarded a plane for Washington and exchanged greetings with the flight attendants sporting Santa caps and jingle-bell earrings. We'd left our families behind on my favorite day of the year for one reason: My husband had to be at his desk at five in the afternoon to help put out the December 26, 2003, edition of "The Nation's Newspaper."

*   *   *

I went back to work before the end of the year, while Congress was still in recess and the streets of the federal city were half-empty, since so many of us Washingtonians are from someplace else. On New Year's Day I caught the president on television at his ranch, taking a ninety-minute walk with journalists in tow and remarking, toward the end of the trek, "Saddam Hussein . . . has got to understand, his day of reckoning is coming."

One day in the office, going through some handouts from Benning, I came across "The Infantryman's Creed," and I clipped out a portion and used a glue stick to attach it to the first page of my Filofax. I was hoping only to toughen myself up for what might come next. The excerpt read:

> I yield not
> to weakness,
> to hunger,
> to cowardice,
> to fatigue,
> to superior odds,
> for I am mentally tough, physically strong
> and morally straight.
> I forsake not—
> my country,
> my mission,
> my comrades,
> my sacred duty . . .
> I am relentless . . .
> I am the queen of battle.

Things were heating up by mid-January, when Pentagon officials called a meeting with the chiefs of news bureaus from all over town; I went in place of my boss since it was clear by then that the war was my story. Victoria Clarke, the Defense Department spokeswoman, ran the meeting in a room wall-to-wall with people. Lots of the top public-affairs guns were out, like the Army's Brigadier General Robert Gaylord and the Navy's Rear Admiral Steve Pietropaoli. Clarke let Bryan Whitman do most of the talking, and he outlined the mechanics of a "very aggressive, ambitious embedding program" that would see reporters "living, eating, and moving in combat" with the military. No enemy country was mentioned; everything was couched in terms of a "potential future combat operation." Yet Iraq, of course, was the invisible six-ton elephant shuffling through the room.

Whitman told us that ideally, journalists would join military units in the States, deploy overseas with them, follow them to a staging area, watch them prepare for combat, and enter the fray alongside them. "You'd march on whatever capital we happen to march on with them," he continued. "You would return to the United States with them . . . and cover the victory parade." I pictured Times Square, ticker tape, and a nation jubilant that its boys and girls were home and the dirty business was done.

Meanwhile, though, Whitman and others were talking about professional gear, proper clothing, the recommended vaccines, and the need to obtain visas for the countries that would be our destination. Members of the press were to supply their own helmets and bulletproof vests, but the Pentagon would give the embeds nuclear, biological, and chemical protective gear, since, as Whitman put it: "If you're embedded . . . you ought to be traveling with the same NBC protection that our folks have. It is an ever-present threat on the modern battlefield."

In addition, the military would offer anthrax and smallpox vaccines, which are not commercially available, but our news organizations would be required to pick up the tab.

In answer to a question, Whitman said we wouldn't all have military escorts—he said there probably weren't enough public affairs officers (PAOs) to go around—and reiterated the ground rules. And he hinted that it wouldn't be long before the military began meting out assignments.

Back in the bureau, I dashed off the high points in an e-mail message to my top bosses, then picked up the phone to set up a lunch with my military escort from Kosovo, Van de Steeg, whose advice had helped me get into boot camp, and out, in one piece.

Fifty years old, the Iowa-raised and Minnesota-educated Van de Steeg and I hadn't hit it off instantly in the Balkans; even my married name, Vanden Brook, seemed to leave him cold. A lieutenant colonel then, he was a by-the-book chaperone bent on keeping us on schedule—and away from hazards such as land mines.

One morning at Camp Bondsteel, the Army's expansive compound in Kosovo, Van de Steeg traipsed into the women's tent five or ten minutes before some 0600 event on our schedule. He was primed to roust anybody running late. I was packed and nearly ready to go; I just had to roll up my sleeping bag, which I did as quickly and expertly as I could, since he was watching me like a hawk. "You did that quite well," he observed.

Damned with faint praise, I thought, so I rolled my eyes and said curtly, "I've camped before, *Sir.*"

Later that day, reporters were trailing soldiers on patrol through a strife-torn village when I stepped on a piece of cardboard big enough to carry twenty-four cans of soda. It was concealing a gaping hole in the street. My right leg plunged into the jagged crevasse until my left knee hit the asphalt street, breaking my fall. Van de Steeg, on the other side of the road, came over like a shot.

"Are you OK?" he asked, genuinely concerned.

I was banged up, but I wasn't seeing stars or anything, so I shook myself off and fell back in line, telling him sassily, "Playing through the pain, Sir."

He slapped me on the back, exclaiming, "You're a good man!"

I found that hilarious, but welcomed a commendation for something more than rolling up a sleeping bag, and from then on, Lieutenant Colonel Van de Steeg and Mrs. Vanden Brook saw eye to eye.

For my lunch in Washington with Van de Steeg, we met at Butterfield 9, a swank place that is kitty-corner from my office. I thanked him for coaching me before Benning, showed him snapshots from my week of training, and gave him a copy of our swan song, which had him guffawing. Then we got down to the business of whether our country was going to war—though if he knew, he wasn't about to tell me. Still, I kept peppering him with questions even as we were saying good-bye in a brisk wind at the corner of Fourteenth and F Streets.

What about weapons of mass destruction? I asked. How likely is it that I'm going to get zapped? He said that it was a roll of the dice; if the Iraqis used them, it would not be a blanket attack against all of the invading forces, but rather, a targeted attack, so I'd be in peril only if I was in the wrong place at the wrong time. He went on to say that chemical agents are difficult to dispense; heat and high winds can scatter them and render them useless. And he said that if atomic weapons were employed, and if I was at Ground Zero, I was shit out of luck; if I was further afield, my NBC gear would afford some protection from the radioactive fallout.

I crossed Fourteenth Street to return to the National Press Building, caught a crowded elevator, and noticed across from me a thick, middle-aged guy, sporting an elegant tweed jacket. He had a black and canary yellow lapel pin I'd never seen before. Prying into strangers' lives is old hat—or maybe I just wanted to shake the prospect of Armageddon—so I asked, "What's the pin?"

"First Cavalry," he answered.

"First Cav," I replied, trying to come off as someone in the know as I examined the pin, which bore the silhouette of a horse's head.

The exchange had me curious. Who was this man with a lined, leathery face, shock of reddish brown hair, and faint smile? He seemed approachable, so I told him my name and reached out to shake his hand.

"I'm Joe Galloway," he answered.

"You're . . . Joe . . . Galloway?" I practically stammered, stunned to meet the coauthor of *We Were Soldiers Once . . . and Young* so soon after meeting General Moore.

Galloway was getting off at the seventh floor, since he had just come on board at the Washington bureau of Knight Ridder Newspapers. "May I speak to you for a moment?" I asked, trailing behind him.

He was somebody I was supposed to look up, the friend of a good friend, Mike Ruby, the editorial page editor of the *Milwaukee Journal Sentinel*. With war in the offing, Ruby had urged me to give Galloway a call. I hadn't done it, though, since I was being spun in circles with suggestions to see this person and talk to that person. Washington—huge, labyrinthine, full of people coming and going, impossible to get your arms around—is like that. And I hated the idea of coming across as a leech.

But there he was, the living legend, hanging his hat in my own building. We talked about Ruby, Moore, boot camp, embedding, and, since I'm a red-blooded American woman, naturally in short order I worked Mel Gibson into the conversation. My favorite movie star had portrayed Moore in the movie. With so much to discuss, I asked Galloway to lunch and he agreed, so I gave him my business card. He had only one card left, and it had somebody else's name, company, phone number, and e-mail address scrawled on the back, but after considering it, he turned the card over to me anyway.

When I got back to my office on the ninth floor I immediately called Ruby, who e-mailed Galloway and praised my reporting abilities but underscored the obvious: she's never covered a war.

A week later I was in the press building lobby waiting for Galloway. I was so nervous that I'd forgotten a notebook, so I bummed some scrap paper from a lobby security guard. When the veteran war correspondent showed up, we walked over to Café 1401 in the venerable Willard Hotel. As if to prove that I wasn't a complete greenhorn, I handed him a copy of my boot camp story, which had made page one of my newspaper. He gave me a three-page memo and dove right into my piece, chuckling every so often, which I took as a promising indicator.

There was nothing funny about his memo, plainly titled, "Some Notes of Being a War Correspondent." It began with this sentence: "There are old war correspondents and bold war correspondents, but no old, bold war correspondents."

Cautionary and concise, Galloway's tips ran the gamut from what to bring to how to get along in the "totally different" military culture to what to do if, as an old editor of mine used to say, the fan hit the shit. He counseled bringing a compass ("so you will know which way to walk if you get left behind"), an extra pair of glasses ("One pair *will* break"), plastic bags for electronic gear ("Where you are going the sand is ever-present and ever invasive"), a big neckerchief ("a sand filter for your mouth as you roar through the wadis in a tank column"), a bottle of Louisiana hot sauce ("MREs taste like crap, generally speaking"), and at least two good books ("Much of war reporting involves waiting . . . and waiting . . . and waiting. Hours and days of waiting; seconds of sheer terror").

He advised that journalists dress like privates so as to blend in and not arouse interest from an enemy taking aim. "If you look different you may thus appear important to someone peering through a sniper scope. If he is low on ammo or short on time he will definitely shoot you first." He pointed out that privacy in a combat zone is practically nonexistent—and not to be desired. "Do not wander off by yourself to commune with nature on a clear desert night. As soon as you are over the hill, your unit will crank up and pull out—Murphy's Law of combat operations." He urged being alert at all times, keeping an eye out for bugs, critters, snakes, and scorpions. "You will have a very painful war if you are nursing a scorpion bite on your butt." Never pick up anything strange, he added. "It will likely blow up in your face." He counseled against lying down or falling asleep near a military vehicle. "It will leave suddenly and run over you. Happens to soldiers all the time."

Galloway, echoing what Van de Steeg had said, further instructed me not to whine, complain, or "huddle in shared misery with other reporters."

"You are there to cover soldiers," he reminded. "Spend your waking hours with them, listening to them. Find out where they come from back home. Put that in your stories."

The average enlisted soldier, he predicted, initially would find a journalist "an item of curiosity" and be interested in how we do our jobs and where our reports are published. "In a day or two you become, in his eyes, 'our goddamn reporter,' spoken with pride, not ridicule. You are the only civilian he will see in the field in a combat zone. You are a sign to him that someone outside the big green machine cares how he lives and how he dies. Do care. At the same time be aware that the GI, the grunt, has a perverse and often black sense of humor. He will pull your chain given the opportunity."

The last two paragraphs put a lump in my throat:

There is no way I can prepare someone who has never witnessed combat for the shock of the first sight of a badly wounded soldier, screaming in pain, begging for his mother. Or the sight of the face of a young soldier in death—a soldier of either side. You will learn to process the images and move on and do your job. But what you see in battle will never leave you.

In combat you may find that those around you need a helping hand. Do not shy away from an opportunity to act first as a concerned human being and later as a reporter. Help the wounded, if called to do so. Carry water or ammo or the dead if it seems needed. None of that violates either the Geneva Conventions or your objectivity as a journalist.

It was signed:

> Joe Galloway
> Vietnam 1965–1966, 1971, 1973, 1975
> Sri Lanka student revolution 1971
> India-Pakistan War 1971
> East Timor 1976

Desert Shield/Desert Storm 1990–1991
Haiti Incursion

His advice was blunter, darker, and more foreboding than anything I had heard during boot camp, when war seemed more "possible" than "probable." If the Army had spoon-fed me survival lessons at Benning, Galloway was ramming them down my throat with a tire iron and, like a concerned host, wondering if I liked the taste.

I was left to blurt out something I've never said to a man while dining alone. "Do you see any deficiencies?" I inquired, practically handing him a pair of scissors and inviting him to cut me into ribbons.

"None. None are apparent," he answered in a deep voice still tinged with a Texas twang. "But everybody is different on the battlefield."

We went on to talk about Pentagon big shots, the sadistic nature of Saddam Hussein, and the pros and cons of the various branches of the services with respect to embedding. I realized as we talked that Galloway was a very important personage—he seemed to be friendly with every general the Army has minted—and before an hour had passed I got the feeling he'd had his fill of a minor figure like me, so I fumbled to find a credit card, summoned the waiter, paid hastily, and headed back to the building with him. When he stopped out front for a smoke, I got to hang out with him a little longer, talking about this and that while he indulged in a small, taupe-colored cigar.

Afterward I thanked him and was off, feeling as though I was stepping down from Mount Olympus after my first and last audience before the guy in charge. But in coming days, I'd see Galloway again and again and again. With every diplomatic belly flop from New York to Baghdad, the war inched closer, and I started smoking again. Outside the building with the other nicotine addicts, I'd stumble into the man I came to call "Zeus" as he took a drag on one of those light brown numbers.

He laughed at my nickname for him, countering, "I think Thor would be more appropriate."

Still I called him Zeus, and privately added him to my war council, which now stood at three: Sando, from Benning; Van de Steeg, from the Pentagon; and Galloway, from south Texas, from battlefields of Asia and the Middle East and from Hollywood's big screen—the only civilian awarded a Bronze Star with a V for valor during Vietnam. He'd won it for rescuing wounded soldiers under fire in the Ia Drang Valley in 1965.

With these three—two officers and one civilian, gentlemen all—I would never lack for advice or encouragement. Entrenched in the military, each made time for a rookie to their game, and what meant the most to me was this: they trusted that I could pull it off.

When I lunched with Galloway, I had no way of knowing that in twenty-five days, I'd be shipping out.

*   *   *

With the Pentagon poised to hand out assignments, I struggled with the same question that naïve, fresh-faced teens confront in strip-mall recruiting stations from Maine to California: Would it be the Army, Navy, Air Force, or Marines?

With Van de Steeg's help, I mentally crossed the Air Force off the list, since he assured me that the living conditions in that branch of the service would be relatively cushy. The Marines gave me a weird, gung-ho vibe. And there was no way I was going to leave God's green earth for a little anchors aweigh with the Navy, not after an encounter I had with some wild animals on leave from a U.S. naval destroyer moored in Zihuatanejo, Mexico. Vacationing alone on the Pacific Coast, I was in a nirvana state on an inflatable raft in the pool at the Sheraton Ixtapa when a bunch of libertine sailors flipped over my float as a way of introducing themselves. I was traveling solo and I ended up hanging out with them for a bit, until it dawned on me that these guys wanted to get laid more than teenaged boys after imbibing a case of Bud Light. My recollection of those sailors—*muy loco*—torpedoed the Navy's chances.

Since both my father and grandfather had served in the Army, the oldest and largest of the armed services was my sentimental choice. Not that Dad ever got behind me; he was, in fact, my biggest antagonist.

"It will be a short, triumphal war," I tried to assure him during a phone call, echoing Washington's Pollyannas. He wasn't buying it, knowing the assignment was risky business. His reply? "We had a saying in the war: 'I'd rather be a living coward than a dead hero.'"

I'd never seen my father lose a fight, but I dug in my heels. While I wanted his approval, I hardly needed his permission. He ended the stalemate by hurtling a verbal hand grenade, snarling, "Even your husband can't control you."

Great, I thought. I'm an idiot and my husband's a wimp. But since my father had been overprotective of me all of my life, I tried to ignore the hurt.

Going to war, I was finding, was like wading into ocean waters, splashing water on my thighs and shoulders until the goose bumps went away, being carried off by currents—and going with the flow rather than deciding to swim back to the safety of the beach.

Soon I found myself giving a couple of interviews about boot camp and indicating to fellow journalists, "Yes, I'll cover a war, if it comes to that." After such declarations I felt that if I backed out, I would be not only weak-kneed (which I could forgive) but a blowhard (which I could not).

One night, with a girlfriend from boot camp, I went to a National Press

Club program on war coverage. Galloway and some other big-name correspondents were speaking, so I brought along his book and asked him to sign it. He wrote: "With best wishes to a fellow scribbler—and soon-to-be war correspondent." Yikes, I thought, that's what I'm going to be, a war correspondent! If nothing else, I couldn't let Zeus down.

Finally I had the long telephone conversation with my mom, spelling out all the things that I had going for me—a track record of foreign reporting, a taste of military life, a modicum of training, and the law of averages. I reminded her that I wasn't getting any younger, remarking, "Mom, when I'm fifty, the Army's not going to take me by the hand and say, 'Hey, Kathy, come to war with us!' "

My mind made up, I still had much to do, and I was continuing to churn out stories on politics and government while preparing for the biggest story of my life. I hated the idea of writing a will for the first time, then deadline pressure kicked in and one day I sketched it out on the subway after work. It took about twenty minutes to divvy up my assets among loved ones and select a few charities; for the latter, I left money to every school I ever attended, from kindergarten at St. Andrew the Apostle School to Harvard. Through a friend, I found a first-rate local lawyer, who coincidentally was from my hometown, and made it official.

At the same time I researched bulletproof vests, telephoning my policeman brother's colleague as well as sources at the Bureau of Alcohol, Tobacco, and Firearms for advice. I even called my dental hygienist's husband, who works on a SWAT team in suburban Virginia. I ended up going with an outfit in Texas that had passed muster with several other news organizations, worrying a bit because it seemed to me that most flak vests weren't designed for people with breasts.

The process of getting my gear together began to seem like a nonstop scavenger hunt. One weekend Tom and I took refuge from the gathering storm at a hotel on Maryland's eastern shore, where a brilliant sun lit up blue winter skies and the bone-cold waters of Chesapeake Bay. We luxuriated in spa treatments, drank Bloody Marys by the fire, and had some ha-cha-cha in a spacious room overlooking the water.

After we checked out on Sunday morning, the afterglow was short-lived. Our getaway was near a Wal-Mart, so we stopped there and I began picking up the odd assortment of items recommended by the Rangers at Benning: cough syrup containing guaifenesin, an antifungal solution containing tolnaftate, insect repellant with DEET, a Zippo lighter, a Leatherman knife.

My boot camp friend, Debby Block from Voice of America, turned me on to a military surplus store in Fairfax, Virginia, where the shelves groaned with desert-camouflage uniforms (DCUs), canteens, and miniature red lights, smaller than a tiny light on a Christmas tree, which I needed for times of so-called light discipline, when any light more powerful was forbidden so as not to tip off the enemy about our location. The DCUs, like the bulletproof vests, were cut for men, and I had only one thought when I put on the pants and the shirt and saw myself in the mirror: "I look like Norman Schwarzkopf." I plunked down a credit card and promised myself that I would take my DCU to a tailor.

More familiar haunts, like L.L.Bean in Tyson's Corner, Virginia, were finding their stores of khaki-colored sportswear and high-performance socks depleted by employees of the Pentagon, the CIA, and the State Department. Bush hadn't declared war, but the massive buildup had begun, and people planning a trip to Iraq were stocking up.

On February 12, 2003, the Pentagon offered my newspaper four choices: the Army's 101st Airborne, the 1st Marine Expeditionary Force, an Air Force base in Al Udeid in Qatar, and an unspecified "maritime" slot with the Navy.

I phoned my war counselors and, if they weren't in, shot them e-mail messages. In short order I'd received a unanimous vote for the "Screaming Eagles." So much about prospective battle plans was published in the papers, practically daily, and the consensus was that with the 101st, I'd go deep into enemy territory. "Tell them you want a far-forward unit," Sando advised. "You want infantry or aviation."

My editors gave me the green light to go with the 101st, while another reporter at my paper opted for the Marines and a photographer toyed with hooking up with the Air Force.

After e-mailing my choice, I stepped outside my building and walked over to an Episcopal church close to my office, a refuge for the rare times I need to talk to God during business hours, just as I did during the week of 9-11, when a memorial service there on Friday, September 14, was so thick with people it could have used a traffic cop.

Afterward I called the public affairs shop at Fort Campbell to introduce myself, but it was late in the afternoon, so the top people were gone. I told a sergeant that I would be e-mailing that evening a letter of introduction, résumé, some military stories I'd written in the past, and a letter of recommendation from boot camp (penned, naturally, by Sando).

The whole process was like an endurance race. First you lobby to get into boot camp; next you try to finagle from Pentagon types a spot in a good unit, and finally, after you've gotten your unit, you introduce yourself all over again, strutting your stuff, thumping your chest and practically letting out a Tarzan scream.

The next day I followed up by phoning the 101st's top public affairs boss, Major Hugh C. Cate III, a West Pointer whose Army lineage is six generations deep. Parroting Sando, I announced: "I want a far-forward unit. I want infantry or aviation." I was trying to send a message that even though I was a woman, I did not want to report on nurses, machinists, petroleum supply specialists, cartographers, computer dudes, or bandage rollers.

Cate, an amiable guy, asked me what I knew about the infantry. Before I could answer, he proceeded to tell me. "They're 'dirt darts,'" he said. "They're 'ground pounders.' We call 'em 'earth pigs.'" He went on to say that trudging through desert sand is tough; it would be no walk in the park. Finally he cut to the chase, asking me what kind of physical shape I was in. I told him that I was in "pretty good shape but no Miss America," so he put me in aviation. Cate and the other public affairs folks at Campbell were coy about when we might depart, but urged us to be ready. "Use the time you have left," he counseled, "to hit the gym."

When I hung up, I remembered Art Kroos, a veteran I'd interviewed years ago in Wisconsin as the fiftieth anniversary of D-Day neared. He had parachuted into German-held territory in Normandy on the wings of the 82nd Airborne the night before the invasion. Kroos, remembering his youthful impulse, explained to me why he'd signed up with an airborne unit, never before tested in combat. He said all these fancy college boys were being trained as pilots, and going airborne would fatten his paycheck by fifty bucks a month, so ultimately he concluded, "Why walk to work when you can fly?"

The bulletproof vest ended up costing my company $1,800 and the helmet, $295. They arrived in a big box via FedEx one Saturday morning, and I hauled the parcel into a spare room and shut the door. I was curious about whether they fit, but I didn't dare try them on in front of Tom, fearing the look on his face. Much later in the day I asked him if he minded if I put them on. We placed the heavy, protective ceramic plates in the front and back of the vest, and I tried it on for size. It fit, but the damn thing was heavy: twenty-two pounds. It was a weird yellow green, like an old Crayola color that was retired because it matched no natural creation on earth, except perhaps for seaweed suffering from acute anemia.

As I was fretting about the war, my gear, my safety, and my uncertain departure date, Tom was doing his own thing. He was training hard for the American Birkebeiner, a fifty-one-kilometer cross-country ski race in northern Wisconsin. Frequenting the gym, sometimes with me in tow, helped him to get in shape and take his mind off of his increasingly nervous wife and her war preparations.

It was Tom's twentieth year competing in the race, which was to be held on Saturday, February 22—the weekend before I was to report to Campbell. I contemplated asking him to skip it, wanting his company and some major-league hand-holding, but there was no way that I could suggest he call off a weekend trip to Wisconsin when I was heading off to war in the Persian Gulf for God knew how long.

As my departure date grew near, I e-mailed Galloway and told him that I'd gotten an assignment with an aviation unit within the 101st. He seemed pumped, replying, "Yee-haw. You go, girl. Have a good, safe war."

His response startled me. If the assignment got Galloway's juices flowing, what was I in for? And I wondered why he used the adjective "good" in front of the noun "war." What kind of company was I keeping? I asked myself. I thought war was evil.

Next were exchanges with my other two war counselors. Van de Steeg issued a no-nonsense send-off. "Don't take the counsel of your fears regarding your ability to keep up with the young soldiers. You can't. And you don't have to." Sando reminded me that whatever happened, I should look around from time to time and savor the memories, since I'd be making history. As part of the 1st Ranger Battalion, he'd taken part in the surprise invasion of Grenada to put down a left-wing coup in 1983, and an older officer had given him the same advice he was giving me now.

Sando went on to say that I should do whatever I wanted before deploying, but before my mind could really run wild with that idea, he added: "If you want a cheeseburger, have a cheeseburger, because you won't have one for a while."

I don't even like cheeseburgers that much, but with Tom gone I started eating them—in between smoking Marlboro Light 100s.

I'm a climb-every-mountain person who confronts new challenges by devouring information. So during the weeks before deployment I carted home an armload of books from the public library in McLean, Virginia. The fact that it's just down Dolley Madison Road from the CIA might explain why all the Saddam Hussein biographies and every book on Iraqi geopolitics were checked out. In their place I toted home books such as Sun-tzu's *The Art of War* and what little I could find on travel in Iraq, mostly picture books but none past the level of a sixth grader, since Frommer and Fodor apparently weren't setting foot in the place.

Paging through the military tomes, I learned that war never goes according to the textbook—not a comforting thought. Still, I kept leafing through the books, since doing so gave me an excuse to lie on my couch in the quiet solitude of my living room and avoid thinking about the Kuwaiti visa and the digital camera and the power-of-attorney documents and the dozen other things I was waiting to have settled.

Packing should have been my number one priority, but I kept putting it off; I'd just haphazardly stuff things like high-performance socks and bungee cords and canteen covers and a camouflage poncho into a backpack in the spare room.

Instead of loading up and preparing to move out, I whiled away chunks of my last weekend at home, lying on the sofa and reading or watching the HBO series *Band of Brothers,* based on Steven Ambrose's book (which my managing editor had recommended). Occasionally I dashed off e-mail messages to my siblings and friends, speaking from the heart in these quick good-byes—"You're one of my favorite friends of all time" or "You know I really love you"—and usually tearing up before hitting "Send," pondering whether this would be the last time I'd communicate with my siblings Tom and Steve and Nancy and John and friends like Jeff and Diane.

When Tom got back from his ski race on Sunday night, I made dinner for him. Putting on an apron was a nod to normalcy and a way of pretending that I could do it all—while preparing for battle, I could still manage to turn out a respectable chicken almandine.

Only on the morning of my departure to Fort Campbell, where I would be staying for an unknown number of days before deploying, did I finally get around to packing. I set the alarm for four o'clock, in fact, and was soon amazed at the sheer stupidity of my waiting so long to count out tampons and pour Pepto-Bismol into plastic travel-sized bottles and rummage through my compact discs.

Tom saw me in high-anxiety mode and volunteered to help. When he eyed the poor excuse I had for a sleeping-bag pad, he tore out the door to a camping-equipment store to buy a state-of-the-art, self-inflating thing that set my newspaper back $80.

We'd blocked off enough time before my flight to make love, so I swept the boots and backpack and bulletproof vest from our queen-sized bed for what was, give or take a few minutes, a quickie—more than a Hallmark greeting card, less than a scene from a Harlequin novel. I clutched Tom so tightly I might have left marks. Tears raining down my cheeks and dampening the sheets, I was transfixed by one heart-breaking worry: Will this time be the last?

3

Band of Brothers

The three of them were huddled in a booth in the Horseshoe Steak House, a white clapboard joint a few paces off Highway 41A in Hopkinsville, Kentucky. An old-time place—"Family owned and operated since 1968"—it featured a jukebox, a badly worn carpet, plastic tablecloths, and attentive waitresses with syrupy drawls who said, "Thanks, hon," an awful lot.

Raucous sounds emanated from a bar in the back, but the dining room was practically empty, since it was getting on nine on a Tuesday night. As I took a seat at a table, I couldn't help noticing the fortyish woman washing down beer straight from a bottle, stopping now and again to snap pictures of the young man with a shaved head, whom I took to be her son. I figured he was about to ship out with the 101st Airborne to the Middle East. A rail-thin woman in a Harley T-shirt and long, stringy dark hair, she was more voluble than the thicker, gray-headed stoic who sat across from her, whom I took to be her husband, perhaps the soldier's father.

I was by myself, content to unwind in a homey little place after a taxing day that had begun with the near-fiasco of my packing before dawn on the very day of my departure. Tom had driven me to Reagan National Airport, where our parting hug and kiss were brief and disappointing—although how romantic could I expect a curbside farewell to be, especially since I was the one walking away from my husband, albeit temporarily, in the name of career?

Once Tom drove off, I could have used a Sherpa, since I had practically enough stuff to fit in a small U-Haul trailer. This fact did not escape the notice of U.S. Airways, whose agent nailed me for $50 for excess baggage. I was traveling on Flight 4031B to Nashville, about fifty miles from Fort Campbell, where the 101st Airborne Division makes its headquarters. My plane was stuck behind several others awaiting takeoff, prompting a flight attendant to get on the public-address system and announce, "We should be airborne shortly."

"Airborne, indeed," I said under my breath, wondering how she divined that I was about to "marry up," as some in the military called this stage of the game, with the 101st. Arguably a curious phrase, the expression meant a journalist would meet and attach to a particular outfit.

It was twilight when I landed in Tennessee, and as I drove a rental car up Interstate 24 through the Cumberland River Valley, I reveled at the sight of limestone bluffs and dense forests. When I put on the radio, some honky-tonk song was on—which was fine by me, since my nerves were beginning to settle for the first time in days. There was no turning back now—and that brought a wave of relief. No more anxious waiting for the digital camera shipped from the newsroom in Milwaukee, for the visa from Kuwait's information office in the Watergate Hotel, and for the penicillin-allergy medical-alert necklace from the jeweler, who had to engrave a second drug, "sulfa," to make me good to go. Nor would there be any more wrenching good-byes.

I was staying in a Holiday Inn that had seen better days in Hopkinsville— "Hoptown" to soldiers—a city of 33,000 and the seat of Christian County in the southwestern reaches of the Bluegrass State. I knew better than to complain about the cheerless accommodations, seeing them for what they were, the last place I'd enjoy plumbing and pillows and a big bed for weeks. As soon as I'd gotten into my room, I telephoned the 101st's public affairs shop, whose staff had been, up until then, hush-hush about just where I was supposed to be the next morning to begin the orientation program for embedded journalists. At last the details were divulged: I was to be in place at eight o'clock at Shoney's restaurant just down U.S. 41A, a stretch known as Fort Campbell Boulevard. It seemed like a strange place to join the Army, and, being spoiled from some elegant morning meals with Washington newsmakers, I had to ask, "Is this a breakfast meeting?" Negative.

At the Horseshoe that evening, I was grateful for the solitude and the Middle American menu and the Patsy Cline songs, but I found myself ineluctably drawn to the booth where the two people I judged to be parents were bidding farewell to their son, especially when the mother stopped snapping her camera. That's when the family got down to brass tacks.

What if the son died? Where did he want to be buried? Would he prefer to be cremated? Did he want full military honors, with a twenty-one-gun salute, at Arlington National Cemetery?

The son settled on Arlington—in the Virginia suburb I'd just left—though the conversation clearly was pained, not the usual banter over charbroiled porterhouses and loaded baked potatoes. "It's not easy for me, either," the mother protested at one point.

The older man, as if to make peace, steered the conversation away from the specter of his soldier's remains being flown home in a body bag. He imagined him returning to a hero's welcome, saying to the younger man, "You could get the Congressional Medal of Honor."

"Well, let's just not try to get that one," the mother rejoined.

"There's the Bronze Star, too," the older man said.

I began cryptically jotting down notes, gathering string for a story I would try to weave together before taking off for the Middle East, though my departure date remained very much up in the air. No matter how poignant this triptych, I couldn't bring myself to mosey over to the family, merrily introduce myself, and mention that I, too, was deploying, and had they heard about the embedded journalists tagging along?

It seemed gauche to butt into this family's farewell dinner and funeral planning session, so I kept my mouth shut, fed a dollar into the jukebox, and waited for my salad and queen-sized filet mignon and baked potato with sour cream—selections I deemed suitable in light of Lieutenant Colonel Sando's prescription: "Do whatever you want."

Some people think reporters behave like scavengers, just flying in circles over humanity's Dumpster and regarding every scrap beneath their claws to be fair game. But that's not true. We do have standards; they just vary from person to person. I remember turning up my nose when I was covering the schoolyard shootings in Jonesboro, Arkansas, in 1998 and overheard a woman from the *New York Daily News* bragging to other reporters that she'd bought a dress in town just so she could sneak into a funeral home—expressly off-limits to the press—for a memorial service for one of the four dead girls. I thought her move was tasteless, and wondered why she'd taken the trouble when all she seemed to get for trespassing was the fact that some teen bubblegum song was played that made people cry buckets. Compounding the reporter's poor judgment was her stupidity: here she was, guilelessly coughing up details of her exclusive for the rest of us, though I wouldn't touch it.

The threesome left the Horseshoe before I did, but I bumped into them several minutes later in the parking lot, where the parents were transferring boxes from the son's truck to their minivan. His Ford F-150 was next to my rental car, and he seemed to be handing over his television and stereo equipment—maybe everything he owned, for all I knew. He and I came face to face as I was about to slide into my car, and I could only think to say, "Be safe," just as a freight train trundled down a distant track and its melancholy whistle pierced the cold, moist night.

The next morning, Wednesday, February 26, a snowstorm dropped giant, feathery flakes over the region—icy crystals so lush and gorgeous they seemed straight out of a televised Christmas special. It was a curious meteorological statement since, by then, I knew sandstorms were ahead for me. After I brushed the snow off my car, I rushed over to Shoney's with only minutes to spare. When I entered the restaurant, dozens of reporters and photographers were jammed in the waiting area, all of them wearing insouciant faces and pricey all-weather gear. Sizing up the square-shouldered assemblage, I practically gasped. "It's all guys," I thought to myself. "Where are the girls?"

Some soldiers in desert camo fatigues mingled among us, shaking hands, while one with a clipboard crisply checked off who among the fifty-six embeds had shown up, since a few journalists already had left for the Middle East. The mystery of why we were to meet at Shoney's was revealed when one of the minders explained that it was chosen for its huge parking lot; we'd be boarding buses to take us past the guardhouse at Fort Campbell and dropped off at day's end to retrieve our vehicles. Like other military facilities, Campbell was placing a high premium on security at the installation, especially during the run-up to war.

Once on the buses, we rumbled through Campbell to the Eagle Conference Room, where we sat for photos for our identification badges and gathered at a U-shaped table, where the good-natured Major Hugh Cate was poised to welcome the volunteers who had signed up for the ride of their lives, in my case, at least, without so much as hazardous-duty pay. Thirty-eight years old, Cate was tall and husky with a low, booming voice. Physically, he brought to mind Hoss Cartwright from the old TV show *Bonanza*, and that's how I came to regard him—beneath a tough exterior, he seemed to empathize with his new charges and understand their line of work.

"I am your tour guide for the next six, eight, ten months, however long you want to stay with us," he began, extending the timetable for embeds that the Pentagon had suggested, which was a minimum of three to four weeks.

"We're glad you're here. We want to get the story of the 101st out. We're going to be moving fast and furious for the next seventy-two hours.

"We have forty-nine chartered aircraft taking soldiers to the area of operations. On Thursday afternoon, you will meet up with your unit, and at some point after that, you will leave with your unit.

"I consider you part of the team starting today."

The embeds ran the gamut from television and radio broadcasters to newspaper reporters from the *New York Times* all the way to Hopkinsville's *Kentucky New Era*. There were writers for wire services, such as the Associated Press and Reuters, plus foreign correspondents from England, Germany, Norway, Japan, Singapore, and Peru. I had met some of my new colleagues earlier, like Rick Atkinson of the *Washington Post*, a reporter turned military historian. I also knew two of the women from boot camp, Kirsten

Scharnberg from the *Chicago Tribune* and Kimberly Hefling from the AP in Evansville, Indiana; and at Campbell I met another woman, Chantal Escoto from the *Leaf Chronicle* out of Clarksville, Tennessee.

Cate urged us to speak up and ask questions during the briefings, boasting, "I'm bulletproof. I can take anything you shoot at me."

I was at that point examining the large black-and-white photos on the walls that depicted some of the 101st Airborne's finest moments. One shot featured General Maxwell D. Taylor, who commanded the unit during its baptism by fire at D-Day and whose son, Thomas, an author and former colonel with the 101st, I'd heard was going to be embedded. It made me feel small: "My dad was an enlisted man and restaurateur. Your dad was a two-star general, chairman of the joint chiefs of staff, and ambassador to South Vietnam."

Cate left stage center so we could watch a short film, *When We Were Needed,* whose grainy black-and-white images recounted the history of the Screaming Eagles, with music intended to get your blood pumping. The film quoted the division's first commander, Major General William C. Lee, Taylor's predecessor, telling his men that while the unit had no history, it had "a rendezvous with destiny," a phrase that remains the motto of the 101st.

We saw footage of a multitude of paratroopers descending from the treacherous skies above Normandy in the hours leading up to Operation Overlord as well as scenes from the Battle of the Bulge, the last major Nazi offensive during the Second World War. During that fight, the Screaming Eagles found themselves low on food and ammunition in Bastogne, Belgium, where they were surrounded by German troops. The Eagles' dire straits led the enemy commander to deliver an ultimatum for their surrender, prompting Brigadier General Anthony C. McAuliffe of the 101st to famously reply, "Nuts!"

We watched scenes from Vietnam, where in 1965 the 101st was one of the early units to deploy and during the next six-plus years, its soldiers engaged in heavy fighting in more than fifteen campaigns, contributing a lingering image from the war: soldiers scrambling out of the division's Huey helicopters and into the fray.

There were scenes from the first Persian Gulf War, with a salute to the 101st's star player, Richard A. Cody, who, as a lieutenant colonel, fired the opening salvo in Operation Desert Storm. Now a four-star general, Cody, with other Apache attack-helicopter pilots, had launched Hellfire missiles to take out two Iraqi early-warning radar sites, opening a twenty-mile-wide corridor into Baghdad so 100 U.S. Air Force bombers could commence a punishing air campaign.

And we saw video from the humanitarian, disaster-relief, and peacekeeping missions that have dispatched the 101st to places such as the Sinai

Peninsula, Somalia, Panama, Haiti, Bosnia, and Kosovo. Only one major fight, the war in Afghanistan, was missing, since the ink still was drying on the story of that conflict. Some Screaming Eagles, in fact, had been home for only twenty-two days from a tour of duty rooting out al-Qaida operatives before shipping out for Kuwait, the primary staging ground for the invasion of Iraq.

By the time the film was over, I was furtively brushing tears from the corner of my eyes. God, country, sacrifice—that stuff invariably choked me up, especially when set to patriotic music. I don't know where I picked that up; maybe it was from Dad, who served a term as commander of the American Legion Post 330 when I was growing up in Calumet City, Illinois.

After the film we were given the lowdown on Fort Campbell, a 105,000-acre facility whose beginnings, as Camp Campbell, date to 1941 when the United States entered World War II. Its namesake is William B. Campbell, who was a hero of the Mexican War (1846–1848), member of Congress, judge, Tennessee governor, and briefly a brigadier general for the Union during the Civil War. Although nearly two-thirds of Fort Campbell lies in Tennessee, its address is Kentucky, because that's where its post office stands. The base's premier runway, we were told, stretches two-and-a-half miles, long enough to handle the space shuttle—but since the *Columbia* had blown up five weeks earlier, hosting the shuttle surely wasn't in the cards.

Next, another briefer took the floor to discuss anthrax. He told us it was "the most likely biological warfare agent. It's odorless, colorless, tasteless, and difficult to detect. And one good breath is enough to kill you." Then soldiers distributed our gas masks and NBC gear.

Later we turned in liability waivers, which held the United States of America harmless if we were wounded or killed while embedded, and reviewed the ground rules. Cate said he wanted us to have as much access as possible to precombat briefings and actual operations, but there were some restrictions. The commanders of our units would decide how our datelines—which announced where we were—would read. We weren't to release specific troop counts or the number of aircraft as well as the names of the soldiers who were injured or pilots who were downed.

We were advised that conditions in the Kuwaiti desert would be primitive, with MREs for meals, showers maybe once every twelve days, and, at the outset, possibly not even tents. And we were reminded to check our boots every morning for scorpions.

In recent weeks, roughly 3,500 soldiers a day had been departing from Campbell on commercial aircraft. Altogether, the division was sending about 14,500 men and women, joined by support elements from other active-duty and reserve units, bringing the total number under the banner of the 101st to approximately 24,000. Meanwhile, 5,800 pieces of equipment had been sent by rail to Jacksonville, Florida, for transport on freighters by sea to the Middle East—including, I later learned on my own, a helluva lot of firepower. The division had shipped enough ammunition to fill eighty-one sixteen-wheel semi–tractor trailers.

"If the president decides to take action, the 101st will be deep inside the enemy's territory," Cate assured us. "I don't know what the president is going to do, but if we get the order, we're going to hit the ground yelling and screaming. If not, we're going to have a good training exercise."

If there's action and you feel you're in too deep, finding yourself unable to keep up with twenty-year-olds carrying seventy-pound rucksacks, we'll talk, Cate said. Meantime, "take a big bite of out the 'patience cheeseburger,'" he advised, since (in my words, not his) hurry-up-and-wait is practically an Army mantra.

Once back at the Holiday Inn, I had plenty to do. I needed to telephone my photo editors for instructions on how to use the camera, which had arrived at my home via FedEx the very day I left. I also wanted to test the satellite phone, which had shown up about a week earlier than the camera but seemed too scary to try out, like I was being asked to conduct brain surgery. And I had a story to file.

First, though, I thought I'd clear my head and grab some food, and on my way out I made a detour into the hotel bar, not for a drink, but for a book of matches. I needed a smoke. In the lounge I saw a vaguely familiar face. It was Matt Cox from *Army Times,* whom I'd sat next to all day. He was a smooth-skinned, thirtyish guy with brown hair and glasses, of medium height, and ultrafit. Cox asked me if I wanted a drink—that took a nanosecond to decide—and fetched me a gin and tonic. After a bit of conversation, he invited me to join a group of embeds who were about to leave for dinner. My to-do list can wait, I thought, opting to join his lively, all-male group for food, drink, storytelling, and a post-mortem on the first day.

Two of our tablemates were television journalists from Britain's Sky News. The youngest in the group, a twenty-three-year-old from the United States, provided the evening's entertainment by regaling us with the story of the year he spent in college living in an apartment with four women, bedding down three of them one by one—and getting kicked out by the fourth. "She didn't want to be last!" Cox bellowed. I wasn't surprised to discover that the raconteur was a photographer; I'd learned long ago that some lensmen fancy themselves real Romeos.

That night, I suspect, you could have gone around the table and squeezed a tantalizing confession out of each of us. But the rest of us were too savvy to play "Truth or Dare?" with professional colleagues who were strangers, really. So we refused to take Romeo's bait and talked instead about where we'd been on assignment before and what we anticipated embedding would be like.

Cox, I learned, was thirty-five years old and newer to journalism than I, but what he lacked in newspapering he made up for in soldiering. He was a veteran of the Army's 82nd Airborne Division and, as a civilian journalist, had made several reporting trips to cover the U.S. military, notably during the war in Afghanistan.

All in all it was a fun night and I was happy for the unexpected company and glad to be turning in at a decent hour.

The next morning I had an early wake-up call. Getting dog tags was my priority before going back on post. I stopped at U.S. Cavalry, a military store across from Gate Four, one of Campbell's main entrances. The store hadn't even opened, but a small crowd of soldiers—some in fatigues, some in civvies—were milling around outside, many of them having a morning smoke. Everybody seemed just like me, pressed for time and desperate for one more thingamabob.

As I waited, I peered through the windows and studied the merchandise. I noticed a T-shirt depicting three soldiers, one of them apparently dead. The fallen man's rucksack was split open and the two comrades, carrying rifles, charged past him on either side. Quoting the pair of gung-ho survivors, the shirt read: "If you die first, we split your gear." The cartoon had me snickering: I liked the dark humor; I also admired the fight-to-the-death spirit.

At precisely eight o'clock a clerk unlocked the doors and I rushed over to get dog tags, not wanting to be a minute late for Day Two. The woman doing the engraving misspelled my name—"CATHERINE"—but it hardly mattered; she got the important things right: my Social Security number, blood type, and rekindled religious preference (Catholic).

Next I tried to find a camelback, which one of Cate's colleagues had recommended. Sort of an ultramodern canteen, the device consists of a plastic water pouch in a carrier that runs down your spine and a long tube that lets you drink hands-free. There wasn't a single one left. Many of the shelves, in fact, seemed eerily empty, like when there's panic-buying before a major storm and the milk and toilet paper and bread vanish. I considered buying the funny T-shirt, but had second thoughts, remembering what David Wood, a veteran war correspondent from Newhouse News Service, had recommended the embedded journalists write down on the cover of every notebook: "I am not one of them."

Back in the Eagle Conference Room, I breezed past the lascivious photographer and called out something provocative, like "Hey, sexy!"—probably a bit too loudly in light of all the paid, professional observers within earshot. My name-calling was a joke—it was the opposite of how I thought of him—but heads were turning, so I slunk into a seat next to Cox and put on the demeanor of a bright-eyed reporter, hungry for the breakfast of military champions: more briefings.

Cox and I, after a single day, were friends. As we sat in the conference room, we began to trade murmurs about the material being presented; before long, we were discreetly dissecting our classmates and handlers in whispered asides. This being the South, we judged some people "hee-haw," and this being a group that took in some professional heavyweights, we decided others were "pretentious." Cox could barely contain himself when I tilted my head toward one of the female embeds and muttered, "She looks rode hard and put away wet." He didn't disagree.

The topics on Day Two were a mixed bag: Iraqi geopolitics, desert health hazards, and incidentals, like General Order Number One, which forbade, among other things, the "introduction, possession, sale, transfer, manufacture, or consumption of any alcoholic beverage" while deployed. Informally it was known as the "If it feels good, don't do it" order.

Afterward we traipsed over to Dreyer Field House and stood in line for the immunizations that were not available to the general public. After talking to my family doctor, I was dead set against getting an anthrax vaccine; instead, in case I got whacked, I had with me a sixty-day supply of the antibiotic Cipro. Still, Colonel Stephen Jones, a cardiologist who commands the base hospital, was persuasive about the protection being important and the shot having no ill effects. So I signed another liability waiver, holding Uncle Sam harmless if I had a bad reaction, slapped down $94.96, and waited my turn. Minutes after being injected, my upper arm stung, but it was nothing I couldn't take. Kirsten Scharnberg, from the *Tribune,* was next in line and asked me how it was. "Not bad," I said.

Scharnberg was a pretty, petite blond not yet out of her mid-twenties. The minute she got her shot, she tumbled onto the floor and I watched as her face turned ashen. I went over, sank to my knees, and asked her what I could do as the medical staff attended her. She groggily asked me to call her boss, the *Trib*'s foreign editor, which I did, trying to give him the facts in the "Oh it's no big deal" way a kindergarten teacher reports a concussion on the playground. In truth, I was worried.

Her swoon sent John Partipilo, a photographer for the *Tennessean* out of Nashville, into action. He began shooting one photo after another of Scharnberg spaced out on the floor. Ten minutes or so went by before she was sitting up on a stretcher and her cheeks were rosy again. Once she was back on her feet, Partipilo played back the digital images stored in his camera—shots that prompted Scharnberg to roar at him and the other lensmen, "You god-damn jackals!" Perhaps she was still too woozy to note the irony of a newsperson taking umbrage at news coverage in a business where it's some-times said, "If it bleeds, it leads."

Colonel Jones pronounced the fainting spell a vasovagal reaction, a re-flex triggered by pain, as happens to some people when their blood is drawn. The heart rate goes down, the vision grays out, and sometimes the person experiences nausea. Trying to be more discreet than Partipilo, I began tak-ing notes to include Scharnberg's misfortune in my story.

The episode threw us off schedule, making us late in returning to the con-ference room, where we were to meet with representatives of our units, such as infantry, artillery, or aviation. I was joining the 159th Aviation Brigade, a helicopter-heavy unit that flies infantry soldiers into combat and supplies and equipment to the front lines. The brigade's liaison, Captain Sean Con-nolly, a lawyer with the Judge Advocate General Corps, did not appear pleased to see me. He was peeved. I tried to tell him that I thought a battle buddy came first, but he just looked at me icily.

Eight of the fifty-six embeds on hand were assigned to the 159th, and fol-lowing Connolly's instructions, we followed him in our cars (by then we'd gotten passes allowing us to drive onto the base) to the brigade's spare, one-story headquarters a couple of miles away. There an old Black Hawk was chained to a tall pedestal, enshrined, so to speak.

Colonel William H. Forrester, the brigade's top boss, had already left for the so-called area of operations, or AOR, leaving other brass, including Major Alex Covert, Forrester's Number Two man, to greet us.

We sank into chairs at a conference table. Just as the meeting was about to kick off, a balding, bespectacled, moon-faced man in fatigues entered the room, waving an arm theatrically and calling out an oversized hello.

"Hello, Father George!" Covert returned the greeting. Everybody in uni-form assembled in the room seemed pleased to see Major Jerzy Rzasowski, who was introduced as the brigade chaplain.

I'd never before seen a Catholic priest in desert camouflage, but I knew an opening when I saw one. Up until then most of the officers I'd met seemed like Captain Connolly: tamper-resistant and schmooze-proof. That left me, one of the new kids on the block, with very little room to maneuver beyond springing for the tab for a sergeant or major when we broke for lunch at one of the Burger Kings dotting the base. So I blurted out a foreign-language greeting to the chaplain, trying to speak Polish, then realizing I was jabber-ing in Russian before managing to spit out some Polish. The others in the room gazed at me quizzically—it probably didn't help that I was the only woman among the eight reporters and photographers—as if trying to decide whether I was a spy, a showboat, or a freak.

Father George answered me in Polish, and then resumed speaking English. "I am praying for support for the troops," he told us. "My boss, the pope, is praying for peace. And if the Iraqis don't want peace, we'll make it."

Good quotes, I thought, taking down his remarks. A Polish-American priest would play well among my Milwaukee readership.

Covert, a barrel-chested man with a wrestler's build and crew cut, then got down to business. "We look forward to the adventure we're about to go on," he began drily. "It should be interesting."

He told us that the 101st was the world's only air-assault division and the brigade was one of its quick reactionary forces; as such, its soldiers could deploy worldwide in thirty-six hours, supporting three infantry brigades. Forty percent of the soldiers from the 159th bound for Kuwait already had deployed, and ninety of its Black Hawk helicopters were on ships nearing port in Kuwait. Covert said the eight embeds would fall in with the so-called trail party when the last of the brigade departed. Our departure time still hadn't been nailed down, but he indicated that we'd leave as early as 7:30 a.m. Saturday. The major then gave out Connolly's cell phone number, told us to be packed and ready to go, and to wait for word from him.

The announcement signaled that our planned seventy-two-hour orientation was being shortened to forty-eight. Read: Friday was a free day—and nobody groused about that. What an unexpected pleasure, I thought; now I'd have a whole day to finish my story and preparations.

After Major Covert concluded his remarks and dismissed us, I sought out Father George for an interview. Sizing up his heavily lined face and tousled white hair, I thought he looked older than forty-two. He said he was from far southwestern Poland, from a place called Walbrzych, which is closer to the neighboring capitals of Prague and Berlin than to Warsaw. In an earlier life, the priest was a chaplain to Poland's Solidarity union, which I knew was a dangerous undertaking. After decades of Soviet domination, the labor movement prodded Poland to shed Communism for democracy and free enterprise in 1989, but first came martial law and state-ordered violence, and priests were among the casualties.

When I asked Father George about the prospect of war, he said that Saddam Hussein was "just acting like a Communist, like Mao and Stalin and the others." "I just can't stand Americans not defending their country," he added, seeming to allude to the fact that America's streets from coast to coast were teeming with people demonstrating for peace. "I was living under Communism too long."

Afterward I made a point to speak privately to Major Covert; I felt it was important to win him over. We sat down in his nearly vacant office; he'd already cleared out his quarters since somebody else would be holding down the fort once he left. I began with my sentimental sound bite—"I'm daughter and granddaughter of Army"—and handed him a dossier that included a biography, a summary of my military reporting experience, and a copy of my letter of recommendation from boot camp. He seemed pleased to have the book on me. Then I told him that I understood the regulations governing embeds—and that I played by the rules.

Covert was an unpretentious forty-one-year-old from Geneva, Ohio, an officer too modest to boast about his prowess at the controls of a helicopter; I learned only from others later about his capabilities as an aviator. Once our business was concluded, we made a little small talk, and he asked me the inevitable question: "Do you have children?"

"No," I replied. "If I had children, I don't think I would be doing this." It was not only true, but seemed to be what most soldiers wanted to hear, especially the men, since their faces betrayed relief that I was not a she-devil so callous as to leave behind little ones while pursuing a dangerous story.

The fact is, I had wanted children more fervently, and desperately, than just about anything else in life, but Tom and I couldn't have them, even after some high-tech medical intervention. I didn't dare tell that to Covert; very few people knew the painful facts, except for the Skibas. I hadn't even been able to tell my husband's mother and father, they being the parents of seven.

Covert told me that he and his wife were expecting their first child on July 31, leaving me to wonder, privately, how a man could leave his wife at a time like that. But he was in the Army, so he had no choice. Orders is orders. I felt bad for his spouse having to go it alone during a pregnancy, especially her first, and told Covert that I hoped he'd be home by then.

As the brigade's executive officer—"ex o" for short—the major had people waiting to see him, so I thanked him for his time and left. On my way out I remembered something else on my to-do list and tracked down Father George, hoping to do something I hadn't done in ages: make my confession. The door to his office was slightly ajar, and I noticed a sullen-looking soldier sitting next to the chaplain's desk. Father George saw me and stepped outside, but when he heard what I wanted, he brushed me off. Maybe his plate was too full—or maybe my face suggested nothing more sinister than "has missed 1,532 Sunday Masses." As I walked away, I tried to remember how Catholics received absolution for their sins nowadays, wondering, "If you just think about them and pray, is that the equivalent of using Clorox on your soul?" If I was destined for the pearly gates, I wanted to show up a five-foot, six-inch tabula rasa.

As I walked down the hallway, the chaplain stuck his head out of the door and called after me. "Watch out for the aviators," he warned, leaving me clueless about what that was supposed to mean.

I phoned Tom from the hotel to give him the latest developments and afterward banged away at my keyboard, the words spilling out like a cloud had burst. I was typing at warp speed when the phone rang. It was Cox, suggesting that it was chow time. I agreed. We discussed whether to scare up some of our colleagues until I ruled it out, saying, "I'm all peopled out today." So we struck out on our own.

As Cox steered his rental down Fort Campbell Boulevard, he rifled through his CDs and asked me if I liked heavy metal. Nope. So he shoved the soundtrack from *The Last of the Mohicans* into the CD player. It was stirring music—and I nodded in approval. "It's what I listen to before every deployment," he told me, raising the volume and navigating on this wintry night past the pawn shops and neon-bedecked strip joints that seemed to creep right up to Campbell's perimeter. I looked straight ahead, turning a blind eye to these ragtag enterprises lest I envision broken-down soldiers trading in wedding bands or class rings for cash, or lonely, liquor-fueled men stuffing dollar bills into the glittery G-strings of naked women with large chests and small prospects. I preferred to believe that soldiers were straight out of recruiting posters—the walking, talking embodiments of Army values: loyalty, duty, respect, selfless service, honor, integrity, and personal courage.

Cox and I sought out the Black Horse Saloon, a brew pub popular among folks from Campbell—Major Covert had recommended it—and there we launched into a discussion about our spouses and how they regarded our assignment. He spoke admiringly of his wife, Heather, a high school English teacher and crew coach, leaving me with one overarching thought: "Great, this guy is safe." And since my gym-toned husband loves good books, too, I thought he and Heather could become friends, just as Cox and I had, especially since our significant others now had time on their hands. But when I proposed that Tom give Heather a call, my new battle buddy cut me off cold, saying, "I don't want my wife hanging out with guys."

After some small talk, Cox asked point-blank why I wanted to cover a war. At first I gave him the expected career blah-blah but then found myself in fast-rewind mode, talking about my childhood as the oldest girl in a family of three boys and two girls. As I spoke, it dawned on me that I had had my own band of brothers. I was born in the late 1950s surrounded by Tom, Steve, and John and Nancy, a tomboy if there ever were one.

I'd played touch football with the boys and shot hoops with them and learned to throw a hardball, and, following their lead, took pride in keeping score at Chicago White Sox games. I'd watched my brothers catch flies and, for sport, drop them in spider webs and squeal with delight as the predators menacingly crept toward the trapped insects and polished them off. I'd watched them build forts in the snow, blow up stuff with M-80 firecrackers, and occasionally pound the shit out of each other. Once Tom threw Steve against the wall in our living room, busting a hole in the plaster the size of a watermelon, right down to the lathe. It took a few days for a plasterer to show up; meanwhile, the collateral damage was a painful emblem of brotherly love gone sour, though, mercifully, their fisticuffs were few and far between.

The boys couldn't roughhouse with me—my parents were emphatic about that—so they indulged in low-intensity torture, like borrowing some hot tar from the roofers who were working in the neighborhood and smearing it all over one of my favorite dolls. Such antics were rare, but by the time I reached seventh grade and was caught up in my first crush, they saw an opening. My eighth-grade beau (an accomplished kisser) was the son of a couple who owned one of the two funeral homes in town. He and his family lived adjacent to the mortuary, which all of us kids found ghoulish. My oldest brother, Tom, invented a method to make my life miserable: he'd offer to take me someplace in his Pontiac Firebird, then drive into the funeral home's parking lot and honk the car horn nonstop, sending me ducking for cover and pleading for mercy. Then there was the Christmas when my brothers tricked me into believing that I'd won a fortune in the Illinois lottery. They'd filched a ticket out of my apron pocket, copied down all six numbers, pretended to have called in for the prizewinning picks, and, with straight faces, announced the results to the entire family. I fell for it, squealing with joy until they could no longer contain their laughter.

Sometimes I managed to achieve payback, like when I trapped Steve in our backyard playhouse by wedging a piece of lumber against the doorknob. He decided to free himself by punching his way through a glass window, cutting himself so badly he wound up in the emergency room for stitches. This was my introduction to the Law of Unintended Consequences, though in truth I secretly enjoyed the power I'd felt in exacting retribution—and above all I was grateful to have escaped a scolding from my parents. Another time I found a cache of love letters in Tom's bottom drawer written by a girl heartsick for him during a semester of study in England. The discovery led me to devour every last morsel, but just a few missives at a time, lest I be caught in the act.

All told, the beauty of growing up with brothers is that it left me with no fear of men, and fewer misconceptions about them. I'd seen them bathing, peeing, battling acne, and busting their knees on the gridiron—just as I'd watched them collect trophies, court girls, and stride off to college.

I didn't recite this ancient history for Cox. I only said that having brothers left me competitive, made me feel a little like Annie Oakley singing in the Broadway musical, "Anything you can do, I can do better."

Cox and I kept up the Doctor Freud act on the way back to the Holiday Inn, peering into each other's psyches with the practiced nonchalance of a professional in search of, if not the truth, then at least a good yarn. For a reporter, being interviewed is as obvious as having a tooth drilled and occasionally as painful, but I didn't mind his questions. Cox struck me as genuine—and a good guy.

"I want this story," I told him. "It's important for people to stand up for a free press, no matter what the stakes are. If you're young enough, and strong enough, and have a little courage, you have an obligation to do this. War is the most important story out there."

Maybe it was the *Mohicans* soundtrack affecting me, but I was sitting tall in the saddle, having crafted my own battle cry: "Youth + strength + courage = obligation."

Cox was hip, handsome, and eleven years my junior, but he was a married man, and clearly not on the prowl, so I wasn't wracked with guilt. I rationalized hanging out with him by telling myself it was as innocent as having an "office husband"—that male coworker with whom you happen to be emotionally intimate. Our encounters never went beyond dinner, drinks, and errands, like a trip to Batteries Plus, where he helped me pick out a power inverter, a device roughly the size of two videocassettes stacked one on top of the other. If my laptop ran out of power, I could use the equipment to replenish its power source using the battery of a Humvee.

Inside, I was a bundle of nerves, and relieved to have Cox as a sounding board and running buddy. He and I and the other embeds, scattered in midpriced hotels up and down the boulevard, were twiddling our thumbs in a bizarre waiting room, preparing to kiss our old lives good-bye, and knowing we might die running after a story.

The next day, Friday, I finally made progress, forging ahead on my Sunday story and figuring out how to send text to my news desk using the laptop and satellite phone. My trial run—only a test—read like this:

[FROM]Iraqtest,skiba,natl,Miljsp/

Baghdad—The U.S.-led coalition completed its mop up of the Iraqi capital today, setting a date for democratic elections, settling all tribal disputes and lastly, unleashing an unprecedented campaign to liberate women here from thousands of centuries of male dominance.

Under the new regime, men will be required to do all housework and will be beheaded for disobeying.

"Where does my wife keep the Windex?" one stunned Iraqi man wondered aloud.

—30—

This brought a chuckle to my longtime editor, Carl Schwartz, who directs national and international news coverage, and who either appreciates, or tolerates, my whimsical side.

Late that afternoon, I checked in by phone with the brigade, hoping to get the skinny on the date and time of our departure. Captain Janel Aleman answered the phone. I remembered her from my visit to the 159th Brigade the day before. She was the unit's chemical officer, which meant that it fell to her to keep us from being slimed—that is, advise commanders on the enemy's WMD capabilities and recommend appropriate countermeasures.

Aleman told me we might leave Saturday or Sunday, so I took the occasion to chat her up, blathering about nothing in particular, hoping to butter her up. Finally I asked hopefully, "When we deploy, we'll be roommates, right?"

"No," she responded. Her tone of voice seemed to imply that I was pitifully out of date and out of step if I imagined women had separate sleeping quarters in the field.

Astonished, I pressed her. "Isn't there a women's tent?"

"No."

"What do you mean—there's no tent for women?"

"The tents are co-ed," she said plainly.

"What?"

"The tents," she repeated, "are co-ed."

My mind flashed back to boot camp at Benning and to the DOD trip I had taken to the Balkans, both of which had a common, much-appreciated amenity: single-sex accommodations. Co-ed military showers—which, I learned in Bosnia and Kosovo, meant separate, designated hours of use for men or women—I could handle, more or less. Nukes and nerve gas, I was ready. But saying "Nighty-night" under canvas to dozens of men I didn't know?

Why, I wondered, hadn't the Army briefed me on this? Now the fog was lifting over the chaplain's murky warning. Good god, the aviators—I'll be sleeping with them. I'll be sleeping with a bunch of strange flyboys!

I wasn't sure whether Tom could cope with the idea. More to the point, I wasn't sure I could. And I said exactly that in my Sunday story.

Cox, over dinner, tried to put me at ease. "It's a battlefield. Nobody cares. Everybody is just a soldier."

On Saturday, Captain Connolly, the liaison to the journalists attached to the 159th Brigade, finally had definitive news. He directed the eight embeds to show up at brigade headquarters at 3:45 p.m. Sunday, saying we should expect to wait several hours while the soldiers underwent final processing, after which time we'd be on our way.

Cox, meanwhile, heard his departure was being postponed. The delay resulted from the hours-old death of a twenty-one-year-old infantryman who lost his life in a motor vehicle accident outside of Nashville. The fatality, at 5:30 that morning, had capped a night of predeployment partying involving the soldier and some colleagues. So before my friend from *Army Times* could leave, first he'd attend a memorial service at Campbell for the soldier.

The irony was inescapable. Here you are, prepared to die overseas for your country and its Constitution, and you're taken out after a night on the town before even leaving the States.

After getting the news about our departure, I dashed out to Wal-Mart, picking up a camera case, credentials holder, and Marlboro Lights. While in the checkout line I noticed a young, anemic-looking Screaming Eagle in fatigues ahead of me. He was dropping $160 on cigarettes and chew, leading me to wonder how long he planned to be gone. Not only was I just an occasional smoker, but mentally I was stuck in the "short, triumphal war" mode. I bought two packs.

Afterward I stopped off at Cox's room to drop off the bungee cord he'd asked me to pick up for him. Noticing his room was immaculate and his gear compact and trim, I was amazed and, more than that, envious. At that moment some street people in cities across America were better organized than I was. My clothing was stacked in little piles on the couch in my room and things such as plastic canteens and Oreos and Post-Its and scrunchees were haphazardly tossed in dresser drawers, which also held my stash of Band-Aids; I had enough bandages to support a Boston Marathon.

Cool and collected, Cox had his act so together that he was left to flip contentedly through a stack of greeting cards that his spouse had presented to him before his departure; she'd even numbered the envelopes so that he would open them in the order she intended. It seemed sweet and touching and wifelier than anything I could have dreamed up. I felt like an absolute shit. My husband's birthday was just days away, and I hadn't even gotten around to ordering him a gift from Nueske's, a Wisconsin purveyor of meat smoked in applewood.

"How come you're ready? You're not leaving for days!" I blurted out, confessing to Cox that I still hadn't finished packing. Funny how I ostensibly could stare death in the face, but was neurotic about packing for the trip.

He volunteered to give my belongings a once-over and help me finish the job. He told me to get a head start, and about an hour later he showed up at my room, where my gratitude at having helping hands vanished as soon as I realized that all of my possessions were on display, right down to the cotton panties and sports bras and super-plus tampons secured in Ziploc bags. I was mortified, and quickly stuffed the unmentionables into the first bag I could put my hands on.

We made haste going through the rest of my stuff, packing it as tightly as we could and setting aside anything not absolutely essential. Since I planned to toss or ship home what I didn't need, I kept pestering Cox about whether he wanted anything I would jettison, but again and again, he turned me down. I felt remorse for accepting his help and giving nothing in return, so I started rattling off what I could spare and offering it up.

"Double-A batteries? Hand cream? Highlighter pens?"

My guilt was assuaged when he accepted a slim leaflet of Catholic prayers I'd brought along. Amen to that.

Before he left, Cox took it upon himself to inspect the canvas bag that carried my gas mask. When he pulled out a Screaming Eagles ball cap—a gift Major Cate, the 101st public affairs chief, had given the embeds—Cox was furious.

"Never, *ever* put anything in there besides your mask and your atropine shots," he barked, in a voice so bellicose I practically shook. "You have to be able to get your mask. Fast!"

Was I in denial, or deluded, or stupid? I really hoped that I wouldn't have to use the gas mask, but Cox knew better, and now smoke was pouring from his ears. Pacing in front of my desk, he announced, "We're going to practice right now—until you get this right."

And so Room 319 of the Holiday Inn in Hopkinsville became the site of chemical-attack drills, which had Cox hollering, "Gas, gas, gas!"—the standard warning—while I held my breath, slapped on the mask, tightened the straps, and checked the seal so no stray toxins would seep in. Cox, meantime, was counting out how many seconds it took. "One thousand one, two thousand two—"

"Gas, gas, gas!" he cried out again. We did it over and over and over until my head throbbed and I insisted that I'd gotten it down. That may or may not have been true, but his intensity was beginning to creep me out.

Then he changed the subject, inquiring, "Are you bringing booze?"

"No, I'm not," I answered, thinking back to my war counselors. I'd only had the nerve to ask Sando and Van de Steeg—not Galloway—about whether to bring something to drink, and the result was a tie vote.

"You're not taking alcohol?" Cox asked.

"No, I'm gonna follow the rules. I'm not bringing anything to drink."

He glared at me as if to suggest that I was making another big mistake, but dropped the matter.

That night over dinner, we talked about everything and nothing, sharing new confidences, disclosing things to each other that normally take longer than four days for one human being to divulge to a stranger, particularly in the Washington area, the land of strivers we'd left behind.

To cap the night, he took time for some last-minute lessons in soldiering, making fundamental points about timing and pacing. "There are two kinds of soldiers: the quick and the dead," he instructed. I took it to mean that speed was important if I came under fire; his counsel stuck, and I walked briskly throughout the war.

He further advised that I shouldn't go at my work balls-to-the-walls every day, saying that if I tried to, I'd burn out. "You've got to take 'down days' every so often, or you won't make it," he said. "It'll be hard to do, but make yourself take a day off every once in a while."

As the week progressed, the hotel had filled up as reservists streamed to the Campbell area to prepare to ship out. The morning I left, I ate alone—Cox and I never met for breakfast. There was an officer from the Army Reserves at the table on either side of me. Soon all three of us were chatting, and after the initial pleasantries, the two reservists weighed in on the Pentagon brainstorm to place journalists in never-before-seen numbers into military units. One of the officers was for it; the other, vehemently against it. "I'll tell you what's gonna happen," the second officer said to me. "One of my guys is going to play to one of your cameras—and get himself killed." His remark stung, but I wasn't buying it.

"I'm pencil press," I said, trying to extract myself from his gloomy prophecy by pointing out that writers move about unobtrusively relative to broadcasters, who come weighted down with video cameras, microphones, and satellite equipment much bulkier than the tools of my trade.

My observation didn't end the debate, but I had neither the time nor the desire to continue making the case that I didn't intend to get a U.S. soldier killed. Taking a swim seemed a better thing to do, so at last I made it to the hotel pool, frolicking like a dolphin and kicking myself for being so obsessed with work that I had ignored the hotel's best amenity until the last day of my stay.

Afterward I showered and dressed in my room. I decided that the desert camo pants were passable, but the matching shirt looked ridiculous, so I changed into another top.

Cox showed up at my room at an agreed-upon hour to get me to the base, clutching a bottle of Dasani water at my door. "Here, take this," he said.

At first I thought he wanted me to stay hydrated during the long flights (how kind of him), but he disclosed that the plastic bottle was filled with vodka. He had transferred his hooch into two Dasani bottles, but felt that he had room in his gear to carry only one.

"I don't want it," I told him.

"Take it."

"No."

"You'll need it."

This went on until I caved in, squeezing the Dasani into a filled-to-the-brim duffle.

On the ride to Campbell, he put on the *Mohicans* sound track again. The two of us knew the score: he was heading out with the ground pounders and I was going off with the flyboys, so we probably wouldn't see each other in the Middle East. Maybe we'd never see each other again.

If I felt a tug at my heartstrings, saying good-bye to a guy with whom I'd practically become attached at the hip, I couldn't—or wouldn't—show my feelings. My "Action Girl Reporter" persona kicked in; this was no time for small talk or big good-byes.

Outside the 159th's headquarters, officers in fatigues milled around, along with their spouses, who were dolled up in their Sunday best. Some of the wives were clutching infants bundled in blankets. It was the "kiss and cry" hour, but nobody was bawling; instead, everybody was putting on a brave face. If you looked closely—I tried not to—you could, from the damp, reddened eyes and flushed faces, tell that some people had been weeping earlier, but not now.

Cox and I unloaded my gear far enough away from the entrance to allow him to get in and out inconspicuously. We traded thanks and a quick hug, simultaneously mouthing the two words I'd spoken to the soldier at the Horseshoe restaurant: "Be safe."

Covert, the brigade's executive officer, the one with the pregnant wife, was out on a front stoop dressed in full battle-rattle. Several other officers were with him. As I approached the group, all of them impassively gave me a once-over. "Katherine," Covert announced matter-of-factly, "you have your helmet on backwards."

"Today, Sir," I answered briskly, "I'm sure I have a lot on backwards."

As everybody snickered, Covert told an underling to fetch some "cat's eyes," a narrow woven band that wraps around a helmet and features two tiny reflective strips, hence the name. The ex o fitted it around my headgear, explaining that the "eyes" went at the back; that way, at nightfall, a soldier behind me would be able to detect that I was ahead.

Next I was given the opportunity to disgorge much of my gear into the back of a truck, which would carry it off to the plane. I kept only that with which I couldn't part: all my professional gear (laptop, satellite phone, camera), my Army stuff (flak vest, helmet, gas mask), and a carry-on bag—taken together, still more than an armful.

With time to kill, I asked a brigade clerk if I could use a computer to pull my Sunday story off the Internet. I wanted to prove my bona fides—that I was a reporter, not just a hanger-on—so I passed out copies of my story to the people I knew the best, including Captains Connolly and Aleman, Major Covert, and Father George.

We left in vans for the hangar, where I got down to business, interviewing soldiers and taking their photos. My piece on deploying from Campbell as an embed had landed on page one of my paper that Sunday morning; but working for a daily means "feeding the beast," as we sometimes grumble, since there's always tomorrow's edition to fill.

The noisy, high-ceilinged hangar was wall-to-wall with hundreds of soldiers in desert camouflage fatigues. Most of them simply lounged on the floor with a rifle or machine gun draped alongside them. Some held hands in a prayer circle. And some stood in line for shots, since soldiers who had small children at home had been told to wait until the eleventh hour for their smallpox vaccination so as not to risk spreading the virus to their little ones. And women, I found out later, had the chance to take a urine test to see if they were pregnant—since that would keep them off the front lines.

As I went about my work, I learned that the words *"Milwaukee Journal Sentinel"* practically guaranteed that someone would know someone from Wisconsin and shove him or her—and they were mostly men—my way.

The first was Specialist Jonathan Hendon, a twenty-year-old who worked as a heavy-wheeled vehicle mechanic. He told me that he landed in the Army because he hadn't done too well in high school—not an uncommon answer—and pronounced himself ready for his first deployment, saying, "Whatever's going on, I'm ready to do my job."

"My family is going to miss me," he continued. "They wish I never came into the military. I feel I did the right thing. I can get out in four years and start over."

When I asked about his relatives, he named his parents, two brothers, and a sister—plus a fiancée, Nicole Cross, who was attending the University of Wisconsin–Madison, my husband's alma mater. But Hendon had second thoughts about how to characterize Nicole. "Don't put 'fiancée' in," he told me. "My mom doesn't know yet."

His instruction made a darling quote, so I asked him to go on the record. With his buddies egging him on, Hendon agreed.

Next up was Private 1st Class Frederick Jolly, a twenty-two-year-old supply specialist from Milwaukee who had enlisted "for the challenge" and "to get away and do something different." How did he feel about the prospect of war? "It's my job," he answered. "I don't make no decisions. I support my leaders."

His view of the potential conflict was practically identical to what every soldier answered, though usually more grammatically—and I'd come to expect nothing more. I rather admired their fealty, in fact, reasoning that battlefields aren't the place for debating societies.

The material was just what I needed, since my editors had asked me to produce short profiles of the troops from Wisconsin for a periodic feature we planned to call "Postcards."

I took a break, lining up for some chicken soup that was being doled out and palming through the boxes of used books being given away. When Father George began blessing and handing out medals of St. Michael—"the patron saint of air assault"—I gladly took one, attaching it to the chain around my neck next to my own patron saint, Catherine of Siena.

Later, when I reached Tom by phone, he was at work and seemed distracted and distant, sending off a vibe suggesting that after four or five good-byes, enough was enough. So I reminded him that I loved him, promised that I wouldn't take any foolish chances, and assured him that I'd be home before long.

Then I called my mom. I put the chaplain on the line, encouraging him to speak to her in Polish as if to assure her that if I was at death's door, one of our own would be there to give me the last rites. Then I called my sister. Then I called an old friend in San Francisco, figuring that even though it was practically midnight in Kentucky, the time difference meant he'd still be awake.

Suddenly everybody in uniform began springing up and standing at attention. A very important person with a small entourage was striding into our midst. It was Brigadier General Benjamin C. Freakley, one of the 101st's top bosses, arriving to deliver an official farewell. The forty-nine-year-old Freakley, the assistant division commander for military operations, reminded the soldiers that they were "going into tough conditions" and counseled them to be alert and prepared. He said there were people in Kuwait who meant to do them harm; he also cautioned that soldiers accidentally had discharged their weapons in theater. "You don't want to be the soldier that shoots a brother or sister," he remarked.

"You have to be vigilant until you get back to Campbell. You've got to be ready. You are not training anymore. You are going to combat. If required, we will invade Iraq and remove weapons of mass destruction and remove Saddam Hussein from power."

Referring to their Screaming Eagle patches, the general told the soldiers they were carrying an "unbelievable tradition" on their left shoulders. He urged them to maintain the honor and heritage of the 101st, intoning, "We will not let those who came before us down."

For me, never having been to war, it seemed so much like the movies: the military flags, the baby-faced troops in formation, the truculent sergeants, and a give-'em-hell general.

When Freakley finished, I dashed over to him for an interview, catching another rare civilian in my peripheral vision. I couldn't believe my eyes. Cox wasn't supposed to be leaving for another day or two. I couldn't help but grin as he and I took turns eliciting more comment from Freakley, and when the general moved on, I asked Cox expectantly, "Hey, are you on my flight?"

Cox wasn't. He explained that no sooner had he returned to the Holiday Inn than he got a call about an empty seat—but not on my flight—so he wasn't sticking around for the memorial service after all.

Deflated, I stood around, chattering with Cox about my backward helmet and his mad dash to Campbell as somebody in the distance shouted that it was time to move out. I kept up the banter with my friend, stashing away my camera and notebook, gathering a bottle of mineral water and some of the hand-me-down paperbacks—not lollygagging, really; at least I didn't think so. But Captain Connolly spotted me and came swooping down like an irate father who discovers his daughter after curfew on the front porch with a beau. "Katherine," he scolded, "you're going to miss the freaking plane."

Now Connolly, from East Hartford, Connecticut, struck me as a proper, precise, lawyerly fellow, so I was surprised to hear him utter even a euphemism for "fucking" and even more surprised to find it hurtled at me. Strike two! I thought, remembering I'd let Connolly down when I'd shown up late for our first meeting since Kirsten Scharnberg had passed out after her anthrax shot. I hustled onto the dark airfield, carrying so much stuff that I violated my own lifelong credo against littering, ditching the hand-me-down paperbacks right on the tarmac before clambering up the steps of a waiting Northwest Airlines B-747/200.

The jumbo jet was carrying 352 officers and enlisted soldiers and eight embedded journalists. By the time I boarded, most of the seats were taken. The brass had commandeered first class; the burly, young soldiers who loaded baggage and equipment into the belly of the plane were rewarded with seats in business class; and the rest of us were sardined in coach. I squeezed into a middle seat between two soldiers right behind business class, hoping, for naught, that one of the plush oversized seats ahead would go empty.

By the time we left, it was 1:54 a.m., Monday, March 3. As the plane roared down the runway, dozens of soldiers whistled, hooted, and hollered things like, "Let's go!" It was like being caught in the middle of the cattle drive in the John Wayne movie *Red River*—only scarier. What did I expect? I was leaving for a showdown with Saddam Hussein with hundreds of armed men and women—trained killers all of them—and no doubt they were as tired as I was with worrying and writing a will and making lump-in-your-throat good-byes. I'd heard some call this their Super Bowl, so I took the cacophony to be rational exuberance.

Before long the noise died down and people began settling in their seats, giving me the chance to meet the soldier on either side of me and to study others nearby. Some had fallen asleep so abruptly that they had to have popped sleeping pills. Others were zoned out in front of Game Boys or DVD players. Still others rested their chins on their fists, staring into the distance, undoubtedly thinking about the mission ahead.

One soldier showed me a little paper sack like the kind old-fashioned candy stores give out. It held a tiny American flag and little sundries with big meanings. A spouses' network known as a Family Readiness Group had prepared the parting gifts for the troops. There was a piece of LifeSavers candy to "remind you that is what you are," some gum to "help the unit stick together," a wad of cotton to "cushion the rough roads," and a penny minted in 2001, a reminder of the 9-11 attacks and the "shining beacon of freedom our nation represents."

Nice color for my story on deploying, I thought; and after getting it all down, it seemed time to sleep, something I'm practically expert at on airplanes. But even with a sleeping mask and ear plugs, I was never out for long. Every few hours on the no-alcohol red-eye, the flight attendants offered us the same thing, a ham omelet.

At one point a pretty stewardess pranced down the aisle in a desert camouflage boonie cap, the floppy, wide-brimmed hat favored by soldiers for blocking the sun. For some reason, that bugged me. "You're not going to war," I said to myself. "You haven't earned that hat." Maybe I was just jealous of what she had and what I had relinquished—a dress, pantyhose, and pumps, for starters.

There was to be a two-hour layover in Amsterdam's Schiphol Airport. That happened to be where I'd landed on my first trip to Europe, and I recalled two disparate images from the terminal: exotic tulip bulbs for sale in the shops and stern-looking security forces brandishing machine guns. Now I imagined having the chance to sip a café au lait and peruse the silk, porcelain, and perfume in the duty-free shops—but those turned out to be complete fantasies, now that I was, while not quite in the Army, getting a flavor of their playbook.

The military attaché from the U.S. embassy welcomed us on the jetway, joined by two Dutch plainclothes security personnel. Our group then was hermetically sealed in a glassed-in, amenity-free waiting area and banned from going anyplace else. Lots of people lit up smokes. I made my way to a women's room to wash my hair and clean up. Captain Aleman, my hoped-for roommate, walked in and spied me with enough little bottles scattered around me to fill Aisle 3 at Walgreen's, and when I saw her I braced myself for another Army scolding, but, to my enormous relief, she only asked to borrow some moisturizer.

Returning to the waiting area, I scanned the room, strode over to the pair of tall, good-looking Dutch security men, and introduced myself using my married name, "Mrs. Vanden Brook." As we talked about this and that, I gazed admiringly into their matching sets of azure eyes—until the little voice inside my head said, "Stop flirting! You have a handsome Dutch husband at home!" Simultaneously I spied Major Covert studying me studying the Europeans, so I said I would be going, proceeded to find a gaggle of troops having cigarettes, and lit up.

As we reboarded, the airport personnel operating the jetway enthusiastically said good-bye and good luck. They knew we were heading to Kuwait City and inching toward harm's way, and their farewells seemed touching, particularly since most of Europe would be sitting this war out.

The plane's crew had changed during our layover, and after the jet climbed to cruising altitude, the new captain came on the public-address system. "It's an honor to take you guys down there," he said. "We wish you good luck in all you do. We'll be back in sixty to ninety days to bring you back."

I found it a moving tribute. The captain went on to invite passengers to visit him in the cockpit and take in the sights, like the brilliant lights that made Rome at night look radioactive. Wanting his name, I took him up on his offer. There was a long line of soldiers ahead of me, so while I was waiting I chatted up flight attendant Tammy Bryant and asked her what it's like to deposit U.S. troops into the Gulf.

The thirty-year-old Bryant, a native of Jacksonville, Florida, began to tear up and sniffle. She'd gotten to know some of the soldiers. Some had even showed her wallet-sized family photos, often laminated, just one more sign the troops were prepared for a harsh environment ahead.

"On your normal businessman flight it's 'Have a good day,'" Bryant told me. "Our quote now is, 'We're coming back to get you.' And their quote is, 'We hope so.'"

"The hardest part," she said, "is closing the doors and leaving Kuwait."

I later learned that the flight crew were volunteers. They were being paid generously to work the flight, given the risks inherent in ferrying U.S. soldiers to the Persian Gulf, where some were not prepared to roll out a red carpet.

Bryant showed me letters and drawings collected from Minnesota schoolchildren that would be distributed to the soldiers through a program called

"Operation Smile." The flight attendants handed out the messages, like one from Tyler, of Farmington Elementary School, who wrote, "I like Army gies."

Ahead of me in line was Specialist Alan Scottsboro, a mechanic, who was so voluble that he was allowed to use the PA system. "This is 'Peacock' speaking," he announced. "Me and Tater are in the cockpit. You better come and get us." Tater was his buddy from the motor pool, Private Ryan McCauley, a native of Idaho. Mr. Peacock and Mr. Potato Head cracked me up, providing the only belly laugh of the flight—and the first Fellini touch of the journey.

When it was my turn to meet Captain Loren Lindo, the plane was sailing through the night skies, with lights from an unknown metropolis shimmering below us. I didn't stay long, but made sure to thank the fifty-three-year-old pilot from Anchorage, Alaska, for his encouragement.

Back in my seat, I looked up wistfully at the monitor, which showed the plane's location relative to major European cities—Paris, Hamburg, Warsaw, Vienna, Rome, Milan. All the names glimmered suggestively. Any of them was preferable to where I was going. I'd been to all of those countries—France, Germany, Poland, Italy, and Austria—but now I was bound for a new place about which I knew painfully little. My thumbnail sketch of Kuwait had it a desert emirate where alcohol is verboten and only men vote.

My seatmates weren't much for conversation; when they weren't slumbering, they were listening to CDs, like the Bloodhound Gang. "They're just way out there," thirty-three-year-old Staff Sergeant Ronnie Daniel enthused. "They're rude."

I tried hard to get some rest and managed a few winks before we landed in the Kuwaiti capital just before dawn on March 4. We couldn't leave the aircraft right away, though, since a soldier had lost a "sensitive item"—part of his rifle, in fact—and people were crawling all over the floor in search of the missing doodad.

We strode down the air stairs at 5:27 a.m. and boarded luxury coaches with dark velour curtains covering the windows. Apparently we weren't anxious to advertise the prospective coming attraction—as a T-shirt that had flown off store shelves at Fort Campbell called it, "No Slack with Iraq: The Sequel," with the "o" in "No" depicting the crosshairs of a weapon.

Covert was the trail boss on my bus, taking a seat in front and asking for a head count. My eyes were riveted to his olive-colored flak jacket, which carried the symbol for his blood type, O+, etched crudely into the fabric with a black marker. The two small characters spoke volumes. I fretted about Covert's pregnant wife and whether he would live to see his firstborn. He and the rest, regardless of their personal circumstances, were prepared to shed their last drop of A Positive, O Negative, AB Positive, and all the rest, as their flak jackets attested. It struck me that people in Washington could be so full of themselves, mouthing sections of the U.S. Constitution with so much self-satisfaction you'd think "We, the People" had spilled forth from their own quill pen. My new companions seemed infinitely more courageous than the political class I'd left behind.

The bus belched forward for a short and serpentine trip to a place called Camp Wolf, which borders Kuwait International Airport. It was time for "in-processing," which meant that hundreds of soldiers from my plane and others were herded into a tent, seated cheek by jowl on several long benches, and instructed to wait for another "brief."

By then I'd been informed that Iraq has forty-six varieties of poisonous snakes. I'd been cautioned about exotic diseases that I'd never heard of before, such as tick-borne Crimean-Congo hemorrhagic fever and the sand fly's revenge, leishmaniasis. And I'd picked up bits of advice, such as, watch where you pee at night because night-vision goggles can afford soldiers quite a show. But only when we arrived at Camp Wolf did someone mention a new potential hazard: we were on alert for incoming Scud missiles.

"The threat level is high. I repeat, high," a full-throated, no-nonsense briefer announced. The military assesses security conditions as Normal, Alpha, Bravo, Charlie, and Delta, in increasing order of alarm, and the briefer disclosed that conditions were at "Charlie-Plus."

Sluggish from the flight, and scared at the prospect of someone taking aim at us, I stifled my professional instincts to seek clarification—Who? What? Where? When? Why?—about the Scud alert.

After the briefing I stood in line with the soldiers and gave my name and Social Security number to an Army clerk seated behind a desktop computer. Then someone took the embedded journalists aside and explained a software program called "Civ Track," which was intended to let the military keep abreast of the comings and goings of civilians in theater. Every time we moved to a new camp, we were supposed to log in and record our whereabouts. After the last Gulf War, we were told, it was considered an "embarrassment" that some civilians were never accounted for on the battlefield. The sight of my dead body sprawled on a lonely desert expanse, complete with buzzards picking off what flesh remained on my skeleton, flashed through my mind. Then I remembered what John Cosgrove, one of the old-timers in Washington, had told me. A retired journalist, Cosgrove had signed up with the Navy the day after Pearl Harbor was bombed and was impressed with me for embedding. "Don't worry," he'd said. "If you die, your family and friends will be sad for a while, but that won't matter to you. You'll be dead."

Finally, after the rigmarole, we got to leave the tent for some fresh air. With the temperature climbing, the winds picking up, and sand lashing at my contacts, my thoughts drifted to other trips I'd taken overseas. Think about it: when you travel to a foreign land more often than not there's a hotel room waiting for you at the other end, and maybe a goose down comforter and some soft pillows. Chances are, you'd have the opportunity to take a hot shower and lather yourself with a heavy bar of soap, possibly hand-milled, maybe scented with jasmine. Then you'd leave your high-ceilinged bedchamber, exchange some currency at the reception desk, and hop aboard a $25 sightseeing bus for a preview of all the glorious moments ahead. After the tour, you might amble down some swanky *rue* festooned with baskets of hot-pink geraniums, then pause at an al fresco café for a caffeine derivative delivered in a demitasse by an indifferent waiter who just might have finished the final chapters of his Ph.D. thesis on Nietzsche at the Sorbonne had a darkly beautiful woman not shattered his heart like a Limoges teacup discarded from a third-floor walk-up into traffic on the Boulevard Saint Michel.

Nobody at Camp Wolf offered us so much as a styrofoam cup of jolt. As the temperature inched upward, the instructions kept changing. It went like this: Get on the bus with all your gear. Get off the bus with your gear. We're staying. We're leaving. Ultimately, during the sweltering heat of midday, I followed the lead of my companions from the 159th, collapsing on the floor of the bus, cradling my head in my crossed forearms on one of the seats, and descending into sleep.

Whenever the plans changed, I did as I was told, lugging my unwieldy gear from Point A to Point B to Point C across the hot, treeless sandscape, trying to be a good soldier and firing up a cigarette every chance I had. But I was so not loving Army life. I was whipped.

"I can't take this," the little voice inside my head announced. I wondered how I could endure another hour of embedding, much less days or weeks.

We were told that in light of security conditions, we couldn't leave Wolf until a convoy of vehicles was assembled for the trip to our next stop, Camp Victory.

At twilight, new instructions had us staying put for the night. At last, certainty. I dumped God-knows-how-many pounds of gear into a pitch-dark tent and traipsed over the sand to find a portable toilet. By the time I returned, no more than five minutes had passed, but the orders had changed again. We were moving out.

It was going on ten o'clock at night when the bus pulled into Victory and snaked through the camp, depositing weary travelers at groupings of tents that housed the various elements of the 159th Brigade's 101st Aviation Regiment. The regiment was comprised of the Fourth, Fifth, Seventh, and Ninth Battalions, and I was assigned to the Fourth, as was Robert Dollar from the *Kentucky New Era,* the only other print reporter among the eight embeds.

When we entered the large, sand-colored shelter it was dark except for a few tiny lights twinkling here and there. Several cots were placed perpendicular to the sides of the tent, and a row of them stretched down the middle. Almost everybody seemed to be asleep, judging by the big lumps of humanity hidden underneath the drab-olive sleeping bags. I could hear one or two people snoring. A few of those still awake reclined on their sides with reading lights aglow. All of a sudden somebody hollered at somebody else by name, instructing that two cots should be set up for the embeds. These words were the most endearing sounds I had heard in a long stretch of time. Somebody was going to do something for me—and it didn't involve a ham omelet.

I dumped my bags, pawed through my gear to track down my self-inflating mattress pad, ear plugs, and eye mask, and rolled out my sleeping bag. After I crept inside, I sank into the goose down, rapturous at being horizontal for the first time in fifty hours. As I crumbled into the fetal position, the loud man spoke again, bellowing so vociferously at his tentlings that he must have awakened every troop already transiting in the Land of Nod.

"Now go," he roared in the darkness, "to sleep!"

4

Sandblasted

As the new day broke, easterly winds hopscotched across the desert and buffeted our tent, sending the flap over the entrance floating backward into the shelter as if it were a magic carpet. There was a rhythm to it. Each time the flap reared, a gust of cool, crisp air swept in, while the silvery blue light of dawn seductively crept in and out with each rise and fall.

Few people were stirring, but I was too restless to stay on my cot, which, while not even seven feet long and three feet wide, was surprisingly easy on the back. I couldn't wait to see what Victory looked like, so I slid out of my sleeping bag, sat up, raked my fingers through a grungy, tousled head, and laced up my boots willy-nilly.

The tent felt chilly when I stood up, so I grabbed my beige rough-weather jacket, which, with its multitude of pockets, was a foreign correspondent's classic; privately I called it the "Dan Rather" model. I checked to make sure there were cigarettes in the pocket, locating a rumpled half-pack and calculating that I'd gone through several Marlboro Light 100s while enduring Camp Wolf's welcome mat.

Pushing aside the tent flap, I stepped outside and drank in the serene surroundings: the vast expanse of golden sand, with creases left by the wind; the pale blue skies overhead, a star or two still twinkling; and the sun creeping over the horizon behind a cloudy plumage, a magnificent morning coat the colors of lilac blossoms, orange sorbet, and cotton candy.

I had had enough rest to feel revitalized, not that I'd slept like a baby, not in a tent full of strange people, sounds, and smells. At one point I awoke in a mild panic at the sound of boots crashing down on the wooden floor. I blamed a sleepwalker, coaxed myself back into slumber, and learned later that soldiers rotate guard duty on the hour to watch out for infiltrators, fire, and other hazards.

Only a few soldiers were milling around as I lit a cigarette and sized up the camp. It had rows of big, biscuit-colored tents, fringed with gravel; a few odd vehicles here and there; new-looking, forest-green plastic latrines; and some wooden contraptions resembling sawhorses. The devices, which held water bottles and soap, both dangling from ropes, functioned as hand-washing stations. "Very Boy Scout," I thought.

I returned to the tent to retrieve the satellite phone and parked my derrière on the gravel, far enough away from the snoozing masses so as not to wake anybody up. The device, called a "sat phone" for short, was a heavy, clunky old thing. Using its built-in compass, first you pointed the satellite dish toward the southeast skies, then you hoped to catch a strong signal, dialed the number, and crossed your fingers. After a few false starts, my call seemed to be going through.

"Tom Vanden Brook, *USA Today,*" my husband answered crisply.

"Hey, honey, it's me! I'm here. I'm in Kuwait."

What joy I felt at my husband's voice. Not only did the phone work—leaving only one other worry, the laptop—but for a few precious minutes, it was just me and Tom. No Army, no minders, no scoldings, no missile scares. Our telephone connection was strong, and I felt near to him.

In Kuwait it was seven a.m., Wednesday, March 5; on the East Coast, it was eleven p.m. Tuesday night. Tom and I spoke only a short while because I wanted to catch my editor, Carl Schwartz, before it was unreasonably late in Milwaukee. His wife, Barbara, who edits the *Journal Sentinel*'s Sunday opinion pages, answered the phone, and before handing the receiver to her husband, she told me the newsroom was proud of me and praying for me. Her remark left me surprised and touched.

Carl was heartened that I'd arrived safely and planned to file a story right away. I proposed recapping the journey to the Middle East and setting the scene with the soldiers of the 159th Brigade encamped in a region more suited to Bedouin herders than Black Hawk helicopters. I cautioned Carl that all was contingent on getting my telephone and my computer on speaking terms. "Sounds like a plan," he said.

Back inside the tent, dozens of soldiers were shaking off sleep. But I was cooking with gasoline now. I was a reporter on deadline—a woman in labor, so to speak; as unlikely to lose my focus as a gal chasing a new love or walking down the aisle or grabbing a confection from Vera Wang marked 75 percent off.

I was paging through my notes, seeing what I had and what I needed, when a man a few cots away called out to me. "Would you like to have an MRE?" he asked.

I turned toward him and saw that he was tall and tan and looked a little like George Clooney. Breakfast suddenly seemed like a wise choice, so I fished a granola bar out of an MRE bag and went over to meet Lieutenant Colonel Robert T. Ruiz, a flight surgeon with the Fourth Battalion.

"Does that mean you're a physician?" I asked. He said it did.

Ruiz looked to be in his late forties. He had a toothy smile and a salt-and-pepper thatch of hair. He said he was married with two kids and that he'd grown up in L.A. It wasn't long before we learned that both of us as undergraduates had been schooled by the Jesuits; Ruiz had gone to Creighton and I'd gone to Marquette.

I told him a little about how I came to be embedded, prompting him to remark, "I feel like I'm embedded, too."

I shot him a quizzical look. "Overly friendly," I told myself, recalling the chaplain's warning. Perhaps it was only the military's unfortunate choice of terminology—the word "bed" is embedded in "embedded"—but a little alarm bell rang in my head, so I missed the point I think Ruiz was trying to make. He, too, was an outsider; unlike the vast majority of the 159th Brigade, who came out of Fort Campbell, he was from Fort Rucker in Alabama.

Ruiz was easygoing, well-spoken, and smart, so I decided to take advantage of the situation. "Do you know how to use a shortwave radio, Colonel?" I chirped.

He did, so we walked over to my cot and I began rummaging through my things to find the palm-sized Grundig Mini World radio I'd buried somewhere. The day was getting warmer, so when I came across a bottle of Dasani water, I took a big gulp out of it—and practically gagged.

It wasn't water. It was the vodka that Matt Cox had given me as a parting gift. And it was strong stuff—I felt like I was breathing fire. It wasn't even nine o'clock in the morning, and there, four or five feet away, was Ruiz, a senior officer and potential eyewitness to an infraction that might have gotten me booted out right then and there.

I needed to cover my tracks, so I started rifling through my gear for gum or a mint—anything to mask the fact that I'd just imbibed. The only thing I could put my hands on was Nicorette gum, but it would have to do. Hence I'd jump-started my day with a cigarette, a snort of booze, and a piece of gum laced with nicotine. My head began pounding like I'd been standing too close to a howitzer, but Ruiz didn't look at me funny or anything, so I figured I'd dodged a bullet. Plus, operating the radio turned out to be a no-brainer.

Most of the officers and enlisted men and women I met that first day, like Ruiz, were welcoming. Many seemed intrigued about having a reporter along for the ride. I think they figured that if they spoke to me and made the news, their mom and dad, Aunt Meg and Uncle Fred, and their spouse, friends, and neighbors could have a window into their faraway world in an austere desert enclave.

Specialist Ronald Hancock, a Black Hawk helicopter crew chief, sounded like many of the others. Already a veteran of the fighting in Afghanistan, he expressed no qualms about taking part in another war in Iraq. "We've been living with the turmoil of Saddam Hussein being in power for too long," the twenty-three-year-old remarked.

Hancock had been at Victory for five days, so he had the lay of the land, and when he and I were finished talking geopolitics, he added a postscript. "Tell people we need silver bullets," he said, using the slang for large coffee urns. "And a popcorn machine."

Overhearing Hancock, a twenty-six-year-old medic, Jeremy Gilbert, added to Camp Victory's wish list: "And phone cards," he said. "And baby wipes. And toilet paper."

Only once that first day was someone less than cordial. A tall, muscular lieutenant colonel crossed paths with me in the tent, glowered, and demanded: "WHO are *you?*"

I said who I was, and he introduced himself as Lieutenant Colonel Anthony Sabb, commander of the Fourth Battalion. I realized that he was the one bellowing the night before, telling somebody to set up the cots and yelling at the entire tent to go to sleep.

I made a mental note to try and stay on Sabb's good side, then went back to my cot, which was doubling as a desk. As I combed through my notes, the plain truth about our odyssey emerged. It had taken sixteen hours to fly from Fort Campbell to Kuwait City, a distance of about 7,100 miles—and, counting from the time we stepped off the airliner, just as long to reach Camp Victory, which was no more than thirty miles from the Kuwaiti capital. No wonder I'd been ready to throw in the towel. Accompanying twenty-first-century soldiers, I'd endured a 1940s' military throwback: a snafu ("situation normal, all fucked up"). Apparently the delay was due to the need to travel with a military escort in a convoy; rumor had it that others had been in line to travel in this fashion ahead of us, hence the insufferable wait.

Captain Adam Kamann, the Fourth Battalion's personnel chief, also was doing public affairs duties now that Dollar, the reporter from Kentucky, and I had shown up. Kamann came to fetch me since a VIP visitor was due at the camp. The guest was Lieutenant General William Wallace, who led the Army's 5th Corps, making him one of the top U.S. military commanders in the Persian Gulf.

The tanned and chiseled troops, most in their twenties and thirties, stood in the sand under the sun, waiting for the general. For them, the event was mandatory. Wallace stepped out of a helicopter and was swarmed by strapping soldiers in buzz cuts, making him seem older, grayer, and more rumpled—but wiser.

Pacing back and forth, he spoke commandingly, if a bit theatrically, as if to parrot the late Scottish patriot who shares his name. "There's a knucklehead up in Baghdad who has been less than friendly to all of his neighbors. And it's time for him to go," Wallace thundered. "If the decision to go north is made, then by God, I'm going to be ready. God bless your families, and God bless the Screaming Eagles."

I took notes and snapped photos as I yanked from my hair one big beetle after another; they seemed to be dive-bombing my head. Wallace, after his presentation, looked straight at me and announced to the group, "Now I'll take any questions—except from reporters." It seemed like a dig, but at least I'd gotten pictures and a usable quote: he'd strongly hinted that war was in the offing.

Before I'd left Washington, a Deep Throat had assured me that war would occur sooner rather than later. At Victory, the average grunt didn't seem to have a clue. One predicted it might be July before the armed forces invaded Iraq; another was betting on November. Such guesstimates made me wonder how long my editors would be satisfied by stories about "girding for war" and how long my husband would tolerate my absence—certainly not for that many months.

After General Wallace left, I tried to find Father George, since it was Ash Wednesday and he'd said he'd be dispensing ashes to mark the holy day. Someone pointed out the tent that doubled as a chapel, but I found nary a soul inside.

Later, while finishing up my story, I saw soldiers pop in and out of my tent with black splotches on their foreheads. I'd had the time wrong: the service was at three o'clock, not two. When I bumped into Father George later, he asked whether I remembered from my catechism the hour that Christ had died. I did; it was 1500 hours.

The day's high point for me was sending my story to the States without a hitch. Nothing else compared—not the subtle grandeur of a desert morning, not even the sweet nothings with Tom. After I filed my piece, a soldier mentioned that there was hot chow being served in a tent on the other side of the camp. I trudged over the sand in the dark to the "chow tent" and thought nothing of it when I learned that the food prepared for dinner had been gobbled up. Apologetically, the cooks began bringing me breakfast fare: white bread and jam, raisin bran cereal, and ultrapasteurized, nonrefrigerated milk. "This is fine; it's real food," I assured these solicitous young women barely out of their teens.

As they wiped down serving tables and packed up napkins and paper plates, they asked me who I was, where I worked, and how long I was planning to remain with them. Was I staying for weeks—or months? Would I be here just for the buildup of U.S. forces—or stick with them if there was a war?

I said that I was planning to be with them for a while and that I was prepared to cover a war. Then one of the women began saying things like "Please don't leave us" and "You can't leave us." Finally she let the cat out of the bag, announcing, "If you leave us, he'll be mean to us again."

The young woman was from Fourth Bat—and so I gathered she was talking about Sabb. He struck me as hard-core, but I didn't have anything against him. It was the girl talk that made me squeamish, since I was only a journalist—not a mediator, referee, or human rights observer.

I capped the night by returning a call from Howard Kurtz, media writer for the *Washington Post*. Carl, my editor, had said that Kurtz wanted to speak to me since he'd seen the story I'd done on deploying from Fort Campbell. He'd left a bunch of phone numbers, suggesting he was keen to hear from me.

Kurtz was curious about objectivity, access, and other issues. I told him that nobody had a gun to my head, demanding good stories about the troops. I described access to sources as good, adding that, should war erupt, we were promised a front-row seat.

When he asked me about my surroundings, I said I was sharing a tent with forty or fifty others; that ten feet away from me were smelly feet; and that twenty feet away, somebody was snoring. He ended up using the atmospherics as well as cribbing a line from my story, questioning whether my husband could cope with the idea of me in a co-ed tent.

After my first full day, I was one happy Camp Victorian—until I ran into Rob Dollar, the reporter from Kentucky. He informed me that all of the 101st Airborne's embeds had been summoned to a meeting in Kuwait City the next morning. Departure time: 0700 hours. Postscript: Don't forget your gas mask.

Now my game plan had called for me to ignore the desert's morning song and sleep in; to slumber for as long as I possibly could; to luxuriate on my drab-olive cot until people worried that I was dead and considered nudging me with the butt of a rifle; to ignore my husband, my editor, my calling, and to take a "down day," as Matt Cox had counseled, which is to say, catch up on my rest, shoot some photographs, and practice sending them overseas.

But I was learning, in fits and starts, that what I wanted didn't matter. I was no longer in control of my destiny; Uncle Sam's Army seemed to be driving that train. Still, I took the news from Dollar in stride, thinking a trip to the capital could be fun, and hoping that I'd see Cox.

*   *   *

Talk about Ku-waiting: the seven o'clock bus was seven hours late. Amid anxious phone calls to Major Cate's public affairs shop and assurances that the meeting was still on, Dollar and I took turns in front of the tent, watching for the bus. Once in a while Ben Senger, a reporter for the NBC television affiliate out of Nashville, who was covering the Ninth Battalion, would stop by to see if we'd heard anything in Fourth about the delay. All the while the winds were kicking up, and when Senger complained he was cold, I lent him my gaiter, a stretchy garment that serves as a neck-warmer and can be pulled up over your mouth to keep the blowing sand out.

During the numbing wait, I sat for a while next to Ruiz alongside our tent, out of the wind, as he dug into MRE menu number twenty-two, pork chow mein.

We weren't exactly alone, because even though the camp had designated times for sick call, I was learning that soldiers came up to him at all hours, wanting his opinion about some malady or asking him to examine their smallpox scar. In the second case "Doc," as he was known, would eyeball the dark, crusty scab on somebody's upper arm (while I was thinking "Yech") and would pronounce it "Perfect. A textbook case." I thought he had a lovely manner.

With little else to do, I pulled out my notebook and asked Ruiz why so many people in the battalion were sneezing, sniffling, and hacking. We're acclimating to the desert, he said, since even the granules of sand carry microbes and viruses foreign to us.

He said that at Victory he'd chiefly been treating colds, sore feet, and anxiety, but every so often something more serious popped up. "It's a little like playing 'Where's Waldo?'" he quipped. "Out of the fifty, sixty people you see, you look for the sick one."

So he was droll, too. And he seemed sensitive. He spoke proudly of his brainy wife and teenaged son and daughter, noting that the girl, Chelsea, had just gotten her first suit because she was interviewing for a spot in a prestigious school specializing in math and science. That told me he believed in girl power.

Ruiz seemed impressed when I told him about my chat with the *Washington Post* and asked me what I'd said. I answered slowly, for effect: "I told him that these sorry excuses for soldiers were the saddest sacks I've seen in my entire life," I deadpanned.

He laughed. The lieutenant colonel knew it was hyperbole and bullshit, and I was glad that he'd gotten the joke. By then I knew that I would not, and could not, warm up to the military's bellicose, by-the-book ballbreakers; Ruiz, to my relief, seemed nothing like those men. I decided to propose a feature on the Fourth Battalion's flight surgeon—an "evergreen" story with a long shelf life, one my editors could run anytime.

It was about two in the afternoon when the bus finally arrived, a Kuwaiti charter with a third-country national as its driver. It had been delayed by the strong winds, bad directions, and who knew what else.

Only a week had gone by since I'd seen my media colleagues back at Campbell, but each one I spied on the bus already seemed transformed. People had on hip, rugged-weather clothing, as if bound for a safari, and had begun to sport suntans. After a short time in the desert, everyone seemed coated with sand and drenched in sangfroid.

But my companions were hungry, and grumbling about it, since they'd endured a long wait too, traveling from camp to camp before the last pick-up of passengers at Victory. I asked an officer in Fourth Bat for permission to share our MREs and, with Cox's help, hauled two boxes onto the bus.

Then I slid into the seat next to Cox so we could catch up during the ride to Kuwait City. I launched into the story of my misadventure with the vodka, laying the blame for my blunder entirely at his feet.

The bus windows, again, were shielded with dark-colored velour curtains, giving me pause about the prospect of a trigger-happy anti-American and preventing us from seeing what Kuwait looked like.

The meeting was held at a five-star hotel, the Fahaheel-Hilton Kuwait, which housed the Coalition Forces Land Component Command public affairs desk. The command—CFLCC for short, which everyone pronounced "C-Flick," oversaw ground forces, the Army and Marines (but not the air, maritime, or special operations elements).

First we posed for photos for CFLCC media badges. Mine had Carl Schwartz's name and phone number on the back; if I was hurt or killed, he as my immediate supervisor would be the first person to get the word. Then we went over some new ground rules and forked over $35 to have our Kuwaiti travel documents adjusted. I'd come with a visa good for up to three months; when a sergeant with the 101st returned my passport a few days later, it seemed I'd been granted residency (something I avoided telling Tom).

As the meeting wound down, Cox jabbed me with his elbow and asked, "After this, do you want to get a martini?"

I gave him a thumbs-up, imagining a nice, strong cocktail in a frosty glass and a pair of olives on a tiny, yellow plastic sword. Cox responded with a burst of laughter; he was pulling my leg. The hotel's ubiquitous luxury had me forgetting that I was experiencing a first: I'd been in dry counties, but never dry countries. It was small consolation to have no-alcohol beer over dinner with him that night.

After eating, we had time to kill, so we strolled outside on the hotel grounds amid the palm trees, manicured lawns, and shallow pools of water that surrounded the buildings like moats. As was our custom, Cox and I prattled about everything and nothing, and while we were walking and talking I failed to notice a decorative pool of water in my path. Ker-plunk! My reflexes allowed me to save the Nikon around my neck from a watery death, but I was drenched from the knees down.

Cox doubled over in laughter, since now I looked like a veteran clam digger, not a fledgling war correspondent. I ruled out going back into the hotel to find a restroom and dry off, since I'd have to run a gauntlet past reporters and photographers and military officers. With my trousers still on, I wrung out my pant legs as best I could, resigned myself to having waterlogged boots and socks, and hurled a few expletives in Cox's direction so he would stop chortling.

He wasn't chancing another long ordeal on the bus; he'd finagled a ride on a Humvee back to Camp Doha, where his infantry unit was based. Although I had no way of knowing it, I wouldn't see him again for a long while.

Cox was wise to blow off the bus ride, since the winds were becoming more vigorous, rocking the vehicle back and forth and sending sheets of sand cascading across the road.

I knew things were dicey, so I turned to the relaxation techniques I'd picked up in a yoga class. Placing my fingertips together, I breathed in and out and made up meditations.

"S-o-o-o-o-o-n," I told myself, "I'll be ho-o-o-o-me.

"S-o-o-o-o-o-n, I'll be c-o-c-o-o-n-ed in my s-le-e-e-e-e-e-ping bag.

"S-o-o-o-o-o-n, I'll be s-le-e-e-e-e-e-ping."

The self-talk knocked me out, briefly, but I awoke to the sound of our driver nervously squawking in Arabic as he battled sand drifts blocking sections of the road. Then I noticed that the military escorts on board were ripping apart the cardboard MRE boxes to fortify the ceiling hatches, the rear emergency door, and other spots where sand was seeping in.

I tried not to worry, reminding myself that I'd survived blizzards on Chicago's Dan Ryan Expressway.

"S-o-o-o-o-o-n," I told myself, "I'll be ho-o-o-o-me.

"S-o-o-o-o-o-n, I'll be c-o-c-o-o-n-ed in my s-le-e-e-e-e-e-ping bag.

"S-o-o-o-o-o-n, I'll be s-le-e-e-e-e-e-ping."

The onslaught of wind and sand kept up, with near zero-visibility conditions by the time we reached Victory. The embeds with the 159th were disgorged at the front gate and ferried in a minivan to our tents. Wind-strewn pebbles and rocks flew and paper debris deposited in plywood garbage containers spun in every direction like whirling dervishes.

It was about eleven thirty when I entered my dim tent, home to the Fourth Battalion's headquarters company. My eyes darted to my cot, which was supporting two large plastic "tuff boxes" in which Ruiz stored medical supplies—with my belongings scattered helter-skelter on the floor.

As the soldiers scrambled to keep the tent standing, I imagined sailors on a nineteenth-century tall ship that was pitching and yawing and struggling to stay afloat under darkened skies during a wretched storm at sea. The tent's cotton canopy and side panels were flapping wildly and the tall, interior metal poles jumped up and down, clanging and clattering while knifing holes in the roof. They seemed like pogo sticks on methamphetamines.

As I was taking stock, and deciding that things were going from bad to worse for the Fourth Battalion, Command Sergeant Major Don Gregg came up to me, shouting over the din, "Put on your K-pot!"

"What's my K-pot?" I asked.

"Your Kevlar," he replied.

"What's my Kevlar?"

"Your helmet."

As I complied, a voice cried out from the opposite end of the tent, "Can anybody sew?" I hastened down there and announced meekly, "I can sew," but nobody heard me over the wind and confusion. It was just as well because when I looked closer, I saw flashlights trained on the soldiers who were "sewing" with a machete and rope. They were trying to affix the top of the tent to the sides, but once I caught the size of the knife, I buttoned my lips and stepped backward.

"We need help outside!" somebody hollered next. I headed out with a half-dozen others, each of us grabbing one of the ropes holding up the sides of the tent and holding fast while our faces were pummeled with sand, dust, pulverized rock, and debris.

Flanked by more than a dozen soldiers, I was securing a rope in the corner, proud to be doing my little part, when Sabb got in my face. "WHO are *you?*" he bellowed, phrasing the question exactly as he had a day earlier.

"I'm Skiba, your embed," I answered.

He stomped off without a word. Couldn't he have used the magic words "Thank you"? I wondered. Would "team player" have been too much to ask?

It impressed me that everyone was pitching in. There wasn't a single slacker—and nobody was complaining, either. Next to me, Lieutenant Michelle Carron, an intelligence officer, held fast to her rope and took the wild weather in stride. "Soldiers eat dirt, wear dirt, and sleep in dirt," the twenty-three-year-old woman called out.

The storm was much too severe for me to commit her slogan to paper, so I vowed to remember it.

Minutes later, Sabb was back, declaring the tent a lost cause and ordering us to relinquish the ropes and let it come down. Hoping to keep the shriveled-up canvas from blowing away, he instructed the troops to throw sand bags on top of it to secure it. That was distressing to me. I watched mutely as a fusillade of the ten-pound bags slammed against the tent, cringing with each new "thud."

There goes my laptop, I thought to myself. Farewell, digital camera. Sayonara, sat phone.

I snapped out of my stupor when I saw Carron, plus other lieutenants and captains, some of them West Pointers, scramble toward another tent to take cover. Like a gosling in need of Mother Goose, I quickly fell in behind them. Once inside, I grabbed a chair, slid up to a small folding table, pulled out my weather-beaten notebook and wrote:

Thursday, March 6, 12:45 a.m. My hair feels like a dirty floor mop. My teeth are coated in sand. The corners of my eyes are clogged with sand. This paper is coated with sand.

During forty-eight hours at Camp Victory, I've had one tick, one hot meal, one shower and one sandstorm.

Sabb entered the shelter, walked to its center, and announced: "Listen up, people! You have just experienced your first squall."

"No shit, Sherlock," I thought. I was pissed at him. The boor had been in my face during the height of the storm, treating me like an infiltrator. I wrote down Sabb's blinding flash of the obvious and privately corrected him: "Not true, Sabb, *you* were my first squall."

I and the other refugees—men and women, most of whom I barely knew—claimed narrow spaces on the wooden floor. I thanked God for my fanny pack, since there was Motrin stashed inside. As I downed two orange tablets, I wondered why my meditations ("Home," "Cocoon," "Sleeping Bag," "Sleep") had been so abominably jinxed.

With only the Dan Rather jacket for cover, I tossed from side to side in search of comfort, shivering since my feet still were cold and wet from my accidental dip at the Kuwait Hilton. I began cursing the name of Matthew J. Cox.

Being a reporter, I've covered disasters—tornados, floods, wildfires, explosions, bombings, you name it—and I know what happens after disasters. With a cheerful toot-toot of its horn, an American Red Cross truck tools into town, and earnest volunteers hand out black coffee, powdery doughnuts, and rough-hewn blankets. So as I tried to fall asleep on what was my third night at Victory, I wondered what was taking the big, white truck with the red insignia so long to deliver the goods. "You're in the Army now," the little voice in my head reminded me. "Ain't gonna happen."

The next morning, I straightened my spine and staggered out to survey the damage as soldiers disassembled their M-4 rifles, cleaned them, and knocked sand out of their ears. When our old tent went up, temporarily, I stepped into the goulash of sand-coated, olive-colored gear now scattered on the floor in disarray and located my professional equipment, which, to my amazement, had survived.

In the tent I ran into Ruiz, who was taking stock of his medical supplies and personal belongings. "Where were you last night?" he asked me. "I was worried about you."

"Oh, I'm OK," I fibbed, stunned that somebody cared.

But now was not the time for idle chatter. My inauguration into Army life had been a roller-coaster ride, but I knew a story when I saw one, so I got to work reporting on what was being called Kuwait's worst sand-storm in fifteen years. At Victory, fifteen of the forty-five tents had come down. Sustained winds were recorded at forty-six miles an hour and gusts at fifty-nine miles an hour; the readings likely were higher, but the storm was too intense for a military meteorologist with a Kestrel 4000, a weather-monitoring device about the size of a cell phone, to remain outdoors for very long.

Air Force Technical Sergeant James Karr, a meteorologist assigned to Victory, told me that it had been impossible to forecast the storm because much of the sophisticated weather-reading equipment bound for the camp still was on supply ships coming into port.

I called my editor, Carl, telling him what I'd endured. He knew about the storm from the wire services, but wanted the inside dope. "What was it like?" he asked.

"It was like that scene from the movie *The English Patient*," I answered, "but without the romance."

As I hung up with Carl, 1st Lieutenant Jamey Trigg, who works in communications for the Fourth Battalion, strode past with a mischievous glance and asked how I was. "Just fine," I insisted.

Trigg retorted, "You ain't seen nothin' yet. Just wait until the war starts."

The repair of our tent fell to local contractors, who crawled atop the downed fabric, cigarettes dangling from their lips, realigning what they could and replacing what they couldn't. Meanwhile I moved, with several others, to the second of two headquarters company tents within the Fourth Battalion. There a drop-dead-gorgeous captain, the affable Carlos Goveo ("I'm the smile of this battalion"), was the company commander.

Getting out of Sabb's tent meant moving down a rung, in a sense, since my new home housed fewer commissioned officers and pilots and mostly enlisted soldiers—cooks, vehicle mechanics, aircraft refuelers, and such. The mood was much more relaxed, since there wasn't a warden like the lieutenant colonel looking over people's shoulders 24–7. Soldiers were doing their work and filling in down time by talking smack, telling jokes, and catching movies on their DVD players. I liked the tent's lighter mood, especially after I grew accustomed to tiptoeing over and around the M-249 light machine guns loitering in the aisles. It took me a few days to get up the nerve to ask the soldiers whether their weapons were loaded; they weren't.

I set up a cot across the aisle from Ruiz and next to Trigg, on whom I'd begun relying for help editing and sending pictures. Ruiz and I privately called him "Jimmy Olson," since the slightly built former student of photojournalism seemed eager to be my legman.

Meanwhile hot food started showing up in the morning and evening; that was a treat compared to a steady diet of MREs. And every so often we got permission to use the showers, though the hours were always limited, and it took me time to acclimate to being stark naked in a steamy trailer loaded with gun-toting women; but, in any case, we soon lost one of the women: she had tested positive for pregnancy, so she was shipped out.

With so little in the way of diversions—no television, Internet, or post exchange—I just tried to enjoy what there was: a cigarette, a conversation, a picture-postcard sunset, maybe a glimpse of Goveo at night wearing only a T-shirt and running shorts. I wasn't the only admirer of the amiable Puerto Rican native with coffee-colored eyes; he was *un hombre guapo*.

I got two unexpected perks: one of those long military addresses (HHC4-101 AHB, 96129, APO AE 09325-6129) and the chance to send letters home for free.

By this point everybody was asking to use my satellite phone, but I was pretty stingy with it, unless (a) you were my friend; (b) you had done something for me, like lent me a table and chair outside of the elements long enough to write a story; or (c) you really needed it. That first week, the battalion chaplain, Captain Kerry Greene, announced that his wife was in labor; the words "She's dilated four centimeters" were all it took for me to hand him my phone.

If I guarded my lifeline, it had to do with the cost of making a call ($2 a minute), the time (it took a five-minute tutorial to instruct a person on its use), and the size of the outfit (2,300 soldiers). I had to draw the line because I had my hands full; I was reporting, writing, taking photos, transmitting material, and, every so often, speaking to the sister radio and television stations that my company owns in Milwaukee.

All in all, just a few days into my stay at Victory, life seemed good, but it turned out that I was on a teeter-totter, and, on that day, happened to be riding high.

On Sunday morning, March 9, Dollar and I were invited to a meeting of the top officials of the 307-person-strong Fourth Battalion. A brainy, thirty-six-year-old major, Michael Shenk, the battalion's operations boss, ran the session, which we were told was to be off the record. Though I had no clue what the meeting was about, I quickly learned: it was on the brigade's role in the impending invasion of Iraq. There was talk of aircraft, personnel, rehearsals, missions, which locations would be seized, and what the threats from the enemy were. Some of the discussion was so loaded with jargon, I found it incomprehensible. Meantime I did what I've done for years: I took notes.

"We're cramped for time, constrained for resources, and facing a force that none of us is going to take for granted," Shenk told the group. Plans for the air assault indicated that "we're going to go further in one day than Patton did in his entire campaign."

Nobody had warned me not to take down what was said; and nobody around me suggested that I should stop scribbling.

But at the conclusion of the meeting, when Sabb got wind of what I had done, I was ordered by one of his subordinates to hand over the pages of my notebook that dealt with the meeting. I was told that I'd get them back after the mission was accomplished.

The whole thing rubbed me the wrong way, for a few reasons. First, I knew the ground rules and was hewing to them; we were supposed to have access to precombat briefings, though we were forbidden from leaking battle plans. I totally respected that. Second, I found it odd that written notes from the meeting retrospectively were deemed taboo; had it not occurred to anyone that at least some of the stuff was now etched on my gray matter? Third, the idea that scraps from my notebook would be preserved in the hubbub of this primitive outpost—and later returned—seemed to me as improbable as the Lipizzaner stallions flying. Finally, I knew that there were military journalists practically embedding with certain generals, and I was sure that these scribes were not being "mushroomed," which is to say, fed bullshit and kept in the dark.

So I stood up to Sabb. Take the whole notebook, I told his emissary, while I take this issue up with Major Cate, the public affairs boss, who was then at Camp Doha, elsewhere in Kuwait.

Looking back, Sabb and his minions may have been stunned that I didn't capitulate. They were used to people following orders; had I been a soldier, what I had proposed as a compromise might have been called insubordination.

But I knew I had to stand up for my rights—and I won the battle. Cate said my notebook should not have been seized, that it should be returned, and that he'd make a phone call to set things right. It had fallen to Carron, the intel officer, to review my scribbles, and when she returned my spiral-bound notebook, she noted that nobody could really make out my chicken scratches anyway.

The word spread that a divisionwide planning meeting was being held at Doha, so I jumped at the chance to go. I wanted to find out what was going on, and I relished a change of scene, too. A number of reporters joined me at brigade headquarters, waiting for a seat on a bus, on a space-available basis, for Doha.

I bumped into Father George; he suggested that I accompany him and the others bound for Doha and not take no for an answer. I ran into Ruiz, too, but found him beside himself. Word had just come in that two of his young medics, who had gone to the port to bring back a Humvee and medical supplies, had been injured—one seriously—in a motor vehicle accident on the way back to Victory. The man who was seriously injured, Sergeant Jeremy Gilbert, was said to have been pinned in the vehicle, possibly with a severed foot.

"He could bleed to death," Ruiz told me.

I told the flight surgeon that he needed more information before jumping to conclusions and suggested he hope for the best. Cupping his hands, I added, "Modern medicine can make miracles."

Instantly I was taken aback by the words that had sprung out of my mouth. Who was this woman? So what if I picked up a few tidbits about trauma when I had dated an E.R. doc? Just three months ago I was at Fort Benning, where I was, in my own words, "no Florence Nightingale," and fighting back tears over make-believe casualties during combat first-aid training.

I took a seat on the bus next to Ben Senger, the TV reporter from Nashville, and we traded notes about camp life, our careers, and where we'd gone to college. Ben was from East Grand Forks, Minnesota, and had gone to the University of St. Thomas in St. Paul. He was only twenty-four, but as two Midwesterners, we hit it off. I used to work for the *Minneapolis Star,* so we had run in some of the same precincts. I got an earful from Ben that day, his life story, in fact—a drama populated by his divorced mother and father, his sister, and his old girlfriend. Maybe because waiting for a war to start is like teetering in the wind on the ledge of a tall building, some people just ran at the mouth; if nothing else, it animated life in the desert.

Senger seemed mature for his age, and I felt I could trust him, so I recounted my run-ins with Lieutenant Colonel Sabb: the "WHO are *you?*" on my first day and the "WHO are *you?*" during the sandstorm, and this morning's demand that I cough up my notes.

Senger was astonished. He and his photographer, Eric Oliver, had been welcomed into their battalion, which, like mine, was a Black Hawk helicopter unit. The Ninth Battalion's commander early on had thanked them for taking the assignment; he was so accommodating, in fact, that he'd told Senger and Oliver, "I hope we don't talk your ears off."

Altogether, there were four aviation battalions within the brigade: the Fourth, Fifth, Seventh, and Ninth. It seemed just dumb luck that I'd drawn Sabb's unit, but after listening to Senger, I began thinking about voting with my feet.

The meeting at Doha was closed to the press, as it turned out, but the day wasn't a total loss, since I got to hit the post exchange (after a warning that, as in the old Soviet Union, half the shelves would be empty, and the stuff missing is what you really wanted) and to visit the American Red Cross (where a little cajoling got me on the Internet, for copies of my latest stories).

Night had fallen by the time we were back on the bus, waiting to return to Victory, when the commander of the 101st Airborne, Major General David H. Petraeus, came on board to say hello. The decorated two-star came with a reputation. He is a fitness fanatic, a scholar, having a Ph.D. in international affairs from Princeton, and a survivor. In 1991 he was accidentally shot in the chest at close range by a soldier during a training exercise; Petraeus credits heart surgeon Bill Frist, then at Vanderbilt University Medical Center in Nashville, now the U.S. Senate majority leader, with saving his life. It wasn't Petraeus's first brush with death. He once survived the collapse of his parachute during a free fall, breaking his pelvis but living to tell the tale.

Petraeus wanted to know how the embeds were holding up, quipping, "As somebody said, nobody promised you sheets." It was the first and last I'd see of him. Ruiz got on the bus, too, but only to collect his things. While Gilbert's prognosis was not as dire as first thought, the flight surgeon was heading downtown to the Kuwait Armed Forces Hospital to help oversee his care.

"Before you go, tell me what you know about the accident, and tell me about Gilbert," I said to Ruiz. "I'll probably be writing about this."

There on the bus he gave me the scant details he had: about six a.m., Gilbert and others had gone to pick up equipment and supplies being offloaded in a Persian Gulf port. The medic was bringing back a Humvee and a trailer with the battalion aid-station equipment when the accident took place. Little else was known, but Ruiz ruefully noted that Kuwaiti traffic signals tended to be taken as mere "suggestions."

Ruiz went on to say that Gilbert was the first person he'd met when he had arrived in mid-February at a Fourth Battalion aid station back at Campbell. "He is a solid man," Ruiz said. "He knew what he was doing. He had combat experience in Afghanistan. I don't think he was ever scared of anything. He is physically strong and mentally strong—unshakable." He added, "He's married with no kids. He and his wife wanted to start a family soon."

The whole thing struck ominously close to home. The genial medic from Flippin, Arkansas, was one of the first people I'd met, too. He was the one who'd asked for phone cards, baby wipes, and toilet paper. During cleanup the morning after the sandstorm, I'd photographed Gilbert in his black Army gym shorts and fleece top. And the night before the accident, he'd wound up in Goveo's tent, taking the empty cot next to mine.

So is this what happened in war? You get to know a person—put a face with a name, share something about yourself, call it a night in side-by-side cots—and then he's gone? I told myself to save the melodrama until we knew more; besides, something Ruiz had said about the twenty-six-year-old medic made an impression.

"Physically strong and mentally strong—unshakable." At that moment I pledged to start behaving that way myself. This was war. This might take every ounce of the courage that I purported to have back at Campbell.

I was distressed, though, to see Ruiz take his leave, since he'd already become a comfort, a friend and daily presence. Of course I knew that he had better things to do than to teach me how to use a shortwave radio, translate military jargon into English for me, and laugh at my wisecracks.

Still, it stung, so I tugged at his sleeve and whispered coquettishly, "Do you mean to tell me that I'm going to be Bob-less?"

Smiling back at me, off he went.

By the next day, the facts surrounding the crash involving Gilbert and Brandon Null, a twenty-one-year-old from Chesterton, Indiana, were clearer. Sabb had visited the pair in the hospital; according to his and other accounts, the two medics had been traveling on a two-lane road in a convoy led by a Kuwaiti police officer. When the vehicles slowed at a checkpoint, the police escort stopped to make sure that all of them got through, then drove down the wrong lane of the highway to return to the head of the convoy. But a motorist in a Crown Victoria was traveling in that lane, reportedly at a speed of sixty or seventy miles an hour; the Crown Vic swerved on the shoulder of the road to avoid striking the policeman, lost control in loose sand, and careened into the Humvee that Gilbert was driving. The medic now was awaiting surgery and, later, transport to a U.S. military hospital in Landstuhl, Germany. Null had broken a few fingers and was coming back to camp shortly.

When Sabb returned to Victory he told a battalion meeting that he was moved to tears by Gilbert's insistence that he still was up for the mission. "The first thing he said to me was, 'Don't let them send me to Germany. Just let me stay here. I want to get better and come out,'" the lieutenant colonel said, adding: "He's one tough S.O.B."

At the same meeting, Chaplain Greene led a prayer for the two soldiers, one of whom was getting a ticket home.

Command Sergeant Major Donald Gregg, a wiry, unflappable fifty-year-old, was among those who filled in some of the details for my story on the mishap. As the battalion's command sergeant major, he was the senior enlisted soldier in the unit. It's a classic middle-management position: Gregg advised Sabb on everything from the soldiers' training and professional development to their health, welfare, and morale and, at the same time, made sure the battalion commander's edicts were implemented.

Gregg, a native of Fort Lauderdale, had been in the Army for "nineteen years and four months," or longer than some of his younger charges had been alive. He was a been-there, done-that kind of guy and a straight shooter. Almost every afternoon I found myself taking a cigarette break with him; before long I began inviting him to these sessions by asking, "Is it time for psychotherapy?"

The next day, when the battalion's collective mood had calmed down, I decided to sit down with Sabb and try to make amends after the battle of the notebook. I began by saying that the two of us never really had had a proper introduction; that I was sorry that I hadn't gotten to meet him at Campbell; and that it was unfortunate we pulled in so late that first night that I hadn't made his acquaintance then.

I told him that I'd written a number of stories about the military, that I'd been to media boot camp, and that I'd brought along a dossier for him to read, if he'd like. Sabb dismissed the idea of reviewing my file. "I *know* who you *are*," he snarled, like when the Wizard was trying to intimidate Dorothy on their first meeting in Oz.

With respect to Sunday's meeting, I told Sabb that nobody had advised me not to take notes and that it was second nature for me to write things down after being a reporter for twenty-five years. I made it plain that I knew the ground rules and did not plan to leak battle plans or act in a manner that would jeopardize a soldier or the unit.

I detected his stone face softening a bit. "I guess I haven't met that many reporters," he admitted.

I went on to tell him my father and grandfather had served in the Army; that I was an American first and a reporter second; and that, just like him, I was wearing dog tags—trying to make the point that I too was prepared to die in the line of duty. Maybe because it dawned on me that enemy spies might also be willing to make the ultimate sacrifice, I finished my spiel with this: "Besides, if I did something to screw up your mission and people got hurt, I'd go down in history as an idiot."

Sabb and I then shook hands. I stood up, feeling that I'd done my best—then walked away with a god-awful headache.

When I ran into Ruiz, I told him what I'd done. "I just had a man-to-man chat with Sabb," I said. "I think everything's OK now."

Still, Sabb tended to inspire either fear or loathing. Plenty of people said the entire battalion looked forward to June 12, the day Sabb's two-year command ended and he'd move on. He had a reputation for forgetting people's names, I was told, and often summoned his subordinates by shouting out their alphanumeric specialty—"S-1" for personnel, "S-2" for military intelligence, "S-3" for operations, "S-4" for logistics, and "S-6" for communications. It seemed callous.

One morning I was telling my troubles to a rough-and-tough pilot in the chow hall, and he bucked me up. "Tell Sabb you're here on DOD orders, and if he doesn't like it, it's his problem, not your problem." That turned my head around. Another time I ran into a veteran pilot from Fourth Bat, asking him if I should switch battalions, since Sabb seemed so difficult. "If you want to be where the action is, stick with the Fourth," he advised.

By now the skies over Victory had begun thundering. The "birds"—that's what everyone called the helicopters—were being off-loaded at a Kuwaiti port, Ash Shu'aybah, and flown in so the pilots could commence drills involving landing and taking off in the sand. Particularly during landings, the rotor blades kick up so much sand and dirt that brownout conditions result, meaning that the pilot has little or no visibility—and little margin of error. So they rehearsed: upwind and downwind; during the day; and, using night-vision goggles, after dark. Joining the ninety Black Hawks were fifteen medevac birds and thirty-four gigantic Chinook helicopters

Meanwhile two-and-a-half-ton trucks were loudly streaming in, metamorphosing my serene, pale desert paradise into a military staging ground crowded with vehicles coated in dull green paint.

From Gilbert, the injured medic flown to Germany, I'd inherited a pair of size 12 galoshes, since the ones I'd been issued as part of my chemical-protective gear were too snug to fit over my regular boots. While happy to have a pair that fit, the gesture made me think only of the T-shirt back at Fort Campbell: "If you die first, we split your gear." Now it didn't seem so funny to me.

Before long somebody, apparently at Sabb's behest, ordered me back into my original tent, saying it was for "accountability," or to keep track of where Dollar and I were. When I returned, I cajoled Carron and a few other female officers into carving out an all-women enclave of four or five cots.

Instructions came down to set our watches back three hours to "Zulu time," or Greenwich Mean Time, and Father George quietly provided the reason behind that, telling us that the Army was synchronizing its clocks with the U.S. Air Force. In other words, war could be around the corner.

One morning a cook called out to me, heralding that lobster tail was on the menu for dinner. "That is bullshit," I shouted back, thinking she was playing me for a fool. She wasn't. And that night when two tails showed up on my plate, I got a Death Row vibe and wondered if this was going to be the brigade's Last Supper.

Ruiz by then was back at Victory, since his injured medic had gotten on a flight to Landstuhl so that he could be cared for at the U.S. military hospital there. That night the flight surgeon and I ate al fresco outside the dining facility (which everyone called the D-Fac), and I handed over one of my lobster tails to him. We were enjoying our tête-à-tête, until napkins and empty paper plates and plastic cups began swirling around, sending people racing to collect them. Another storm was brewing, so Ruiz and I quickly headed over the sand back to the Fourth Bat's tents. The gusts got nastier during our quarter-mile trip, and I rued having relinquished my neck gaiter to Senger, who had lost it in the big sandstorm days earlier.

Back at the tent, there were new instructions: Dollar and I would have to leave the shelter temporarily, since a secret military planning meeting was about to commence. It was practically nine o'clock at night—and I had planned on sinking into bed. Couldn't somebody have given me a heads-up about this? Couldn't somebody have proposed a middle ground—say, letting me transport my cot into the furthest recesses of the tent where, on my word of honor, my eye mask and ear plugs would have neutralized whatever threat it was that I seemed to pose? Couldn't somebody just read the damn ground rules and stop mushrooming me?

I had no interest in being shanghaied. I was going to bed, thank you very much, and so, a bit dramatically, I collected my sleeping bag and gear and stormed out of the tent. The winds were so violent that sand and dust and itinerant debris pelted my face during the short hike of several feet to Goveo's tent. I started to care less about the top-secret mumbo-jumbo and more about being unceremoniously booted out in such awful weather.

"I'm b-a-a-a-c-k," I announced to anyone within earshot in the new tent. Dollar had come, too, but was following instructions, planning to stay only for the duration of what turned out to be a long meeting. I found an empty cot near Ruiz's, dumped my things, and let it rip. "Sabb is such an asshole! He is so rude! All I wanted to do was go to sleep! In real life, I have options! I can walk away from a story! I can write a story around somebody who won't cooperate! I can't believe this bullshit! *No one has ever treated me this way!*"

There was nothing discreet about my profanity-laced paroxysm. It's likely that the cooks and mechanics and communications guys heard it all, maybe a soldier assigned to intelligence, probably some lieutenants and sergeants, certainly a warrant officer or two. I didn't care. If hell hath no fury like a woman scorned, then double or triple or quadruple that to gauge how furiously my blood was boiling. I was an embedded journalist trying mightily to play by the rules, taking the biggest gamble of my life, going where most of my colleagues refused to tread, carrying with me at all times injections to counteract a nerve-gas attack—all to let the United States of America learn about this war.

Now it seemed that my man-to-man chat with Sabb had been for naught. "I am out of this battalion! There are other battalions!" I announced to Ruiz. "I knew before I got here that everything would hinge on your relationship with the commander of your unit. But how can you have a relationship with such a twisted freak?"

The doctor didn't say much, except to suggest that I sleep on it.

When I was up and at 'em the next morning, Ruiz took me aside and looked me in the eyes. "Please don't leave Fourth Bat," he said quietly.

His entreaty stopped me in my tracks. I shrugged my shoulders and scanned the soldiers around me, many of them just kids. Plenty of the troops didn't even know my name; I was "Reporter Lady" or "Press Lady" or "Miss Reporter."

By then I'd been with them for ten days. I knew many of their names and ranks and military specialties. I'd learned their home towns, seen their family pictures, heard their coughing fits, and screwed up my face at some of the most elaborate tattoos I'd seen in my life. Once I'd watched a girl stand up and cut her hair with a Leatherman knife, feeling a mixture of revulsion and admiration.

They were soldiers—good people and great copy—and none of them had interfered with my work or been unwelcoming. To the contrary, they'd taught me computer shortcuts, hustled me to the D-Fac when the chow was almost gone, and keyed me in to the rare times the showers were open for business. (Our instructions for showering were: "Turn on the water, rinse, turn off the water. Turn on the water, lather, turn off the water. Turn on the water, rinse, turn off the water.")

Ruiz kept lobbying. "Please don't leave," he said. "If you stay, I'll tell you every day how grateful I am."

He was my best buddy. I wasn't likely to meet his clone in the other battalions—Five, Seven, or Nine. And if I moved to a new unit, whatever inroads I'd made with the Fourth Battalion soldiers would be lost; I'd have to start from scratch with a new group.

So I stayed.

Before too long it seemed like the right thing to do. Word was getting around that the *Milwaukee Journal Sentinel* had a reporter here—and people were volunteering story ideas and telling me about soldiers from Wisconsin to meet. One short feature I did was on Sabb's ordering the Fourth Battalion's Bravo Company fliers to take down a Harley-Davidson flag that they'd hoisted on the flagpole in front of their tent, right beneath Old Glory. The piece caught the eye of the Milwaukee-based motorcycle manufacturer and hog enthusiasts across the United States.

But while I stayed in Fourth Battalion, I knew that I had work to do with higher-ups in the 159th Brigade. Something told me that there was one avenue left to make my life tolerable: I could try to trump Sabb by ingratiating myself with his boss, the brigade's top gun, Colonel Forrester. He struck me as smart and steely, plus word of mouth had him universally respected. Already during an introductory one-on-one the colonel had sized me up from head to toe, buttonholed me on my view of war against Iraq, and lauded my story on the injured medics.

He seemed my only hope.

5

"You've Got Balls"

The burly, towering 1st Sergeant Mark Kolesar welcomed soldiers from the Fourth Battalion to their new home, Camp Thunder Road, with the subtlety and charm of a cowboy wielding a red-hot branding iron over the hind end of a Black Angus calf.

"Unfuck your shit!" he shouted across the tent.

If this was Army jargon, I needed no translation. He was telling his charges to unpack what they needed from their rucks and stow the rest beneath their cots, preferably in double-time. I already was, as the thirty-eight-year-old sergeant put it, uncopulating my excrement; and even before his directive, he'd landed at the top of my shit list.

It was Saturday, March 15, when the 159th Brigade pulled out of Victory and put down roots in another sand-blown expanse, this one near Kuwait's borders with Iraq and Saudi Arabia. The brigade was inching closer to the coming fight, positioning itself to, if ordered, get across the Iraqi border fast.

The new camp married the informal name of the brigade, "Thunder Eagle," and the Bruce Springsteen song. "Thunder is nothing but a road," Colonel William Forrester had told the embedded journalists in a briefing just before moving day. He was exaggerating only slightly.

Indeed, a key feature of the new desert outpost was a long stretch of asphalt that served as a convenient parking place for the brigade's ninety Black Hawks, thirty-four Chinooks, and fifteen medevac birds, though the "road" wasn't spacious enough for all of them. Some helicopters were left to take off, land, and park in the dreaded sand.

I'd ridden to Thunder Road in the back of an open-air truck jam-packed with young soldiers, rifles, gas masks, and a mountain of gear. "Illegal-immigrant style" is how one soldier described our mode of transportation. I ended up squished next to Krystal Carter, a twenty-year-old private from Miami who told me she'd joined the Army with three of her sisters on the same day. My first thought was that that would make a great story, until I learned the military had scattered the Carter Quartet to the four winds, giving me less material with which to work; my second was to feel melancholy, as I tried to imagine how her mother must have felt giving up four daughters in one fell swoop.

On our way to the new camp, the sun bore down on us from azure skies. Carter and I ended up whiling away the time singing hits by Whitney Houston and Diana Ross, inevitably forgetting the lyrics midway through each song and busting our guts laughing. There were many false starts on other tunes; given the gap in our ages, there weren't a lot of artists whose music we both knew.

The frivolity came to a halt once we reached Thunder Road. The camp was surrounded by a steep, sandy berm and, here and there, tall wooden sentry towers, where heavily armed soldiers stood watch. Outsiders clearly were not welcome.

Just inside the berm there was a group of tan-colored metallic boxes angled toward the sky; each of the containers looked as if it could fit on the back of an eighteen-wheeled semi. "There are the Patriots," Carter called out, enlightening me to the proximity of the U.S. surface-to-air missiles. It's not like I studied them hard; they seemed as incidental as umbrellas in a stand in somebody's foyer.

I lugged my gear into Sabb's tent, hoping to set up my cot next to the women there I'd come to know: Michelle Carron, the young intel lieutenant who'd put on a brave face during the sandstorm; Captain Alicia Chivers, a native of Montana who'd graduated from the U.S. Military Academy, the first female West Pointer I ever met; 1st Lieutenant Veleka Douglas, a soft-spoken woman who made sure everybody had been given protective garments in case of WMD; and Sergeant Sherre Maxson, a sturdy, upbeat woman who handled logistics and hailed from the lake-and-cabin country of Eagle River, Wisconsin. I'd vacationed there, beginning in childhood, so I felt I knew her roots.

As I started to settle in with the womenfolk, I was booted out; somebody informed me that Sabb, the battalion commander, didn't want the two reporters in his tent any more. So I left for the second of two Fourth Battalion headquarters company shelters, where, in light of Captain Goveo's temporary absence, Kolesar was playing king. When he spotted me hauling in my things, he blew a gasket, complaining out loud that his tent already was too crowded.

With a Sunday story to finish, I lacked the time and appetite for being treated like a hot potato, so I suggested that Kolesar and I go over to Sabb's tent and resolve the dispute. The result: I was sent packing again and traipsed back with Kolesar to his quarters.

Once we returned, the sergeant refused to let me stake a claim for one of the tent's four corners, which was prime real estate for reasons of space and privacy, both of which, especially the latter, were becoming faded memories. Then he vetoed my second choice, which was to erect my cot perpendicular to the side of the tent; that would have afforded both a few feet of space between me and my neighbors and other privileges too, like the chance to set up an empty cardboard box as a nightstand and to string up bungee cord from the tent ropes so I could have a clothesline.

Nope. I was chopped liver, destined for the big submarine sandwich of humanity being assembled down the middle of the tent, where soldiers were setting up cots end to end, two rows across.

At Fort Campbell I had received written travel orders from the 101st Airborne's headquarters, a one-page directive indicating that I was to be treated, for "billeting purposes," as the equivalent of a major. I got a charge out of that, since having put in a mere five and a half days at media boot camp, it was like being promoted at lightning speed. Not that anyone in the entire battalion seemed aware of this piece of paper.

But being on deadline, which is to say, you finish your story or you're a dead woman, I had scant interest in arguing about creature comforts—even after Kolesar added insult to injury by directing me to reside—for "accountability" reasons—adjacent to my putative competition, Rob Dollar. He and I would sleep head to toe. Just as disappointing was being placed side by side with Specialist Steven Summerlot, who worked in communications. I learned he had finished a degree in philosophy; and nothing against Summerlot, but next to calculus, his major was my least favorite subject in college. The arrangement had me worried that at night I would flail an arm reflexively, as if to embrace my husband, and wind up caressing Summerlot. That night I turned in with my arms pressed tightly against my sides, wishing I'd brought along superglue.

The only good thing about where I slept at Thunder Road was Carter, the young warbler with whom I'd been transported to camp. She ended up in one of the four cots neighboring mine and eventually started calling me "Momma," though I found out later that I was older than her own mother. Based on a silly name one of her friends had blurted out during our overland trip, I nicknamed her "Sha-Nay-Nay."

Carter proved to be a real trouper, not to mention that she had an astonishingly large collection of "chick flicks" on video, and often drew a large crowd of friends during nighttime showings after her cooking duties were done for the day. Judging from the volume of mail she received, I figured she had an infinite number of friends in the outside world, too. All in all, she was my kind of girl.

Heeding Kolesar's dictate, that afternoon I unpacked what I needed and stored the rest; then I took a quick tour of our new, sandy precincts. Thunder Road reportedly had been an Iraqi outpost during the Persian Gulf War. Somebody told me he'd found a decaying foot in an old shoe on the installation. But now, besides us, the camp's only living and breathing inhabitants seemed to be pesky bees, beetles, flies, and spiders. They were everywhere. There were snakes and scorpions in residence, too, according to camp scuttlebutt, and based on the ear-splitting booms I began hearing, there was unexploded ordnance within the berm, supposedly left behind by the Iraqis after the last war. The first few times explosions shook the camp, the hair on my arms stood up, until someone pointed out that the blasts were the work of U.S. soldiers in an E.O.D. unit, which means explosive ordnance disposal.

Wandering around the camp, I hoped to score a sand-free work space, just as I had in Victory, where either the camp's "mayor," a no-nonsense reservist from Minnesota, Colonel Doug McIntosh, or its communications personnel, had loaned me a chair and table space. But Thunder Road didn't seem to have a mayor yet. Nor did it have a spacious "commo tent," just a truck chock full of communications gadgetry. Seeing no alternative, I went back to King Kolesar's tent, located a rare electrical outlet, and set up shop on the floor.

Forrester had indicated that this sprawling camp, with forty-five tents, would be more austere than Victory; he had, in fact, warned us that conditions would be increasingly primitive every step of the way. But Thunder Road didn't seem that bad. While at Victory we'd had outdoor sinks, albeit without plumbing; at Thunder, we still had portable latrines. And although our tents no longer featured wooden floors, in place of them was dirt-cheap all-weather carpeting.

The next morning outside my tent I ran into Sabb, Forrester, and Bill Allen, the brigade's command sergeant major. Shaking their hands, I greeted them in turn, "Colonel, colonel, sergeant major," and they appeared pleased that I'd gotten their ranks right, as if it demonstrated I wasn't completely clueless.

I interviewed Sabb for a bit as he dug into a packet of chow mein noodles from an MRE. We talked about helicopters and his career and his next assignment; he would be leaving the theater of operations on June 12. I feigned ignorance of his departure date, even though I knew well that it was a red-letter day for many Fourth Battalion soldiers, who were counting the days until Mister Angry left. If I was making nice with Sabb, even though he rubbed me the wrong way, it was because he held my ticket to ride. At Victory he indicated that I wasn't going up in a helicopter until he felt the pilots were competent at taking off and landing in the desert. I knew, though, that Ben Senger from NBC already had been up in a bird—and had some good video footage to prove it.

As I bided my time I learned that Black Hawks are built by the Sikorsky Aircraft Corporation, which was founded by a Russian-born scientist, engineer, aviation pioneer, and pilot. Inspired by the drawings of Leonardo da Vinci and stories of Jules Verne, Igor Sikorsky first erected a rubber-band-powered model helicopter when he was twelve.

Headquartered in Stratford, Connecticut, Sikorsky Aircraft has manufactured military helicopters since 1943; the Black Hawk emerged in 1976 in the aftermath of Vietnam after multiple deadly crashes involving its predecessor, the UH-1 Huey, sparked design changes to improve what is known, in aviation lingo, as survivability and crashworthiness. I was informed that every branch of the U.S. Armed Forces uses Black Hawks, which are transport helicopters, or one of their variants; the Army alone has nearly 1,600.

The helicopter—"the bird" was the shorthand everybody used, and God forbid you called it "the chopper"—was designed for two pilots and twelve passengers, but when its portable seats are removed, it can hold more, even when soldiers are fully equipped for combat; or, lacking passengers, it can handle up to 8,000 pounds of cargo.

Facts from Sabb and other pilots came at me fast and furiously: with two engines, the eleven-ton aircraft can climb vertically at speeds of thirty feet per second and fly at speeds up to 184 miles per hour. It can carry enough fuel for a 373-mile trip and is equipped with triple-redundant electronic and hydraulic systems to help withstand enemy fire—although, as depicted in the popular film *Black Hawk Down,* invincible it is not.

The price tag: $9 million dollars each. "It's the coolest ride on Earth" is how one pilot put it, saying he'd read that in *Maxim,* a men's magazine that began turning up so often I wondered if it was required reading.

When in flight, the Black Hawk simply thunders through the skies. At first I found the noise unsettling; it meant an end to the relative peace and quiet I'd enjoyed at Camp Victory. But as more and more of the aircraft arrived from the port and commenced flying, day and night, in and around Thunder Road, the racket just became white noise.

Sabb had 1,300 hours of flight time under his belt and clearly admired the aircraft's capabilities. "The Black Hawk will be here well after I'm gone," he told me.

I left the battalion commander to track down one of his fliers, Russ Toeller, who'd grown up in suburban Milwaukee. I wanted to ask if I could profile him. But when I went over to the Bravo Company tent to find Toeller, I was told to come back at noon; he'd been flying the night before and was dead to the world.

Next I went over to visit with Chaplain Greene, figuring it was Sunday, so a dose of religion wouldn't hurt—plus his Mr. Coffee had a full, fresh carafe of joe. Greene, a captain, had gotten on my nerves at Victory, coming up to me at odd times and feeling he could grasp my hands and commence praying over me. During one such encounter, he beseeched, "Dear Lord, please take away Katherine's fears and anxieties," but I must have wrinkled my face, since he hastened to add, "*if* she has fears and anxieties."

But lately I'd been warming up to him—and it wasn't just his bottomless carafe or the fact that his daughter, Aubrey Elizabeth, had just been born. At Victory I'd admired one of the daily slogans handwritten on his erasable white message board: "Even though our neighbors may seem different or hostile, treat them with respect and pray for them." At the time, I was thinking "Iraqis," but looking back, it might have been directed to our little world, where, especially in light of the stifling heat and privations, infighting erupted from time to time—and I was becoming no slouch at popping off and dropping profanities. I'd also subconsciously begun dividing soldiers—and the other embeds, too—into one of two camps: you were either my friend or my foe.

When I finally caught up with Toeller, he struck me as introverted and self-effacing as much as sleep-deprived. Thirty-three years old, he was small and compact like a jockey—five feet, seven inches and 155 pounds—with brown hair starting to gray. He had a cold sore and couple of tattoos, a panther on his left arm and a "dragon-tiger thing" on his right; he allowed that he was a little inebriated when he sat for the second one. His chin featured an inch-long scar from a teenage motorcycle accident; he said he'd been hurt when he rear-ended a car while "looking at girls."

As Toeller and I sat in the meager shade alongside his tent, I tried not to betray emotion; I just kept writing things down and hoped his mouth kept moving. Reporters learn early in their careers that most people love talking about themselves, and I put on a poker face in hopes that the multicolored stacks of chips would keep multiplying, which they did.

I discovered that while Toeller flew a Black Hawk, his dad drove a Milwaukee municipal bus. As a kid, he felt classrooms were confining and middle-school sports were dull; instead he was drawn to the postage-stamp-sized Rainbow Airport, now defunct, a few miles from his childhood home in suburban Franklin, Wisconsin.

Paying for flying lessons was out of the question, so Toeller kept pestering the airport's owner, Leon Rediske, until the proprietor gave him work. He cut grass, washed planes, and began tinkering with engines. Soon he was conducting the 100-hour inspections that the airplanes were required to undergo after as many hours of flight. He started flying lessons when he was about sixteen. "It's where I belonged, I guess," he told me. "I just loved it."

After joining the Army, he found himself repairing Apache attack helicopters during the 1990–1991 Gulf War, but when the military drew down its forces afterward, he landed in the private sector, turning crashed AH-64s into trainers for use by mechanics. Toeller found life as a "wrench turner" less than satisfying, and being employed then by a government contractor seemed more a gamble than a career path, so he decided to try for a spot in the Army's flight school. He applied three times before he was accepted. He completed the program in 1998 and was rated to fly the UH-60 Black Hawk in 1999. "I was elated," he remembered. "It was what I've always wanted to do. I can't see myself being a civilian pilot. It seems boring."

Toeller, like most of the pilots, was drawn from the Army's warrant officer corps. There are five grades of warrant officers, one being the lowest and five the highest, and he was a chief warrant officer 2.

He'd already had 1,200 hours of flight time in the "Hawk." In addition to the Persian Gulf, he'd flown in Honduras, Venezuela, Panama, and Nicaragua on a variety of missions, including military, disaster-relief, and drug-interdiction operations.

His skills were such that he was designated a lead pilot; that made him first in a serial (a group of helicopters flying together under one commander) of four or five or more birds. The standards for lead pilots are exacting; they must touch down within fifty meters of a target landing zone and within thirty seconds of the intended time.

Waiting at home were his twenty-seven-year-old wife, Danyette, and firstborn son, Nathaniel, eight-and-a-half months old. He said that Danyette was "concerned" about his deployment, but in the weeks leading up to his departure they'd just gotten down to business—having a will drawn up, making sure his life insurance was in order, and signing a power of attorney document in case he was incapacitated. They hadn't stopped to talk much about it, mirroring the way I'd behaved with my own husband as I tackled my to-do list; so Toeller's observation had me breathing easier about how I'd treated Tom.

Toeller wouldn't say much about going to war—"We're not here playing games" was as far as he'd go—although he indicated that he was in for the duration. "I'll be home," he said, "when we're done."

The pilot didn't know whether his infant son was teething or crawling; that seemed unfortunate. In answer to another question, he told me that his parents, Richard and Susan, were worried: "I know just from the tone of their voice the last few times I got to talk to them before I left."

Still, he could see past these bare-bones surroundings and the dangerous drama on the horizon. He had eight years left with Uncle Sam before hitting the twenty-year mark and qualifying for retirement; already he was planning an idyllic future. He imagined himself working for Ace Hardware, owning a 100-acre hobby farm with a pond and river, and rounding out his family with "lots of kids."

As I was scribbling notes, I looked up and saw Ruiz several feet away chatting up David Zucchino, a reporter who had dropped in from the *Los Angeles Times*. I shot daggers at Ruiz, making a mental note to give my friend the flight surgeon grief, and when Zucchino glanced back at me, I smiled smugly, as if to say, "I've got a great story. You don't."

When I wrapped up the interview with Toeller, I had more than enough to work with: the boyhood quest, the elbow grease, the roundabout path to achieve his dream, the refusal to accept rejection, the far-flung missions, and the Currier & Ives future.

All that was left for me to do was shoot his photograph on the flight line and back in his tent and to talk to other Bravo Company pilots—the "Kingsmen," they called themselves—for their views on what made Toeller tick.

I liked the Bravo guys. I'd first met them when I wrote about their short-lived attempt to fly the Harley-Davidson colors at Victory. "The boys of Bravo Company had a brainstorm," I'd begun my story, recounting their effort to plant a reminder of home in a faraway sandbox. When members of the company including its commander, thirty-year-old Captain Jeff Beierlein, a native of Cincinnati, vowed that the flag would fly again after they were ordered to take it down, I liked their pluck.

Toeller, as a warrant officer, specialized in a technical field—in his case, aviation. Talking to him seemed like adult conversation. He and the other warrant officers struck me as professionals; and since careerwise they resided in the region between the officer corps and enlisted people, they were neither get-aheads nor galley slaves.

Interviewing fliers like Toeller was a win-win situation: I enjoyed learning about Army aviation, and they seemed to relish talking about it.

As darkness fell that day, Ruiz came to collect me to walk over to the chow tent that had been erected far across the camp. On the way, I feigned outrage that he dared talk to Zucchino.

"You are all mine," I said. "You are not to help other reporters."

Ruiz: "But I grew up in L.A."

Me: "I thought Zucchino was from Philly."

Ruiz: "He works for the *L.A. Times*."

Me: "Oh, that's right. He's in their Philadelphia bureau."

On a more serious note, I asked Ruiz if he thought it was unusual that Toeller didn't know whether his infant son was crawling. He said it wasn't.

"It's a pilot's personality. They compartmentalize things," the lieutenant colonel said. "They can put their worries aside and press on with the mission, and deal with other things later."

Ruiz said he traveled so much earlier in his military career that he missed long stretches of his two kids' early years, having to catch up by looking at pictures his wife Phyllis took as they sprouted.

"What else can you tell me about pilots?" I asked.

"It doesn't matter what aircraft you fly," he said, "since their traits are the same. They're high achievers. They're not brilliant. They're not the smartest guys in the world. But they're not the dumbest either. They are above average in intelligence, but their ability to process technical and mechanical information is high, with pretty good speed and accuracy. And they're decisive under pressure. There's a certain amount of obsessive-compulsiveness about them—and a bit of narcissism, too."

"When you're a pilot," he finished, "if you don't like your surroundings, you can just fly someplace else and enter a whole new world."

Every time Ruiz opened his mouth, I learned something. And I appreciated how he looked out for my health, thinking nothing of handing out tablets for congestion or cough medicine or eye wash. And we always found something—or someone—to laugh at.

The good-natured physician seemed different from everybody else. Like me, he was classified as a noncombatant; the nine-millimeter Beretta he wore in a shoulder harness was to be fired only in defense of himself or his patients. "I think I like you because you're a healer, not a killer," I told him.

Hot chow in place of an MRE was typically the high point of the day, although water for showers was a close second. The food invariably was stick-to-your-ribs fare such as beef stew or barbecued ribs. Generally there were rolls and a durable vegetable such as green beans; and if you were lucky, the tossed salad bowl hadn't been emptied. Usually there were bananas or oranges; sometimes sheet cake; and always cartons of fruit juice in odd flavors like mango.

The food line typically stretched the equivalent of one or two city blocks, but the wait was tolerable because you could grab a smoke and meet new people while in line, exchanging names, hometowns, wisecracks, and the camp's chief currency, gossip. After your food was dished out, you walked into a scrum of people eating from the floor, since tables and chairs, early on, were scarce. With few lights, the dining section was impossibly dark, and the floor was so lumpy that if you didn't watch it, you could step into a cavity and twist an ankle. It seemed that whoever laid down the carpet hadn't bothered to level the sand first. To compensate for the darkness, I was taught that night to unscrew the head of a six-inch Maglite and stand it up like a miniature candle.

Chow time was a particular treat for me because the cooks, and Carter was one, always made a big show when I showed up with an empty plate.

"Miss Milwaukee!" Heather Denham would greet me, lighting up like a Roman candle. Denham was twenty-one years old and from Kingsland, Georgia. Her effervescence was such that I didn't bother to correct her, even though I hadn't lived in Wisconsin's largest city for a few years. Anybody in the Army who was enthusiastic about me tagging along automatically fell into the "friend" camp.

Before turning in that night I dialed up the BBC on my radio, trying to hear the latest about whether there would be war. About this time, courtesy of one of the officers in the Fourth Battalion, additional news was delivered: Dollar and I were to meet with Sabb the next morning; and at last there would be lift-off and we'd go up in a bird.

I was told to report to the battalion's Alpha Company—their tents were next to Bravo's—and while I waited outside the shelter to catch a ride in a truck out to the flight line, some pilots began spilling out and introducing themselves. These guys had just seen combat in Afghanistan, so they fancied themselves the top dogs of the battalion, if not the entire brigade. The self-styled "Comancheros" even carried business cards, which many of them offered to me.

The cards read: "If you Kill for fun, You're a Sadist. If you Kill for money, You're a Mercenary. If you Kill for both, You're a Comanchero."

The flip side listed "specialties," such as combat assaults and emergency ammo resupply, but more eye-catching were the "sidelines." They spelled out:

> World's Greatest Pilot
> War Monger
> International Playboy
> Social Outcast
> Ladies Man
> Renowned Booze Hound

A sane woman might have run in the opposite direction, fast; but I was not a sane woman—I wanted to be a war correspondent. Being handed the card reminded me of when I was a little girl and boys would trap a spider in a Mason jar, punch air holes in the lid with an ice pick, and proudly show off their quarry, hoping I would flip.

So, like the little girl eyeballing the spider, I merely rolled my eyes, though in my heart of hearts I found these pilots' claims outrageous. Where did they get off thinking I would find militaristic, drunken cads attractive? So what if they could fly? I studied the card furtively while being driven out to the flight line. The pilots' "sidelines," to my reckoning, suggested one thing: AIDS.

The camp's old road was crowded with helicopters; I'd never seen so many aircraft in one place in my life. The Black Hawk, from a distance, was dull and dusty green and shaped like a small-mouthed bass. A Screaming Eagle emblem was spray-painted on its nose, and "UNITED STATES ARMY" was stenciled on its tail boom.

Sabb was the lead pilot on the flight out of Thunder Road, so the trip was strictly business. We were heading to Camp New Jersey, another desert compound housing U.S. troops, where I understood that Sabb had a meeting to attend.

Joining Sabb at the controls was Michael I. Patton, Jr., a thirty-two-year-old who'd grown up in Pittsburgh. I'd already met Patton, a chief warrant officer 2 who doubled as an instructor pilot. Lieutenant Jamey Trigg, who'd helped me edit my photos, had offered me some of his own shots taken the morning after the sandstorm; one of them featured a forlorn-looking fellow in fatigues seated on a cardboard box with Arabic labeling, staring off into the distance. The surroundings explained the dejected look on his face: the sides of the tent were barely standing and its canopy had blown off to God-knows-where. I needed the soldier's name and rank, but I couldn't find him, so it fell to other Alpha Company soldiers to provide the details. A day or two later, Patton, who'd been captured in the photo, introduced himself to me. I asked if he was related to the famous general and was stunned when he replied, "No." I imagined the climbers I had left behind in Washington saying, at a minimum, "I have a great-uncle looking into that. We have reason to believe that he is a shirt-tail relative."

I took a seat in the aircraft next to a window, with Dollar on my right and Staff Sergeant Brad Kitch just ahead of me acting as the door gunner. A thirty-five-year-old from Galena, Kansas, he manned an M-60 machine gun with a menacing, brass-colored belt of 7.62 millimeter rounds at the ready. (These bullets were "full metal jacket," a bit of information I'd picked up from my *Army jTimes* friend Matt Cox.)

Now I had flown in a Black Hawk a handful of times, but never in a desert and certainly not in a war zone. The terrain, from the air, appeared an ocean of smooth, khaki-colored sand; it hosted only scruffy sea-green bushes, about a foot tall, and it was pockmarked with long stretches of tire track, punctuated by the occasional discarded tire. The tracks intrigued me. Vestiges of mysterious desert journeys, they triggered questions for which there would be no answers. Who was driving? What kind of vehicle were they in? Where were they going? Did they make it OK?

Kitch, the door gunner, kept his eyes trained on the terrain, scanning left, center, and right for anything ominous. He wore the mien of a state trooper who'd never in his life been persuaded not to write the ticket.

"Damn, it's flat out there," Patton commented.

After twenty minutes, Sabb brought the bird down on a gravel helipad surrounded by sand. We were on the outskirts of Camp New Jersey, which,

I realize only now, is named for the state where Sabb grew up. He missed the landing zone by a few yards, and in my mind I was doing flying splits again and spelling V-I-C-T-O-R-Y. I found Sabb so imperious that I took delight in the fact that, like the rest of us, he was fallible.

After disembarking, Dollar and I joined other reporters on the ground to watch soldiers from the 3rd Brigade of the 101st Airborne conduct "cold loads." These rehearsals saw as many troops as possible, fully outfitted for combat, cram into a Black Hawk. "Cold" signified that the helicopter wasn't running; "hot" would have made it more dangerous, since if an infantryman didn't duck, he could be decapitated by the main rotor blades.

The curious scene reminded me of the old college prank from the 1960s involving stuffing as many students as possible into a telephone booth. But at Camp New Jersey nobody was laughing; the aircraft was so jam-packed with human beings and instruments of death that I wondered how the young GIs extracted themselves without straining themselves badly enough to require a chiropractor.

Counting the personnel as they piled in and out, an officer called out: "That's sixteen with the water bag." The water, as it happened, was stowed in a body bag; it was the first time I heard those two words strung together in a while, and for a split second I felt knots in my stomach.

Then I noticed Gregg Zoroya, a reporter for *USA Today,* and went over to say hello. He'd skipped the orientation at Fort Campbell for the 101st's embeds because he'd already landed in the Gulf. The first words out of his mouth were: "Your husband's in better shape than I am." I could only nod. Tom, of course, was the man I slept next to—until Summerlot came along.

It was hotter than blazes under a cloudless sky; I was wilting—dripping in sweat, actually—and trying to cover ground in the desert wearing a three-pound helmet and twenty-two-pound flak jacket. When told that some of the infantry guys had loads of one hundred pounds or more, I mentally sent an instant message to Major Cate, the 101st's public affairs boss, extolling his wisdom for placing me in an aviation unit.

On the return trip to Thunder Road—over the sand, sans Sabb—Patton and his copilot, whose last name was Fink, made a refueling stop at Ali Al Saleem Air Base in Kuwait, the looks of which confirmed widely held rumors that the Air Force lived better than the Army.

On the final leg of the trip back to camp, I put away my notebook and camera for the first time in days. As wind ricocheted in and out of the windows, I soaked up the sensation of dancing through crystalline blue skies at twice the speed of a car motoring along a highway. It was late afternoon, as the temperatures were starting to moderate, when I remembered something I'd forgotten during the nerve-jangling weeks spent scrounging for Army gear and battling my father about the assignment and deciding how to divvy up the fruits of my life's labors and tolerating vaccinations for strange diseases and tearfully leaving Tom behind.

I remembered: I love to fly.

The light was so perfect when we landed that I cajoled Patton into posing for photographs in and around his bird. He's a brash, live-out-loud guy, but he put up with it. Maybe if you're in the Army, when someone pays attention to you it means something. Meantime his flight crew got to work, wrapping duct tape on the rotor blades and then spray-painting them, since these movable parts got beaten up with every takeoff and landing.

By the time I returned to my tent, somebody called out, "How was your joy ride?" It was an innocent question, but it annoyed me. I wasn't a college co-ed with a backpack, credit card, and guidebook entitled *Let's Go: Middle East*. Most of my waking hours (when I wasn't smoking) were spent working: thinking about stories, going after them, writing, shooting pictures, and negotiating with Jesus Christ for a satellite signal strong and steady enough to send text and photos back to the States. It took a while for the soldiers to grasp this. In the beginning they thought nothing of trying to engage me in a discussion about politics while I was on deadline; others assumed that as a newswoman, surely I had all the latest sports scores at my disposal and would dispense them as gladly as a U.S.O. volunteer handing over an ice-cold can of Coke.

Nobody ever seemed to get my mission: journalism.

The pace, by then, had picked up for everyone, including Trigg, but I persuaded him that evening to take a few minutes to look over my photographs of Russ Toeller. There were dozens of shots; I planned to submit a close-up of the flier next to his bird as well as an informal shot of him playing cribbage in his tent with a couple of buddies.

Trigg insisted that I shouldn't send the shot showing the card game. "You can't send that," he said. "It'll look like we're doing nothing all day, just sitting in tents and screwing off."

Was it the heat? The loud-mouthed sergeants? The sand so invasive that twenty minutes after I washed my hair in the morning I wondered why I'd bothered? Might it have been the growing stack of excrement I confronted when I stepped into the latrines? Whatever the reason, I snapped. I tore into Trigg, not really caring how many people heard or who they were. "I am *not* an *arm* of your *fucking* P.A.O.!" I shouted in his direction, at a decibel level that had heads swiveling. I wanted these people to know that I wasn't part of their public affairs office, gambling with my mortality to churn out PR material.

Trigg stomped off, leaving me with second thoughts. I had treated my friend as foe. Initially I blamed "Unfuck your Shit" Kolesar for my bad manners, but that wasn't reasonable. I was sorry I'd trashed Trigg, so I tried to make amends by calling out to him, "Cribbage is popular in Milwaukee!" as a way of explaining why I liked the image of the men playing cards.

Trigg didn't bother looking back, and his silence stung.

The next day, Tuesday, March 18, under a blistering midday sun, the entire 159th Brigade conducted a drill involving gas masks and nuclear, biological, and chemical gear. It meant wearing the masks for twenty-three minutes—that wasn't so awful—and spending another forty-eight minutes in full MOPP gear, the acronym for one of the military's better euphemisms: mission-oriented protective posture—in other words, the mask and all the NBC protective overgarments. Midway through the exercise, there was an inspection to ensure we had the injections we were issued, atropine and pralidoxime chloride, which we were to inject into our thighs if struck by a nerve agent.

Having on all the gear in the heat was like wearing a scuba-diving mask and calf-length fur coat in a steam bath. I worried that I might faint from heat prostration and willed myself to remain standing. Finally, somebody called out, "All clear," meaning the ghastly dress rehearsal was over. Afterward Captain Adam Kamann, the Fourth Battalion's personnel officer, who was saddled with being a liaison to the embeds, did me a huge favor: he gave me a spare canteen cap with a little tube that would allow me to get a mouthful of water even if I was "masked"—wearing a gas mask.

Everywhere I looked the activity level was picking up; the drill was one sign, and the 24–7 roar of the birds up above was another. Suddenly freshly dug survival trenches bordered every tent. Officers were scrutinizing maps of Iraq and typing away at laptops, sometimes even banging away at two of them. I told my editor, Carl, that I was collecting material for a story about how, from our little corner of the world, the United States seemed to be on the brink of war.

Then President Bush made it all but certain, giving Saddam Hussein and his sons the now-famous ultimatum: You have forty-eight hours to leave, he said. Failure to comply "will result in military conflict, commenced at a time of our choosing."

I slugged—that is, entitled—the story "Brink." After completing the story, I had one more thing to write. From my cot, fortified with sips of "Dasani water," I began writing a letter to Tom, trying to be the good Girl Scout: prepared. In case I never made it home, I wanted him to have a world-class good-bye letter.

Just as I began jotting down words, I caught a glimpse of David Oviatt, a chief warrant officer 2 and the motor pool boss, who was draping a four-by-seven-foot American flag on the wall behind his cot, which was close to mine. I liked and trusted Oviatt, not least because he was a decent guy from Maine. His patriotic gesture seemed to confirm that war was at hand.

I began my letter to Tom with the news of the day (I'd seen the remains of a snake's jaw in the desert) and, before getting down to farewelling, digressed into a litany of complaints:

"Photos, a disaster. I shoot OK but have transmission woes."

"Yesterday while I was on deadline one knob wanted to discuss his thesis, 'All journalists are leftists.' I was laughing about that later when I had my gas mask on. Me, a 'flower child.' "

"No laundry, shower, cream in my coffee."

"It's so unglamorous here."

"The b.o. of the guy next to me is wafting over every other sentence."

"What doesn't break, you misplace."

"Face it: I'm here on pluck, which has its limitations."

"The frustrations are numerous. The only saving grace is a few friends."

Then I thanked him for letting me see another part of the world; I called him my friend, lover, husband, hero, helpmate, soul mate, and lifelong love; and I told him how proud I was of our eternal bond.

Finally: "If anything happens to me, pls be happy. Marry someone nice. Fish a lot. Forgive me for doing this."

I was silently weeping as my gel pen slid across the paper; it was the first time in the company of the United States Army that I cried. Hoping that no one would notice, I tried to collect the tears as they streamed down my cheeks, but after signing the letter, I grabbed a damp, mangled wad of Kleenex and let out one big honking snort. Surely I was dreaming, but I tried to persuade myself that none of the sixty or so people around me would notice. I hoped that I sounded like someone with a sinus problem; in light of the sand that was waging war with our respiratory systems, every other soldier had a relentless case of the sniffles, called "the crud" if the ailment was severe.

The next morning, March 19, I added a postscript for Tom: "Here's a new one: I *awoke* to a sandstorm. It's now about nine a.m. local time. Very insane. I had to ask the other rptr. what no. sandstorm it was. He said #4. I told him he wasn't counting the littler ones. They are truly ev'y 2–3 days! Now the lights in the tent are blinking on and off like Christmas bulbs."

With war in the offing, a somber mood permeated the shelter, as though death was creeping through the tent flap. There were none of the usual high jinks—like playing baseball with a cardboard tube for a bat and a crumbled wad of legal paper for a ball—and the videocassette and DVD players and boom boxes were hushed. For once soldiers were not jam-packed on somebody's cot for another in the nightly showings of *Saving Private Ryan* or *Black Hawk Down*. Even our resident Playstation 2 addict had miraculously weaned himself from Grand Theft Auto.

As if at the drop of a hat, people got down to brass tacks, wiping the sand off their gas masks, polishing their rifles, and organizing their gear. I drank it all in—and it was sobering.

I rose early the next day, Thursday, March 20—back in the States, it was still March 19—and switched on the BBC. The announcer broke the news in a crisp British voice, intoning, "For all intents and purposes, the attack against Iraq is under way."

I began scrawling down everything he said: the main attack had not yet begun; selected "targets of opportunity" were being hit; these were "decapitation attacks" involving "bombs or missiles"; the intent was to cut off the Iraqis' ability to command and control their military; a burst of antiaircraft fire was reported over Baghdad; and Iraqi radio had gone on the air with songs of praise for Saddam Hussein.

And so it had begun; my country was at war in the cauldron of the Middle East. I scrambled out of the tent with my phone, lit a cigarette, dialed Carl, and as I waited for the call to go through, began recording weather conditions: a full moon appeared in the hazy morning sky and the temperature felt like about sixty-nine degrees.

Carl sounded pleased at hearing my voice and said given the time difference, if I filed a story in ninety minutes, I could still make the paper being readied for Thursday, March 20. He wondered whether or not I could do it.

Could I do it? I held my tongue, thinking this was the biggest story of my career; of course I could do it. I told myself to finish in seventy-five minutes—there was no way I was going to risk missing the edition. I dropped off the phone in the tent, clawed my hair back in a ponytail, and made haste for the brigade tactical operations center, known as the TOC, to find Forrester.

My heart was pounding as I dashed over the sand. The soldiers milling outside their tents seemed like movie characters in slow motion. One sipped an orange-colored drink from a used Al-Rawdatain bottle. Another dragged a razor across lathered-up cheeks. One guy knelt over a laundry bucket, yanking fatigues in and out of sudsy water. Another sat beneath the dull buzz of an electric razor, having his head shaved.

It seemed too prosaic, especially since I was in "Damn the torpedoes—full speed ahead!" mode. I did notice that some people seemed to be heading someplace with more spring in their step than usual, and many crisply sounded out "Good morning" as they passed, a courtesy not often heard on these austere acres.

On my way to the TOC, I spotted Major Tony Fish, the brigade's military operations planner. He was planting a wad of Red Man Golden chew in his cheek as he headed for a latrine. I dashed up to him and practically ripped the bag out of his hand, saying, "I want the brand name—for color." Next I asked for his view of the war. "I haven't thought about it that much, beyond watching CNN like everyone else," he said. "The focus is to make sure we're ready to go."

Outside the center I asked a soldier who was standing guard to tell Forrester I needed to see him. When the commander appeared, I blurted out, "Do you have thirty seconds?" and began asking questions.

Coolly and precisely, Forrester told me, "The orders have been issued, the focus is clear, and we're continuing our preparations for our piece in this. The job is to continue preparations for the mission ahead."

Then he surprised me by inviting me into the TOC for the first time, steering me past officers huddled over briefing books or laptop computers protected by heavy plastic dust covers—men and women working in operations, logistics, legal matters, communications, and personnel—so I could see some of what was on CNN.

"Strike on Iraq," the cable network had dubbed it. "Operation Iraqi Freedom" was what the United States had named the invasion. Hearing that name for the first time, I copied it down on the cover of my notebook.

The network showed a video clip of President Bush announcing, "At this hour, American and coalition forces are in the early stages of military operations to disarm Iraq, to free its people and to defend the world from grave danger. On my orders, coalition forces have begun striking selected targets of military importance to undermine Saddam Hussein's ability to wage war. These are the opening stages of what will be a broad and concerted campaign."

The network then showed footage of F-14 Tomcats and F-18 Super Hornets tearing off the deck of the U.S.S. *Lincoln* in the Persian Gulf on bombing raids.

With a tight deadline, I couldn't stay long. The wire services would give Carl and his deputy editors the war's big picture, our local staff would capture the reaction on the home front, and my responsibility was to convey the activity and views at Thunder Road.

Outside the TOC, I ran into Major Covert, the brigade's Number 2 man, who characterized the Air Force and Navy as "the first players," hinting that the brigade's time would come. He went on to pronounce spirits at Thunder Road "high," parroting exactly what he'd said to me a day earlier. As a fellow optimist, I didn't care, even if he was exaggerating, which I suspected he might be; if somebody had a mind to write *Journalism for Dummies,* it would open with, "Listen to what people say, and write it down."

Don Gregg, the Fourth Battalion's command sergeant major, told me that the war triggered no particular feelings. "Basically, there's no kind of emotion about it," he said. "This is why we came, and we trust our leaders to work their end of this deal, and we'll work ours. Right now, it's just business as usual. We're preparing for future operations, awaiting orders, improving the survival trenches, and preparing our combat loads."

Sergeant Sherre Maxson, the woman from Eagle River, Wisconsin, and the noncommissioned officer in charge of logistics for the Fourth Battalion, echoed the "business as usual" theme. She said the battalions within the brigade were comparing notes to ensure they had what they needed; the priority was ammunition for the M-60 and M-2 machine guns and M-4 rifles. "Ammo is key," she said. "Food and water, we're good on. Toilet paper, we're good on. We're playing the 'Army of One' in the brigade. We're helping one another to make sure no one falls short."

Sergeant 1st Class Eddie Smith, a flight crew chief for a Chinook, was rare in betraying a sense of urgency. "We've just got 101 things to do, no pun intended, and fifty people to do it with," he said. The thirty-eight-year-old soldier described loading helicopters with ammunition, food, water, tents, and cots and preparing a "go-bag" packed with just the essentials, noting, "We may fly aircraft out of here on Friday."

Glancing at my watch, I figured I could fit in a couple more interviews before cranking a story out. "We're glad it's finally getting started," said Captain Darrell Doremus, the thirty-year-old native of Tampa, Florida, who commanded a Black Hawk unit within the Fifth Battalion. "I mean, we've given 'em deadline after deadline, and they never meet it. We're here to do our job and to get it done, and to go home to our families as quickly as possible."

Stating his belief that the Iraqis supported terrorism, Doremus, who had a twenty-month-old son at home, added: "We want to do the right thing for the next generation, for my child and for all children."

Private 1st Class Chad Weins, a twenty-two-year-old from St. James, Minnesota, said he thought it was good that the war had begun—"We need to get Saddam out of power"—but punctuated almost every sentence with a nervous "I guess."

Weins, a "Rakkasan," as members of the 3rd Brigade of the 101st are called, noted that he'd just been assigned new duties. "Now I'm a helicopter door gunner, I guess." He joined the Army "just to serve my country, I guess." He viewed going to war as "just doing my duty, I guess."

Was he scared? "A little bit, I guess." He said, in answer to my last question, that he feared chemical weapons above all; it was one sentence he didn't end with an "I guess."

As I stepped into Bravo Company's tent with my professional equipment, its commanders welcomed me in. It was starting to be my second home; by now my newspaper's Web site was a fixture on the company's message board. While paging through my notes and pounding out a lead, I heard a senior pilot, Ken Ballard, tell somebody that the start of the war was a double-edged sword. "You can get killed doing this," he reminded.

Birds, bullets, and go-bags were one thing; his comment brought home the deadly nature of this undertaking. "Hey, can I use that quote?" I called out, wanting his permission, since the remark hadn't been directed at me. Ballard agreed, and filled in the rest: he was forty-five years old, originally from Pleasanton, California, and a chief warrant officer 4, just one rung below the highest level.

I filed my story with a few minutes to spare, phoned Carl to make sure it arrived, and stood up on the toes of my boots and made an arc with my arms, trying to work the kinks out of my upper back. I was coming off an adrenaline high, congratulating myself for the "quick hit" but knowing the bar would be higher for the next day's paper. I figured I'd do a bigger, better story about how the start of the invasion was affecting my unit.

Bravo pilot Carl Barber, a thirty-seven-year-old from Brooklyn, suddenly popped in as if he were the town crier. He joked that Associated Press had reported that two of Hussein's sons had been captured, adding: "Now the hard part: We have to 'bag dad.'"

Such a punster; he reminded me of my father, who loved inventing gags based on the news of the day. It seemed like a good time to be on my way.

While rounding up my things, I tugged idly—nervously, probably—at the chain around my neck and watched as my patron saint's medal fell to the floor. I got down on my knees and pawed the carpet in search of the pewter medal, which was no bigger than a dime. Before long some Bravo fliers joined in the hunt.

I didn't like the notion of St. Catherine of Siena being AWOL; for years the holy medal had been my talisman, particularly when I felt troubled or needed strength. But after a while, I just called off the search, figuring that I'd be back in Bravo's tent later in the day to write and could resume looking then.

It was time for a breather, and since by then I could detect my own body odor, I thought I'd freshen up, wash my hair, and calm my nerves by straightening up the mess inhabiting my cot. During my break I telephoned Tom, who had his hands full back in the *USA Today* newsroom, but listened to my assurances that I was fine, just working and trying to stay safe.

Forrester, earlier in the day, had seemed hospitable, so I thought I'd go back to the TOC and talk to Thunder's top boss for the next day's story. But as I approached the heart of the camp, where the TOC was located, I heard a loud swoosh overhead in the southeast skies. Two young soldiers were driving toward me in a two-seat John Deere Gator, which is used to haul small loads of cargo. They put on the brakes, craned their necks backwards, and witnessed the same thing I saw: a missile was rocketing through the dull gray skies directly over our camp.

"What was that?" I asked.

"A Patriot," one of them said, sounding like a doctor who's come across a suspicious spot on an X-ray.

"I thought so," I told them, swallowing hard. I knew this spelled trouble, so I looked at my dusty watch and recorded the time: 12:27 p.m.

"There's two more!" one of the young soldiers called out.

As we stared at the sky, one of the missiles exploded into what seemed like a blaze of yellow fireworks. I had little clue as to what was happening; it looked to me like something had been taken out. My mind flashed back to a childhood memory: it was Friday night in Chicago's Comiskey Park, where the White Sox had just finished a double-header and the fans were being treated to an extravaganza of pyrotechnics.

The next thing I knew, somebody at my elbow was wordlessly steering me into the closest tent. There light was low, but I recognized the soldier. It was Lucky Mertes, a forty-four-year-old flier from my unit, the Fourth Battalion's headquarters company, and, like Ballard, a chief warrant officer 4.

Mertes and I crouched near the entrance to the tent; in no time, a soldier called out, "Gas, gas, gas." More trouble, I thought. Mertes strapped on his gas mask and indicated that I should do the same. Suddenly I was all thumbs, so he helped me secure the wide elastic bands over the back of my head and made sure I tested the mask's seal so no toxins could seep in. "Let's go," he said next.

We made our way to the newly dug foxholes that ran in a zigzag pattern adjacent to the Fourth Battalion's headquarters. Once we were in, my mouth felt like I'd been chewing cotton balls. The soldiers around me, sensing that I was hyperventilating, counseled, "Deep breaths," so I inhaled and tried to slow down my lungs. All I wanted was water, so I hoisted my canteen, gulped and kept gulping, privately thanking Kamann for having given me the special cap that let me take in water while wearing a gas mask.

As I got my bearings, I noticed that Mertes was standing not far away, next to another veteran flier, Gregory A. Wood, another chief warrant officer 4. "Excuse me," I muttered to the young soldier next to me, as I planted myself between Mertes and Wood. If something terrible was about to happen, I wanted to follow the lead of two experienced men. This didn't seem the time to take cues from kids.

When I asked Mertes what was going on, he answered, "Ma'am, I'd be speculating."

Turning to Wood, I inquired, "What do I do now?" He told me to square my helmet and brace my back against the trench, so I scrunched down, adjusting my K-pot and pressing my spine against the wall, sending loose sand and pebbles cascading from the sides of the four-foot trench.

I told myself to gather my senses. I lowered my head and silently prayed the Act of Contrition, preparing for the prospect that less than seven hours into the war, I might be a casualty. The loss of my St. Catherine medal now seemed like a very bad omen, since she'd kept me safe all these years. She was gone; I could be, too.

"Please God, get me out of this," I thought. "If you get me out of this, I'll be a better person from now on. I promise. I will. Really."

I toyed with the idea of writing Tom a letter the way one of the nine coal miners in Somerset County, Pennsylvania, did in 2002 before their miracle rescue. If I died, if somehow my notebook wasn't blown to smithereens, if the sand-coated, spiral-ringed, eight-by-four-inch tablet labeled "Skiba, 159—4 Btn HHC—Pls return" made its way back to my spouse, then he could see a last loving good-bye.

But I dismissed the notion of a farewell letter, not only because reaching Tom seemed like a long shot, but because I'd already written it. There seemed to be nothing more to say than what I'd already said: "Pls be happy. Marry someone nice. Fish a lot. Forgive me for doing this."

A young soldier's shouts snapped me out of my reverie. "I hope they bomb the shit out of them," he cried out. "Bomb the whole fucking country!"

Wood, for his part, added commentary in a voice that still carried the lilt of his native Birmingham, Alabama. "This is going to change things," he said matter-of-factly. "They're wantin' to play."

With nothing else to do, I turned to a time-tested mechanism to cope with trouble: I blamed the victim. Why in the hell had I done this? Where did I get off thinking I should cover a war? How could I be so stupid as to think a battlefield would be safe? Why, oh why, was I always such a cockeyed optimist?

Periodically I imagined a huge explosion directly ahead of me, about 100 yards away, give or take. Mostly, I just sat there, studying the wiggly patterns of sand and rock coloring the sides of the trench and remembering that I found geology a bore and archeology painstakingly slow. Mostly I was just plain numb.

Fifty-six harrowing minutes into the ordeal, an "All clear!" was sounded. It was 1:23 p.m.

"I think I just aged fifty years," Wood, the veteran flier, said to no one in particular. His observation comforted me; I was not the only one who'd tasted terror.

I got up, lifted off the mask, and drank in fresh air—too drained to move much. Then Sergeant Sergio Nava, who'd been squatting over a radio near the lip of the trench, said meekly: "Hey, listen up, possible second Scud launch."

He was a slight, soft-spoken twenty-two-year-old and his voice seemed too subdued to suggest peril; I thought he might be testing the radio. But once I saw soldiers slapping their masks on again, I knew Nava meant business. In eight minutes, mercifully, the second alert was over.

Gregg, the battalion command sergeant major, who was standing outside the trench, tore off his gas mask, fired up a Marlboro Ultra Light, and took a long drag. "You've now been under attack by an enemy of the United States," he shouted to his troops. "People, next time run faster, but good job."

After I eased my way out, I approached Gregg with open arms, saying, "I need a hug." If it was unsoldierly, I didn't know better—or didn't care.

Then Gregg spoke again, and nearly as loudly as the first time. He seemed to be addressing not only me, but every man and woman in uniform within earshot.

"Thank you for being here," the grizzled old soldier told me. "You've got balls."

Won't Hurt a Bit. Newly embedded with the Army's 101st Airborne Division, the author gets a dose of military life in the form of an anthrax vaccination administered at Fort Campbell's Dreyer Field House. (Photo courtesy of John Partipilo, *The Tennessean*)

Nodding off to War. Soldiers from the 101st Airborne Division camp out in a tangle of rifles, helmets, and gear in a hangar at Campbell Army Airfield. Theirs was a red-eye flight in early March 2003, so they're escaping into sleep—or a card game—before departing for the Persian Gulf. (Photo by Katherine M. Skiba)

Just Doing My Job. Private 1st Class Frederick Jolly, a twenty-two-year-old from Milwaukee, Wisconsin, awaiting a flight to the Persian Gulf. The supply specialist with the 101st Airborne Division was typical of the men and women going off to war: he voiced no particular view of the impending conflict, saying he was just doing his job as a soldier. (Photo by Katherine M. Skiba)

One More Injection. Hours before soldiers deployed on a chartered airliner from Campbell Army Airfield, more vaccinations were administered in the hangar. Soldiers with small children were urged not to undergo the immunization for smallpox until they had left home to deploy. (Photo by Katherine M. Skiba)

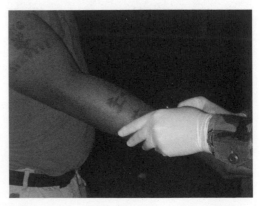

Arrival. The author shown a few days after acclimating to the desert and her new home with the Army's 159th Aviation Brigade, a bare-bones camp in Kuwait with the hopeful name "Victory." (Photo courtesy of Captain Jamey L. Trigg)

Pit Stop. The author, in helmet, goggles, and a bulletproof vest that weighs twenty-two pounds, leaves the aircraft during a refueling stop at Ali Al Saleem Air Base in Kuwait. On her hip is the gas mask the troops were required to have with them at all times.

What So Proudly We Hailed, If Briefly. The boys from Bravo Company, Fourth Battalion, 159th Aviation Brigade, 101st Aviation Regiment, 101st Airborne Division fly the Harley colors at Camp Victory in Kuwait. A commander quickly ordered that the flag be taken down. Left to right: Chief Warrant Officer 3 Bruce Woodmansee, Command Sergeant Major Don Gregg, 1st Sergeant Lance Peeler, Chief Warrant Officer 2 Brian Buol, and Captain Jeff Beierlein. (Photo courtesy of Brian Buol)

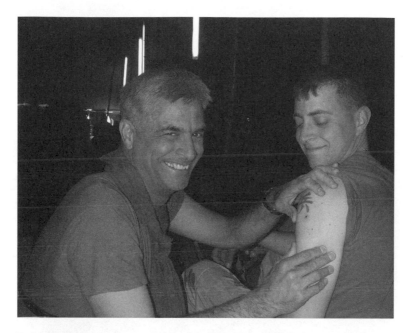

Battle Buddy. Lieutenant Colonel Robert T. Ruiz, a flight surgeon for the 159th Aviation Brigade, was the author's closest friend while deployed. Ruiz, who grew up in the Los Angeles area, is shown with 1st Lieutenant Sean Barrett of Walpole, Massachusetts, who asked the physician to examine the scar left by a smallpox vaccination. (Photo by Katherine M. Skiba)

Tent Down. Major Michael Shenk and Chief Warrant Officer 4 Greg Wood take stock the morning after a vicious sandstorm whipped through their desert camp in Kuwait two weeks before the war. Camp Victory temporarily lost one-third of its tents during the tempest, including this one, which housed Shenk, Wood, and the author, among others. (Photo by Katherine M. Skiba)

Firing Them Up. Lieutenant General William Wallace, one of the Army's top commanders in Iraq, gives a rousing address to the troops at Camp Victory in the days leading up to the invasion of Iraq. The three-star commander was necessarily vague about if or when the United States would strike. (Photo by Katherine M. Skiba)

Big Sky. Chief Warrant Officer 2 Michael I. Patton, Jr., a helicopter pilot from Pittsburgh, looks forlornly into the desert after Alpha Company's tent lost its canopy to the brutal sandstorm in early March 2003 at Camp Victory in Kuwait. (Photo courtesy of Captain Jamey L. Trigg)

Morning After. Specialist Curtis M. Rose, of Oak Grove, Kentucky, cleans his rifle in front of Old Glory after the first major sandstorm that riddled U.S. Armed Forces in the Persian Gulf. (Photo by Katherine M. Skiba)

Black Hawk Pilot. Chief
Warrant Officer 2 Russ
Toeller, a native of
Milwaukee, flew UH-60
helicopters carrying
infantrymen into the war in
Iraq. He later returned and
flew air ambulances there,
transporting soldiers and
civilians injured or killed
during the violent postwar
insurgency. (Photo by
Katherine M. Skiba)

Straight Talk. Chief Warrant Officer 2 Russ Toeller gives an interview
from the helicopter he flies, the UH-60 Black Hawk, as one of his crew
chiefs downs some chow. (Photo by Katherine M. Skiba)

Down Time. Chief Warrant Officer 2 Russ Toeller unwinds in his tent during a game of cribbage with other fliers from Bravo Company. One officer urged the author not to publish this photograph, concerned it would appear that soldiers were "doing nothing all day, just sitting in tents and screwing off." His attempt to censor the picture led to a clash between the author and the officer. (Photo by Katherine M. Skiba)

Tested Twice. Chief Warrant Officer 2 Michael I. Patton, Jr., was among the pilots in Operation Iraqi Freedom who had recently flown combat missions in Afghanistan. (Photo by Katherine M. Skiba)

Black Hawk at Dusk. A silhouette of the Black Hawk UH-60 helicopter at Camp Thunder Road. (Photo by Katherine M. Skiba)

Ready for Anything. Captain Carlos Goveo, a native of San Juan, Puerto Rico, wears nuclear, biological, and chemical (NBC) protective overgarments and carries an M-4 rifle during a drill beneath a blistering desert sun. (Photo by Katherine M. Skiba)

Survival Trenches. Soldiers take cover during one of many missile alerts sounded at Camp Thunder Road in Kuwait. One of the alerts signaled the real thing: an Iraqi missile bound for the camp. A U.S. Patriot surface-to-air missile obliterated the incoming weapon. (Photo courtesy of Lieutenant Colonel James Marye)

Anything for a Story. Soon after Operation Iraqi Freedom kicked off, the author found herself taking cover when an Ababil-100 missile—the crown jewel of Saddam Hussein's arsenal—careened toward Thunder Road, her desert camp. This photo was taken after an "All clear" was sounded. (Photo courtesy of Captain Jeff Beierlein)

Gimme Shelter. Sergeant Maria Buggey, a native of Jacksonville, Florida, adjusts her gas mask at Camp Thunder Road during one of many trips to the foxhole triggered by missile alerts. Her boss, Colonel William H. Forrester, said he "felt like a damn yo-yo" getting in and out of the survival trenches. (Photo by Katherine M. Skiba)

Missile Target. Camp Thunder Road in Kuwait as seen from aboard a Black Hawk. On March 20, 2003, less than seven hours into the war, the camp had the unwelcome distinction of being the target of one of the first Iraqi missiles fired at coalition troops. A hit-to-kill missile launched by the United States neutralized the threat by destroying the Iraqi weapon in midair. Thunder Road then was home to about 2,300 soldiers and more than a billion dollars worth of military aircraft. (Photo by Katherine M. Skiba)

Into Iraq. First Sergeant Tim Nidiffer from Aurora, Colorado, of the Fourth Battalion, holds Alpha Company's colors as he watches pilots depart Camp Thunder Road for their first major mission into Iraq. "As we move through the ranks, it's hard to see our little brothers go off without us there to protect them," he said. Sergeant 1st Class Patrick Hopkins of Augusta, Georgia, is with him. (Photo by Katherine M. Skiba)

The Lord's Work. Captain Kerry Greene, an Army chaplain from Holly Springs, Mississippi, ministered to the soldiers but had his own cross to bear. The war meant he missed the birth of his second child, Aubrey, on March 10, 2003. (Photo by Katherine M. Skiba)

Top Gun. Colonel William H. Forrester, a West Point graduate who hails from Pulaski, Tennessee, led the 159th Aviation Brigade at the onset of Operation Iraqi Freedom. (Photo by Katherine M. Skiba)

Salute and Farewell. Army Specialists Robert Jenkins, of Ripley, West Virginia, and Curtis M. Rose, of Oak Grove, Kentucky, stand atop a Humvee and show their respect for the fliers departing Kuwait for Iraq. (Photo by Katherine M. Skiba)

Kicking It Off. Brigadier General E. J. Sinclair and Colonel William H. Forrester study the airfield at Camp Udairi in Kuwait on March 28, 2003, minutes before the longest air assault in military history, a distinction the 101st surpassed a few weeks later in Iraq. (Photo by Katherine M. Skiba)

Making History. Three Chinook CH-47s carrying troops and supplies take to the skies above Kuwait on March 28, 2003, as Black Hawk UH-60 crews prepare for takeoff. Altogether more than 200 helicopters from the 101st Airborne Division flew 240 miles into Iraq in what was the deepest air assault in military history. The Screaming Eagles broke their own record less than a month later when they advanced into northern Iraq and made Mosul their base of operations. (Photo courtesy of Captain Benjamin Saine)

Screaming Eagle. The emblem of the 101st Airborne is stenciled on the nose of the Black Hawk UH-60. Soldiers wear the emblem proudly, though some jokingly call it the "puking chicken." (Photo by Katherine M. Skiba)

Game Face. The author, in a UH-60 Black Hawk helicopter, was armed with little more than a pen while embedded with the 101st Airborne Division's 159th Aviation Brigade during the war in Iraq. (Photo courtesy of Lieutenant Colonel Robert T. Ruiz)

Mission Accomplished. Chief Warrant Officer 2 Brian Buol had pledged that the Harley-Davidson flag would rise again. After flying without incident into Iraq for the first time, he had a soldier record the moment for posterity. (Photo courtesy of Brian Buol)

Desert Living. This was the scene in central Iraq at a primitive facility known as Shell, a forward arming and refueling point, or FARP, as U.S. Armed Forces advanced northward. (Photo by Katherine M. Skiba)

Dust Landing. Helicopter pilots faced a particular enemy in Iraq: sand. Landings and takeoffs in the desert were dangerous because the rotor blades whipped up the sand, creating brownout conditions. Here a "bird" from the 159th Aviation Brigade lands at Shell. In early April the brigade saw two pilots seriously injured there while sling-loading cargo beneath their aircraft. (Photo by Katherine M. Skiba)

At the Controls. The author strikes a pose in a Black Hawk UH-60 helicopter at Camp Udairi, a major airfield in Kuwait used by the U.S.-led Coalition Forces in Kuwait.

"You Call, We Haul." That's the motto of Chief Warrant Officer 2 Jon Nowaczyk, who stands next to his Chinook helicopter in the desert sands of Iraq after a supply run to Shell. His father, Dick, flew helicopters for the Army in Vietnam, and pinned his aviator wings onto his son at his graduation from flight school. (Photo by Katherine M. Skiba)

Hurry Up and Wait. Three pilots—Chief Warrant Officer 3 Ralph Ferrell, from Bangor, Maine; Captain Jeff Beierlein, from Cincinnati, Ohio; and Captain John Butora, from Murfreesboro, Tennessee—bide their time at Exxon, a forward arming and refueling point, while they await word of their next mission. (Photo by Katherine M. Skiba)

Mail Call. Sergeant Sherre Maxson, who grew up in Eagle River, Wisconsin, displays a drawing by her three-year-old niece. The correspondence, from Lake Villa, Illinois, reached her at Camp Thunder II near Najaf, Iraq, after mail call had been suspended for several days when fighting was brisk. (Photo by Katherine M. Skiba)

Final Roll Call. Command Sergeant Major Don Gregg sounds the final roll call to remember six soldiers from the Fourth Battalion of the 159th Aviation Brigade, 101st Aviation Regiment, who died after two Black Hawks collided over Mosul on November 15, 2003. A total of seventeen soldiers from the 101st Airborne died in the midair crash and five were injured. (Photo courtesy of United States Army)

Reunion. A year after leaving Iraq, the author returned to Fort
Campbell to see the men and women she accompanied to the war.
The trip was timed to the change-of-command ceremony for outgoing
Major General David H. Petraeus, who was replaced by Major
General Thomas R. Turner. (Photo courtesy of Ben Senger)

Pass in Review. Young infantrymen from the Screaming Eagles of
the Army's 101st Airborne show their stuff during a "pass in review"
ceremony, which dates to a time when commanders evaluated which
units to send first into combat. A CH-47 Chinook helicopter is in the
background. The 101st is the world's only military air-assault unit.
(Photo by Katherine M. Skiba)

6

Shifting Sands

I didn't stop to call anyone—not my editor, not even my husband. I just got the facts on the missile attack from Major Alex Covert and hustled back to Bravo Company to plunge into a story about the brigade coming under fire. The projectile that had careened toward Thunder Road initially was thought to be the first Iraqi missile launched in the war. It was an Iraqi-built, surface-to-surface missile known as the Ababil-100, the crown jewel in Saddam Hussein's arsenal. Traveling faster than the speed of sound, it carried an estimated 660 pounds of explosives—or about 160 pounds more than believed was used in the attack against the U.S.S. *Cole* in Yemen in 2000—and when it was taken out in midair, it was only nine miles from Thunder Road's airfield, a high-value target since the military helicopters parked there cost more than a billion dollars.

The missile, with a range of just under ninety miles, was thought to have been launched from the vicinity of Basra in southeastern Iraq. Its velocity meant that it was less than a minute away from its target when it was taken out. It turned out to be the second the Iraqis fired against U.S. forces.

Altogether, three Patriot missiles were unleashed from Thunder Road that afternoon, their inaugural use in the war. The first intercepted and destroyed the Ababil-100; the second one malfunctioned and self-destructed, causing what looked like the burst of yellow fireworks; and the third exploded in the desert.

In my mind, the strike by the Iraqis added up to one truth: I, with Allen and Beierlein and Carter and Denham and the others in the brigade's alphabet soup, had had, if not a brush with death, then certainly a close call. I wrote my story in the first person, sparing little emotion and few details, except for the soldiers' F-words and the specifics of what I'd told the Almighty. I even shared with readers the putative farewell to my husband—a disclosure whose timing was exceptionally poor.

While writing I was so fired up with adrenaline that the words just flooded out, and only when I finished did I call Carl to relay the news. "The story's written. You've got it," I told him, taking him by surprise, since ordinarily an editor gets advance notice on something this big.

I never took the trouble to call Tom that day, in part because the alerts kept coming at us like a weird clown springing out of a jack-in-the-box. Calls to take cover came again at 3:33 p.m., 4:07 p.m., 8 p.m., and 9:33 p.m. Sometimes the warnings lasted only a few minutes; sometimes we waited it out in the trenches for more than an hour.

After returning to my tent after one of those opening-day scares, Specialist Shane Oates must have seen the pained look on my face because he offered me a bag of Gummi Bears. I gnawed through every one of the colorful little candies before the night was out and soon felt sick to my stomach.

Before hitting the sack I made a point to wangle use of a working printer—some had ground to a halt, thanks to the sand—to copy my story for Lucky Mertes. I'd detailed his assistance during the attack in a passage that opened, "Fortune sent Lucky Mertes my way." I sensed that the short, solidly built flier could have looked the other way that afternoon, but instead lent a hand to the rankest amateur in the camp.

"You are a kind and brave American," I wrote by hand on top of the story. "I shall never forget your help to me today." His cot, in Sabb's tent, was empty, so I just left it there.

That night we were instructed to sleep with our protective overgarments and boots on and to have our gas masks at hand. It was a restless night. Three times—at 12:05 a.m., 1:11 a.m., and 2:19 a.m.—we were rousted out of our cots with cries of "Lightning, lightning, lightning," and, fumbling with our gas masks and flak vests, hurried into the trenches and toughed it out, once for a sixty-three-minute stretch. I knew the drill—take cover, square your helmet, brace your back—but by the night's final sinister alert, I just followed the lead of some others, stretching my weary bones across the open trench, my feet on one edge, my head on the other. If it made me more vulnerable, I was too wrung out to care.

So while shock and awe was hammering Baghdad, Thunder Road was feeling the figurative tremors. The veterans in the battalion spread the word that the Iraqis wanted, if nothing else, to keep U.S. troops at a disadvantage by disturbing their sleep. While I can't speak for the others, I was drained, physically and emotionally.

Maybe I assumed, or hoped, that Carl would tell Tom that a missile had been heading my way. Maybe I didn't have the guts to tell my husband myself. Or maybe I was just hewing to my ritual, waiting to telephone him at day's first light.

Tom, by then, had joined USA Today's "war desk," which had geared up around the time of Bush's ultimatum. The move caused Tom's hours to be

pushed back; he was now starting work at six p.m. Eastern standard time and handling news from the war until at least three the next morning. While the hours disrupted his sleep schedule, they were convenient for us, since when I phoned him in the morning, say, at eight, it was midnight back home, and usually he was at his desk.

The story about the missile, like everything else I wrote, was uploaded on the Internet and ran in the morning paper, which meant that by the time Tom read it online in his newsroom later that day, hundreds of thousands of readers in Wisconsin—including his own family—already had seen my would-be last words to him. Only weeks later did the actual letter straggle home to him.

"Hey, they're shooting at Kathy!" he called out loudly as he read my story, worrying—as I was—that the assignment was proving more treacherous than either of us had anticipated. His coworkers on the night crew wandered over and asked what had happened, so he shot them electronic copies of the story, and as in my own newsroom, the anxiety escalated.

On Friday—still Thursday in the States—I apologized to him for my oversight and promised that from now on, he'd hear bad news from me before he read it.

That morning I caught up with Forrester. The tall, wiry, middle-aged warrior looked no worse for wear, and he was candid when I asked about the opening day of the war. "I had probably the same thought you had," he said. "I was tired of getting in and out of the damn [fox]hole. I felt like a yo-yo."

Forrester allowed how the brigade's top brass had given the air-defense artillery soldiers, who operated the Patriot missiles, a standing ovation for their performance. He went on to predict that the Iraqis would play somewhere else today, though as he and I stood there talking, another alert, at 12:45 p.m., sent us scurrying back into the foxhole, with two more at 1:03 p.m. and 2:42 p.m.

As I was finishing a follow-up story about Thursday's missile, someone passed on word that Ben Senger from NBC in Nashville, along with his photographer, Eric Oliver, was pulling out. Rob Dollar was heading home, too, plus a two-man crew from Fox News out of Nashville. That left the 159th Brigade with me and two TV journalists from St. Paul, Minnesota.

Next to Bob Ruiz, Ben was my best friend. We'd kibitzed, traded notes on survival in the Army, and tried to keep each other's spirits up. Some people annoyed me by coming up to my cot day or night and striking up a conversation without so much as a "Do you have a moment?" But Ben was always welcome; once, in fact, when I was resting with a rolled-up towel over my eyes, he just lifted up the makeshift mask and smiled. If it were anybody else, I might have been perturbed, but he and I just picked up where we'd left off: "What's going on? What are you working on? How's your health?"

Since Ben had been ferrying his videotape from the camps back to NBC's headquarters in Kuwait City, he'd return with stories of how the "hotel warriors" in the press corps were living. They were, he said, ensconced in seaside hotel rooms with plush terry-cloth robes (and, even better, bathtubs and toilets) and a miles-long buffet of food and Jell-O shot with tequila to cap the night. I enjoyed his travelogues from the outside world; they let me live vicariously, and made me feel proud to be roughing it. But I was amazed that Ben could ease back into our sandy wilderness with its irregular shower times and latrines so foul you sometimes gagged. Once when the human waste in the honey wagons reached impossible heights, I suggested to the soldiers that Kuwait's topographical maps would need to be redrawn.

The prospect of losing Ben for good was like sacrificing some of the day's sunshine; I knew I'd carry on, but I didn't like the idea one iota. I went over to his battalion's tent to say good-bye, but he already had gone out to the flight line to catch a Black Hawk for Kuwait City. Then I got wind of a van taking the guys from Fox News to the same aircraft and hopped in.

"Did you think you were going to leave me without saying good-bye?" I asked my young confidante when I caught up with him. As we hugged and exchanged business cards, I told him that I would miss him, but I respected his decision.

Alerts riddled the camp again that evening at 7:01 p.m. and 11:15 p.m. The first came while I was giving an update by phone to WTMJ-TV, an NBC affiliate that is owned by the same media group as my newspaper. When we got the alert, I blurted out, "Oops. Gotta go," and hung up and took cover.

That evening, in between responding to the alarms I buried myself in the only book I'd brought along—*Life's Greatest Lessons: 20 Things that Matter,* with chapters on subjects such as a positive attitude, thankfulness, and honesty. I struggled to put my troubles in perspective, remembering the concentration camps I'd visited in Germany and Poland, and, closer to home, the anthrax-tainted letters that hit Washington, D.C., in October 2001, killing two postal workers and threatening lives on Capitol Hill.

Coming so soon after 9-11, the strange white powder had sent all of us into a panic. Then I recalled that a friend, Chris Tuttle, an aide to Wisconsin House Republican Mark Green, had found words of wisdom when he was evacuated from the Longworth building and relocated to the bland, labyrinthine General Accounting Office. Tuttle was given an office used by somebody working from home during the disruption, and in that office he'd found a snow globe. "Bloom Where You're Planted" it urged.

I wrote the axiom in black marker on a hot pink notepad so that I wouldn't miss it, and left it out on my cot, thinking it might inspire somebody else.

I bloomed, all right. After five of the eight journalists left, my head swelled so much it was surprising that my helmet still fit. It didn't go unnoticed that the only woman in the original group of embeds had stayed. And while I hadn't planned on earning my stripes through a close encounter with an Iraqi missile, once it happened, I flaunted my supposed bravery.

"The whole brigade is now mine!" I thought privately, sashaying around the camp and answering to new nicknames, like "Xena, Princess Warrior," which had more pizzazz than "Reporter Lady."

As I passed fliers and crew chiefs outside their tents, they'd ask me, "What happened to the other reporters?" and I'd smile smugly, square my shoulders, and, purring like Mae West, say something like, "I guess it's time to separate the men from the boys."

Such hubris. Maybe I was just drunk on life since the Grim Reaper had almost punched my ticket, but what I didn't know was this: in life, things change; in war, they change a helluva lot faster.

By now I was collecting material on Forrester, telling Carl that while the colonel deserved the ink, the story too might serve as a "beat sweetener." I would give the man his due and at the same time try to improve my standing within the brigade. I wasn't selling out. The colonel impressed me every time I spoke to him—even intimidated me a little, because he liked to put a person on the spot—and seemed held in high regard by everyone. He was game for it. I took my time gathering string, since writing about another human being is like peeling back an onion; with each layer, you get closer to the core. Plus I was not in a terrible hurry; I was still, no doubt, licking my psychic wounds.

On Sunday, March 23, I found out when and where Father George was saying Mass. I'd seen relatively little of him since he was housed with the brigade's staff and nowhere near the Fourth Battalion's tents. I figured it was time to thank God for having survived. I also felt it wouldn't hurt my reputation if people noticed I was getting religion—and people in this doorless universe noticed everything. Once I was examining my face in a Humvee's right side-view mirror—just checking to see if I was sunburned—and I got screamed at by someone who thought I was intent on eyeballing the secret maps left out on the passenger seat. Another time I put on tiny pearl earrings, prompting a female sergeant to demand, "Do you have a date tonight?"

In this world without walls, just as I was freshening up before Mass, Sergeant Willie Jacobs came up to my cot with an older fellow in tow. Jacobs worked as the brigade equal opportunity adviser, trying to ensure that no one was discriminated against because of race, color, religion, or national origin and that rules against sexual harassment were enforced; he was also, at Forrester's behest, told to keep tabs on the embeds for the colonel.

"Katherine, I want you to meet Jack Lawrence," Jacobs said. "Jack is from *Esquire* magazine. I'd like you to show him the ropes."

Curses! Something was interfering with my plan to have the brigade virtually all to myself—it was called the United States Army. Apparently the higher-ups were not going to let the five vacancies go wanting; they were sending in replacements. The nerve!

I studied Jacobs, who looked as eager as a puppy dog, and looked at Lawrence, who seemed older than any embed I'd come across—and cleaner than anybody I'd seen in weeks. Meantime I thought to myself: Help a guy from some glossy men's magazine? I've been eating sand with this brigade for three weeks, thank you very much, and I'm supposed to help out somebody who turns out pretty prose for a monthly?

"What are you smoking, Jacobs? Yours may be the 'Army of One,' but it's every scribbler for himself."

No such bile, of course, sprang from my lips. Instead I said the next thing that came to mind. Addressing Lawrence, I muttered: "I wouldn't drink the coffee here. There are scorpions in the coffee."

That, of course, was bullshit, since every single morning I was helping drain my tentmate David Oviatt's forty-two-cup coffee maker. And if I was trying to establish my credentials as a bitch on wheels, Lawrence wasn't buying it.

"Jack covered Vietnam," Jacobs chimed in.

Great, I'm thinking, I was in the seventh grade wearing a navy pleated skirt being schooled by nuns, diagramming sentences, and writing nothing more significant than entries in my first diary, and you were off covering a long and tragic war in Southeast Asia.

"Yes, I wrote a book about Vietnam," the sixty-three-year-old Lawrence said, copying its name on the back of his business card—*The Cat from Hue: A Vietnam War Story*—and handing it to me.

So began Lawrence's charm offensive. He talked about his book; it turned out my buddy Joe Galloway was in it. Next Lawrence invited me to visit his home in Surrey, divining, somehow, that I'm mad for England. Finally he asked me if I'd heard about the two journalists, one British, one Australian, who'd died the day before—I had—and he volunteered to point out where they'd been killed.

We studied my National Geographic map, and as he indicated the locations, near Basra in the south and Sayed Sadiq in the north, I marked them in pen with crosses, in the way people memorialize automobile fatalities along a highway. I'd heard only sketchy reports about the deaths from BBC and VOA, and I very much wanted to know where my colleagues had fallen.

Now I felt in Lawrence's debt, so I started blabbing about Forrester and Sabb and the missile and the shower times and maybe even "Be sure not to be late when the chow tent opens, Jack, because after a while they run out of food."

He seemed, in the end, like a good guy.

Twenty-three of us gathered to hear Father George celebrate Mass in a tent; and just like the first time I used the shower trailer at Victory, it took me a while to adjust—this time to all the M-4s and flak vests at a religious service, where I'd never before seen weapons. The makeshift chapel was in a combat zone, but the guns seemed out of place, like tambourines at a funeral.

I felt consolation, though, at seeing the blue-eyed, round-faced priest— physically, he reminded me of my maternal grandfather, John Urban—and to hear his heavily accented English. But all was not well. "Let us pray," he began, "for our brothers who were seriously wounded by a brother." I wasn't sure what the chaplain meant; could it have been another instance of an accidental discharge? One such mishap had happened on the outskirts of Camp Victory, and I'd mentioned it in an early story.

Father George went on to say that in light of our hardships, we should show consideration for other people, reaching out and lifting one another up. His words triggered a wallop of Catholic guilt. We're all suffering, I told myself, and since I was older and wiser and more advantaged than many others in the brigade, I ought to show them more compassion; giving out Hall's Mentholyptus cough drops and the occasional compliment wasn't enough.

The chaplain's tent was not far from the medic's quarters—where Ruiz, after an angry run-in with Sabb, had relocated in a bid to keep his sanity— so after Mass I went over to see if I could scare up my battle buddy.

He wasn't around, but I knew some of the people there, including Major Brian Smalley, the brigade physician, and Null, the medic who'd broken his fingers in the Humvee crash. Once I sank into one of their canvas field chairs—an improvement over my fold-up stool—I was so relaxed that I didn't want to move. I stood up only to help myself to some bottled water and an MRE, and afterward, still seated, asked Smalley for a refresher course on how to administer the injections we carried for a nerve-gas attack. Then, for my story, I interviewed Smalley about Forrester.

As we talked, a satellite radio news program broadcast word of an early-morning grenade attack striking members of the 101st Airborne at another camp in Kuwait named Pennsylvania. The report had a U.S. soldier in custody for an assault in the camp's command and staff tents. One soldier was reported dead and fifteen wounded. Only then did Father George's sermon—

brothers wounded by a brother—sink in. Somebody really lost it, I thought. One of the injured was from the 159th Brigade: 1st Lieutenant Terrence Bacon from the Fifth Battalion. He survived, but another one of those hurt did not, bringing the death toll to two.

Back home, the initial stories indicated only that the casualties were within the 101st, sending my husband and parents into a minor panic; the same, no doubt, was true for everybody who loved one of the Screaming Eagles.

The bad news that Sunday morning, though, was only beginning. Another report said the combined U.S. and British death toll had climbed to twenty-eight. And long before Private Jessica Lynch became a household name, it was reported that a large group of soldiers with an Army maintenance unit had taken a wrong turn on the outskirts of Nasiriyah. Some of these troops were killed and others captured; both some of the POWs and some of the dead were being shown on Iraqi TV. In addition, a Patriot missile had accidentally shot down a British aircraft, killing two. And there were reports of mercenaries streaming in from Syria and Jordan to join the fight against the U.S.-led coalition, triggering fears of a pan-Arab war.

A short, triumphal war? The prediction I'd heard voiced in Washington now seemed like a pipe dream amid the reports of Iraqi resistance in Umm Qasr, Basra, and Nasiriyah.

As I studied the faces of the pilots in the camp—experienced guys I looked up to and trusted—I saw drawn, gray visages, suggesting they were worried, too. Their murmurings did little to allay my fears. At one point someone took me aside and asked, "Have you heard? There are female soldiers being captured, raped, and cut into little pieces."

I tried to steel myself to the idea of such a vicious way to go. I hadn't heard this in a radio news broadcast, and I couldn't rule out that my source was one of those men who didn't think women belonged on the battlefield. I could hack it, I tried to tell myself; but my subconscious didn't fall for it. I walked over to the Bravo Company tent, where by now everybody was treating me like a kid sister, and asked for some self-defense lessons.

First Sergeant Lance Peeler was only too happy to comply. I was a novice—theoretically capable of landing a knee into an attacker's groin or jamming my car keys into his eyeballs (not that I'd brought along keys)—and I only wanted two or three ways of getting out of a jam; my brain cells were too fried to absorb more than that.

Peeler, though, introduced me to several techniques he'd picked up studying CQC, close quarters combat, which he'd learned during his years in Special Forces. He showed me at least a dozen ways to disable someone: delivering a blow to someone's brachial nerve; jamming a thumb outside someone's ear or under their nose or Adam's apple; sharply thrusting my boot into the nerve running alongside the femur, as if I were kick-boxing.

He demonstrated these and other action-film moves with great enthusiasm, spinning me around, putting me in one hold and then another, pointing out more vulnerable nerves and pressure points. If it hadn't been so clinical, or important, we might have been disco dancing. In the end, though, all these techniques blurred together; I left the tent unable to remember a single one, much less bring someone down in a fight.

When I told a pilot about it later, he volunteered something that hadn't occurred to me: "Maybe he just wanted to touch you."

Ruiz, for his part, did nothing to ease my nerves about the litany of bad news. "I've always wanted to be part of a desperate struggle," he mused, speculating about something already troubling me, which was the prospect of other Arab countries jumping into the fray.

Miles from the fighting, I kept working on the profile of Forrester, who was being roundly saluted as a "soldier's soldier." An attorney's son from Pulaski, Tennessee, he went to West Point Prep School before being admitted to West Point and graduating in 1978. Then he spent three years as an infantry officer before switching gears and going to flight school. He had considerable experience flying Black Hawks and had established himself as so formidable a commander that for a time he led a battalion of the elite "Night Stalkers," the Army's Special Forces aviators. He disclosed little about his missions then, generically describing the long-range insertion of soldiers into hostile territory and combat search-and-rescue operations.

When the Gulf War ended in 1991, Forrester, by then a major, worked in operations during efforts to resettle and aid 10,000 Kurds in the mountains of northern Iraq. He'd also had stints in Honduras, Panama, Colombia, Liberia, Sierra Leone, the Balkans, Germany, Italy, and Korea.

On the flip side of his business card was a quote from George Orwell: "We sleep safely in our beds because rough men stand ready in the night to visit violence on those who would do us harm."

Colleagues said he put a premium on the well-being of soldiers, telling them it was his job "to make sure you're taken care of and to bring you back in one piece." Forrester told me he tried to give the battalion commanders beneath him latitude, making himself available if they needed him. But he was hard-driving, too, telling subordinates: "If you set the conditions tough, it's easy to back off. But if you start easy, it's tough like hell to push up the standards." By "conditions" he meant the whole shooting match: having enough foxholes in the camp, making sure soldiers had on their flak vests and helmets and kept their weapons cleared and ready, and insisting that safety standards were followed when helicopters were put to the test during takeoffs and landings.

Jacobs, the equal opportunity adviser, regarded Forrester as "a father or a grandfather." Smalley, the flight surgeon, said he was nothing like the commanders bent on climbing the ladder even if it means stepping on others on the way up. "I see him the other way," he said. "He's a genuinely good person." Bill Allen, the command sergeant major for the brigade, put it this way: "He loves soldiers. And he loves the Army. They're the same reasons I haven't retired."

Lean and muscular, Forrester's balding pate and bifocals were the only clues that he was pushing fifty. He struck me as unflappable, except for his cigarette habit and, at the end of a long day, red-rimmed eyes. The colonel had a kind of courtliness about him, too; his Southern credentials were underscored by having a son, an aspiring Army aviator, poised to graduate from the Citadel; a daughter at the College of Charleston; a Labrador named Savannah; and a Weimaraner named Steel Magnolia Blossom. He told me his wife, Nancy, led the Thunder Brigade's spouses group, the Thunder Chicks.

It was a largely flattering portrait, but I wouldn't file the story without getting his take on the bigger picture. What about the U.S.-led coalition's overall progress? Forrester followed the guidelines by "staying in his lane," replying, "I'm not in a position to comment on something I haven't seen. It's out of my sandbox. The brigade's doing super, and there's a whole bunch ahead. As the president said the other night, this isn't going to be a short operation. We're going to stay here until it's done."

The suspected fratricide? "It brings the realism of what we're doing to the forefront. This is a dangerous place," Forrester said.

Then there were the hardships, beginning at Camp Udairi, where, before I arrived early in March, a retinue from the brigade watched a large dining facility go up in flames. Next came the terrific sandstorm at Camp Victory and the incoming missile at Camp Thunder Road.

Now nobody in the Army ever used the word "problem," at least not in my presence, preferring the innocuous term "issue," as in, "We have an issue with this vehicle." Forrester wouldn't even acknowledge "issues."

"Small distractions" is how he characterized the dark clouds that seemed to trail the 159th Brigade from one desert camp to the next. While acknowledging difficulties with communications, transportation, contractors, and living conditions, he maintained, "The job at hand is getting done and meeting my expectations."

If this veteran commander was keeping up a brave face, I can't say that I shared his sunny outlook. I had eyes and ears. Soon after the fratricide, wide coils of concertina wire were installed around the perimeter of the camp's tactical operations center, which now was guarded more heavily. Around the same time, I heard some women jabbering about a female Reservist who'd gone to the medic's tent for a Prozac refill. When asked why she was taking the antidepressant, she responded, "I'm bipolar," and promptly was relieved of her rifle and ammunition. That wasn't the first time I'd heard a story like that. Whenever somebody seemed to be losing their marbles, their weapon and ammo were confiscated; it had even happened in my own tent. (For me the Twilight Zone moments came later, when the same enlisted man was deemed to be better and got his ammunition back.)

Maybe I was sweating the small stuff; maybe I was getting low on intestinal fortitude. I was wigged out when a notice went up in Bravo's tent indicating that some of the atropine, handed out as the antidote to a nerve agent, was defective: "Lot 8T5454, Expires 12/03." I jotted down the information, thinking, "What on earth next?"

Then came a news flash that lifted my spirits, if temporarily. As I waited in line with other women for a rare opportunity to shower, a soldier behind me said the two guys from NBC News had returned. "You mean Ben and Eric?" I asked eagerly, and was told that it was them.

By then the Fourth Battalion's Number Two man, Ralph Litscher, had briefed me on the upcoming mission into Iraq. The helicopters would carry infantrymen across the border to something called a FARP—a forward arming and refueling point. The aim was to have fighters from the 101st in place just west of where the Army's Third Infantry Division had advanced; it was expected that there would be heavy fighting in central Iraq's Karbala Gap, southwest of Baghdad. If I wanted to go along, I was to bring my chemical protective gear, a couple of MREs, some water, and a "day bag" with enough personal effects for a short trip.

Already a small group of fliers from the Fourth's Bravo Company had quietly gone into Iraq on Sunday, March 23, to a FARP near Najaf. Scuttlebutt had them taking fire and having a tough time of it; as one veteran flier still at Thunder Road warned me, "It's Injun Country up there."

I was told to show up at five a.m. on Tuesday, March 25, for a pre-mission briefing in the Fourth Battalion's Alpha Company. Soon after that, we'd be off.

The company's operations center was crowded with fliers and their crews, some still wearing sleep in their eyes, all huddled around a large map spread across a plywood table. Someone rattled off the times each group of aircraft would leave, first for the nearby Camp Udairi, which had a large airfield. There was a briefing on the weather, which was expected to be poor for a few days, possibly delaying the mission; and then the possible threats were enumerated. That's when I really paid attention.

Among the hazards were a possible roll-in; small-arms fire; rocket-propelled grenades; mortars; SA-14s; AK-47s; and what was called the biggest threat of all, 400 to 600 paramilitaries with small arms in the vicinity of Najaf, possibly wearing black, operating out of Bedouin tents and hiding behind women and children.

While I understood most of what was being said, I was clueless about what a "roll-in" was; the same for an SA-14. The former, I discovered, was antiaircraft fire; the latter, a Soviet-made, shoulder-launched surface-to-air missile.

The session ended with Chaplain Greene's reciting the first three chapters of Psalm 18, which added nothing to my peace of mind; he might well have been administering the Last Rites, the Catholic sacrament for someone approaching death.

"I will love you, O Lord, my strength," he began. "The Lord is my rock and my fortress and my deliverer; my God, my strength; in whom I will trust; my shield and the horn of my salvation, my stronghold. I will call upon the Lord, who is worthy to be praised; so shall I be saved from my enemies."

He concluded, in his own words: "Thank you, Lord, for the men and women who are brave and courageous."

The press, rather than travel in the Black Hawks, was invited to go in on Chinooks, and were given the name of a contact person within that battalion of heavy-lift helicopters.

When the session broke up, I was torn. These guys had made a career of doing air moves and air assaults; I was so new to the game that some of their chatter might have been spoken in Mesopotamian.

Afterward I took aside two people I trusted, Ruiz and the command sergeant major, Gregg, and asked them point-blank: "Should I go now, or wait for a later mission?" Ruiz urged me to go; he, after all, was heading off with the fliers. But Gregg advised staying back. That left me to break the tie. I had too many doubts, so I decided to play it safe and remain behind. Then I noticed the white-haired Jack Lawrence striding off jauntily with the flyboys. I felt very small.

As a consolation a couple of young soldiers invited me to ride in their Humvee to the edge of camp and see the helicopters off. The sun was just coming up, making the light perfect for shooting pictures, so I tagged along, watching the momentum build as the pilots fired up the engines, the rotor blades began thwacking rhythmically, and a long procession of helicopters roared in the skies above us and out of sight.

The two soldiers stood solemnly on the hood of their Humvee, crisply saluting as dozens and dozens of helicopters streamed by.

Nearby were two sergeants from Alpha standing on top of another Humvee, one of them vigorously waving the company's teal blue pennant, known as a guidon, back and forth. The ritual seemed like a medieval throwback; I decided to go over and speak to them.

First Sergeant Tim Nidiffer, a thirty-seven-year-old native of Aurora, Colorado, said it was the first time he wasn't going on such a mission in about seventeen years. "As we move up through the ranks, it's hard to see our little brothers go off without us there to protect them," he remarked.

He was concerned about what loomed beyond Iraq's border. "The last war, we were kicking the Iraqis out of Kuwait, and this time, we're invading their country. The enemy is hardened. They're going to pull out every stop they can pull."

Nidiffer said the pilots and crews were concerned, too. "They're confident in their abilities, but there's always the unexpected out there."

"They're scared," said his sidekick, Sergeant 1st Class Patrick Hopkins, a thirty-eight-year-old native of Augusta, Georgia. "I'd be scared, too."

So maybe I was wise to have hung back, I thought.

After the birds left, Litscher, the Fourth Battalion executive officer, sat me down and walked me through the mission until I finally got it. Then he passed on a new tidbit: Thunder Road, in the next several days, would be shutting down as the entire brigade moved forward. If I didn't fly, I'd end up in a convoy with the support personnel; going over land was expected to take forty-eight to fifty-four hours, complete with a host of hazards not unlike those the fliers faced. "You're probably safer in a helicopter than in the convoy," he advised.

He made it seem so elementary. And contrary to what I'd heard, he said Sunday's mission with the first group of aircraft had gone well. He offered me the chance to fly into Iraq on Thursday, so I took it. Suddenly I was raring to go.

As predicted in the early-morning meeting, another punishing sandstorm erupted that evening. During the height of it, my buddy Ben popped into my tent. I was delighted to see him, until I caught the glum look on his face. Yes, he and Eric were back, at their station manager's behest, but they were thinking about pulling out again. Ben's rumor du jour had Saddam Hussein using chemical weapons the next day.

Dead soldiers, dead journalists, prisoners of war, Iraqi resistance, Arab mercenaries—and now I could be slimed.

"Maybe I'll go with you," I told Ben. If the three of us left together, it would make it easier on the Army, which had more important things to do than arrange transportation out in onesies and twosies. Meantime the three of us would have security in numbers and once in Kuwait City, we could regroup and consider reporting the war from a safer vantage point.

Still, I felt that we needed more information, and since Ben and Eric had more sophisticated equipment than I did, allowing them Internet access, the Web seemed like the place to start. He and I headed over to their tent, where

I turned to the *Washington Post* online. A story by Thomas E. Ricks, whose work I respected, seemed to confirm what Ben was hearing:

The battle now beginning between U.S. forces and the Republican Guard's Medina Division to the southwest of Baghdad promises to be a decisive engagement that signals whether the new Gulf War will be over in a week or drag on for a month or more. . . .

If Iraq chooses to use chemical weapons during this war, analysts think it will be in this battle.

The story quoted a former CIA analyst as saying that intelligence reports indicated that Iraq had distributed chemical weapons, mostly likely VX (nerve gas) to the Republican Guard. A retired rear admiral, formerly a chief planner with the U.S. Central Command, agreed: "I don't think you'll see bugs [biological weapons], but you might see gas."

It was chilling stuff, but given the lateness of the hour, the best course of action seemed to be to sleep on it.

It was getting late—most people in their tent had already zoned out—but I asked Ben if I could use his equipment to check my e-mail; I'd been without it since the day I left Fort Campbell. There were 1,700 messages in my in-box, mostly spam. Tom, Carl, and Carl's wife, Barbara, had been my lifelines so far, but in between the junk mail I also found messages from old friends, new friends, my in-laws, and, out of the blue, a source I'd met on a news story more than twenty years earlier.

Sando, my boot camp leader, had written, too, prompting me to hit the reply button and ask, "Will you still be my friend if I tell you boot camp is starting to resemble the Camp Fire Girls by comparison?"

A number of the messages were from the families of the 101st: spouses, mothers and fathers, aunts and uncles, sisters and brothers, cousins, and coworkers too. Russ Toeller's wife, parents, and a cousin sent messages; Toeller was the first pilot I'd profiled, the bus driver's son. Someone from Harley-Davidson told me the story about the short-lived bid to fly its flag had found a spot on the motorcycle manufacturer's employee bulletin board. The mother of a private who had been on board my flight to Kuwait City wrote to tell me, "It made me feel closer to him just reading it."

The wives of Fourth Battalion pilots sent words of encouragement. From Catherine Jarvis, who is married to Adam: "I just wanted to say we are proud of them and love and miss them very much. You have really helped us to stay updated. May God bless you and keep you and our troops safe." From Hedi Brotherton, Erik's spouse: "My first thought is to thank you from the bottom of my heart for the work you are doing. I pray that God will protect you from harm's way and guide you. I pray that your husband and family stay strong and support you in all you do."

"Be careful. God protect you," a retired Navy commander wrote.

"I truly admire your Annie Oakley grit," an infantryman's mother said.

While my editor, Carl, had told me he was hearing good things from the friends and families of the Screaming Eagles, I had had no real sense of how far-flung my readership was.

A number of Forrester's friends wrote, too—like Ted Meyer and Charles Brumback. I copied their names and stuck them in my press credentials holder, wanting them at hand to share with Forrester later.

Scrolling rapidly through the correspondence, I saw an update from a friend and fellow embed, Jerry Zremski, a Washington correspondent for the *Buffalo News.* He wrote that he'd gone into Iraq with an Army supply unit from V Corps Command Rear on Saturday, March 22, and after "four harrowing days" wound up in Najaf. He recounted a "fifteen-hour drive through hell, featuring ambush scares and missiles flying above our heads." He'd seen U.S. soldiers who were wounded and heard reports that two others were killed; meanwhile there was word that more than one hundred Iraqis were dead after clashes nearby.

One Iraqi, he wrote, "still sits dead at his steering wheel, with half his head splattered through the cab of his truck."

"War is the worst thing I've ever seen," he concluded. "Of course, I am trying to make arrangements to get out of here as soon as possible. Believe me, I have seen enough ugliness in the last couple of days to last a lifetime."

The letter gave me a chill. My friend had hit rough shoals, and it seemed like more than a fluke that I'd gotten his e-mail message; maybe it was a beacon, warning me away from danger.

I knew the decision was mine alone, and at the moment there wasn't much more to do than brave my way through howling winds and blowing sand and get back to my tent and sleep on it. In the morning I planned to ask an intelligence officer for a better sense of the day's threats.

At my cot I hauled out a notebook and wrote: "Maybe it's time to leave. (1) Lost my St. Catherine's medal just before the missile attack. (2) Stress. (3) War more dangerous than I expected. (4) Sabb."

I concluded that the positives were good stories and a possible career boost, but these seemed trivial compared to never again seeing the people I love.

Next I pulled out my bedtime reading, *Life's Greatest Lessons: Twenty Things that Matter Most,* and for the first time, turned to Chapter 18, which was entitled "It's OK to Fail—Everybody Else Has." It read:

- Failure teaches us humility. It confronts us with our limitations and shows us that we're not invincible.

- Failure teaches us to correct our course of action. It forces us to look at what we're doing and gives us the opportunity to try a new direction.
- Failure teaches us that we can't always have what we want. Sometimes, even when we do all the right things, it still doesn't work out.
- Failure teaches us about perseverance. It asks us whether we're going to quit or become more determined and keep trying.
- Failure teaches us that we can survive defeat. There's no shame in failing, only in being afraid to get up and try again.

The next morning, the intelligence officer I approached for information stonewalled me, saying, "I don't know what I can tell you." I was furious, and pleaded with her, "I'm not asking you for a story. I'm asking you because I'm worried about my own butt."

I finished with a snide postscript: "If you won't tell me, I'll get it from Forrester."

My frustrating exchange with the intel officer was the last straw. I wasn't planning on going down a dark alley, even with the Army holding my hand.

I called Tom to tell him I was thinking about pulling out. The threats emerging from the briefing, Ben's warning, and Jerry's e-mail message gave me the heebie-jeebies, and though normally I'm not superstitious, I took it as a bad sign that I'd never found my St. Catherine's medal. Then there was some simple arithmetic: If I went into Iraq, it would be the thirteenth foreign country from which I've reported.

Number thirteen, Tom!

My husband said my worries seemed overblown; he pointed out that no news organization had reported that women troops were being taken captive, raped, and cut into tiny pieces. By then he'd seen the work of other embeds, who were taking fire with the Marines and the Third Infantry Division, ripping through Iraq and living to tell the tale. Tom had the strong sense that I'd regret it later if I'd gone to cover a war and gotten cold feet at the enemy's border.

My editor, Carl, knew by then that I was having second thoughts, and after conferring with the paper's top managers, said the choice was mine; since they were so far away, they were not in a position to decide for me. Their refusal to give me guidance was a mixed blessing. On one hand, I appreciated the hands-off approach—I could decide for myself to get out and maybe save my life. But on the other hand, I was mildly cynical about their reluctance to ride me a little harder, thinking that none of them would want blood on his hands.

In the end, just after ten in the morning on Thursday, March 26, Ben, Eric, and I went over to the brigade tactical operations center and delivered the news to Sergeant Willie Jacobs. We wanted out. "We don't feel safe here anymore," I explained.

Our ride out was set for seven o'clock the next morning. There was no ill will about it; I sensed mixed emotions among the troops. For one thing, there would be fewer civilians to feed, shelter, transport, and keep tabs on. But then, we might well have been canaries in a mine shaft; if the journalists were weak at the knees, what did that presage for the men and women in uniform heading into Iraq?

I started packing up, giving away things like duct tape and extra AA batteries; I copied down the e-mail addresses of wives and children whom soldiers wanted me to contact; and I even dashed off a few good-bye notes, including one to Ruiz.

Once I had things in hand, I called Tom again, telling him I had made arrangements to leave. This time my husband wasn't buying it. "The war is going well," he insisted, to my astonishment. "If you leave now, you'll regret it."

"Aren't you worried about me?" I answered him. "I can't believe I'm hearing this. *Don't you ever want to see me again?*"

Meeting my hysterics with his trademark calm, he insisted, "Yes, I want to see you again. And no, I don't want you to die. But you won't." Tom didn't believe that I was truly desperate to get out; nor did he think that I was approaching the breaking point. He thought, mostly, that I was seeing things too narrowly; that the war seen through my keyhole blurred the larger, better story.

"The war is going well," he repeated. "And I know you: if you come home without setting foot in Iraq, you'll never forgive yourself. You've already seen some bad stuff; it's not going to get much worse. When you go to cover a war, you should get in there and cover it."

Everything he said made sense. If I chickened out just miles from the Iraqi border, I'd likely never have the opportunity again. I was back in my high school's indoor pool, where, though an excellent swimmer, I sometimes stood at the edge of the high dive, peering at the water, paralyzed with fear.

"Maybe I'll talk to Forrester," I told him.

"That sounds like a good idea," he said.

Chaplain Greene was waiting for me to get off the phone. After I hung up, he asked to speak to me.

"Hey, listen, I heard you were leaving, and I'm sorry to hear that," he said. "I wish you'd stay, Katherine. You're a positive force here."

A positive force? Did my ears deceive me? Up until then the Army and I hadn't exactly been holding hands around the campfire singing "Kumbaya." I'd been challenged about my identity during the sandstorm while trying to secure my tent and keep it from blowing all the way to Saudi Arabia, had a notebook seized, been kicked out of my tent during another storm, been chided by a lieutenant for having a messy cot ("If you were in the military, there would be wall-to-wall counseling for you"), and been berated for using a Humvee's rear-view mirror to study my face, not some classified maps.

Maybe the Army families back home were supportive, but the kindest things I'd heard so far from an officer—excepting Ruiz, who had begun to call me "Darling"—was that I had testicles.

Greene asked me why I was leaving, and having nothing to lose—after all, I was heading off to the land of terry-cloth robes and tequila Jell-O shots—I unloaded. I unleashed every single grievance, every insult, every slight, and every worry.

The chaplain took it all in but kept insisting that I should stay. He said people liked having me around, that my work was important, and that I was having a positive impact.

I studied him skeptically and demanded, "Why are you doing such a sales job on me?"

"I used to be in sales," he admitted, chuckling.

"Maybe I'll talk to Forrester," I told him.

"You ought to talk to Forrester," he said.

As I had been planning, I went over to Bravo's tent to print out my just-published story on the brigade commander. I'd been around enough officers to sense that Forrester wasn't your average full-bird colonel. Granted, he was the camp's big cheese, but nobody would even volunteer a negative anecdote off the record. Jacobs said he'd never once seen Forrester dress down a subordinate. Smalley remembered the time a soldier back in the States went AWOL for three months; rather than throw the book at him, Forrester felt that the young man could be rehabilitated, so he brought him back into the fold.

"Some military bosses are screamers," I'd begun the story, my ears still ringing after a male sergeant in my tent ordered someone to appear before him by calling out the soldier's last name and bellowing, "Come to your bitch!"

Some are micromanagers. Some are taskmasters who try to extract 24–7 from troops.

People who work beneath Colonel William H. Forrester, the forty-eight-year-old commander of the 159th Aviation Brigade, say he's none of those.

The printer was still spitting out my story when a young specialist came in and handed me a letter from Forrester. I was surprised the messenger had found me, but, in this open society, apparently everyone knew where I hung my helmet.

"Can you hang on a minute?" I asked him, tearing open the envelope. Inside was a commemorative coin celebrating the 101st Airborne, listing all the places where the division had made its name: Normandy, Bastogne, Holland, Berchtesgaden, Vietnam, Iraq, and Saudi Arabia. The other side heralded the 159th Aviation Brigade.

In a handwritten note, Forrester wrote that he'd read my story, suspected that I'd embellished some of the comments from his soldiers (which I hadn't), but was touched by them. "I believe you captured the hardships we've endured and were able to accurately pass along from your foxhole. Again, thank you and I'm glad you joined our team. Respectfully, Bill Forrester."

After a string of bad omens, suddenly fate seemed to be smiling. When I traipsed back with the specialist to the TOC, Forrester was in his private tent with Bill Allen, the brigade command sergeant major.

"I suppose you've heard those untrue rumors about me leaving," I opened. "But my husband tells me the war is going well, and he thinks that I should stay."

Forrester invited me to tell him what was on my mind, so I spoke plainly. "Well, I feel a little like I'm standing on the edge of a high dive, afraid to go into the pool. But I realize if I leave, I'll never be in this position again. Back in Washington, Joe Galloway told us that we should never go on a mission if we didn't understand the operation and its risks. And I know I've been kept in the dark, but when I went to the preflight briefing in Alpha Company, there was a lot of stuff—like roll-ins and SA-14s—I didn't understand."

He nodded, seeming pleased to hear that I didn't know everything that was going on around me.

"But there was a lot of stuff at the briefing, like AK-47s and rocket-propelled grenades and paramilitaries with small arms, that I did understand," I continued.

"And then all of a sudden I'm supposed to go with the Chinook fliers. Well, I don't know those guys. I know the Black Hawk fliers. I'm not afraid of the aircraft, per se, and I'm not a prima donna, but I'd feel more comfortable flying with somebody whose name tape I've seen before."

While I didn't mention names, the Fourth Bat's pilots reeled through my mind: Wood and Mertes and Jarvis and Toeller and Beierlein and Buol—I'd fly with any of them. Beyond quick conversations in a dimly lit chow tent, I didn't know the Chinook guys.

Suddenly Forrester asked, "Why don't you fly into Iraq with me?"

"Fly with you?" I repeated, wanting to make sure I heard correctly.

He nodded.

"Sure, I'll fly with you," I told him.

Next he looked warily at all I had hauled in—a small suitcase of professional gear, plus body armor, helmet, and gas mask. It probably seemed like quite a load for somebody trekking across camp.

"Be sure to pack light," he instructed. "Take an extra change of clothing and some food and water."

He told me to be at the tactical operations center at four the next morning.

Only then did I tell him I'd gotten e-mail messages from his friends; I was glad that I waited, since I hadn't wanted to appear to be dropping their names as bargaining chips.

I might have been ten feet off the ground when I left, exuberant about having been stopped from making an embarrassing career U-turn.

Something about the rough-and-tumble Bill Allen always brought out the devil in me, so on my way out of the tent I looked at him and said, "Yeah, I got an e-mail from your ex-girlfriend, too. She told me to break your kneecaps."

Allen and I laughed, but I think Forrester scowled, so I ditched the bad girl persona and said to the colonel, "Thank you, Sir. I'm grateful. I'll see you tomorrow."

I was still in midair when, on my way back to Fourth Bat, Captain Sean Connolly, the Army lawyer, brought his Humvee to a halt in the sand. "Hey, I heard you're leaving," he said.

"Look at this," I told him, pulling the 101st coin out of my pocket. "I'm staying. Forrester said I could fly with him into Iraq."

Now the old Cadillac ad popped into my mind: "Cadillac, Cadillac, Cadillac style." I figured that the brigade's top boss would have his helicopter in tip-top shape and an expert crew along for the ride.

Tom sounded relieved when I gave him the news. "You're going with the right guy," he told me, privately thinking that the odds of a colonel getting killed in a battle were slim to none.

Now all I had to do was to wash up, and, with the precision of an astronaut, pack for the mission and set out my clothes for the next morning. No more dilly-dallying with my gear like I'd done at the Holiday Inn near Fort Campbell, even though the last forty-eight hours had felt like a dozen consecutive roller coaster rides.

Still, I was practically too excited to sleep. I set two alarm clocks, covered my eyes with my sleeping mask, and shoved ear plugs in my ears for a few hours of rest. *I am going into Iraq!* I thought.

Time passed, and the next thing I was aware of were shafts of light behind my head and a gentle breeze wafting into the tent. God, I feel rested, I thought; then I hit the mental snooze button for a few more delicious winks.

Next I felt a tap on my left shoulder, so I eased myself up off my cot and onto my elbows, lifted my eye mask and said, "Excuse me. I don't know who you are."

The next words hit me like a four-inch hypodermic needle rammed into my backside: "Colonel Forrester."

Only then did I realize that I had overslept. "Oh my God!" I exclaimed. "I'm so sorry!"

"How much time do you need?" Forrester asked curtly.

"Five minutes, Sir!"

Forrester left the tent, and I leaped out of my cot and traded long underwear for real clothes. I missed a few of the loops on my pants while putting on my belt and even more of the notches on my boots as I laced them up. I shot my fingers through my hair, collected my things, and galloped outside in four minutes flat. My teeth were wearing sweaters, my head felt like it was going to explode, and my mother's old reprimand echoed in my every aching neuron: "Katherine, you're going to be late for your own funeral!"

I looked up at the colonel and blurted out, "I understand, Sir, that you're a forgiving man."

Grabbing one of my bags, he said drily, "We're going to have to have a little education about ear plugs," and we marched off to the aircraft.

7
Bad Guy Land

Oversleeping was my first major misfuck in the company of the U.S. military, but two things saved my hide. First, the skies still were hazy from the last sandstorm, and the reduced visibility meant it was unlikely that the fliers would depart that day for Iraq, or "Bad Guy Land," as some commanders called it. Second, plenty of people seemed to be chuckling over the inanity of my setting two alarm clocks and then putting in ear plugs. News that the embedded journalist had to be rousted out of bed by the brigade's top boss was making the rounds, giving everybody a reason to snicker during a fairly humorless stretch.

We were bound for Camp Udairi in Kuwait, where a massive airfield recently had been built for the U.S.-led coalition forces. It was about fifteen miles from the Iraqi border, and, by helicopter, a thirty-five-minute trip from Thunder Road.

Before leaving, Staff Sergeant Brad Kitch, the door gunner who reminded me of a state trooper, shot me a withering look. I didn't mind. I figured that everybody in the Army had made a mistake once, since its rules and regulations if lined up end to end could span the equator two and a half times.

While Kitch and the other crew members readied the aircraft, I turned my back toward them and brushed my teeth and combed my hair. Once I was strapped into my seat, I smeared some foundation on my face and dug into my fanny pack, which was brimming with over-the-counter remedies, for something to conquer my headache.

Forrester said little as he took the controls with pilot Brent Driggers, a forty-seven-year-old from Union Springs, Alabama, who was one of the most senior fliers in the outfit. He'd climbed to the highest grade available to warrant officers, which is 5, and looked as though he'd been in and out of a lot of tough spots. He reminded me of a middle-aged Sean Connery, not least because of the mischievous glint in his eyes.

Rounding out the crew was a back-up pilot, Chief Warrant Officer 2 Matthew I. Hernandez, a twenty-six-year-old from Sacramento, California, who operated a laptop with an imaging system known as "Blue Force Tracker," which showed the location of "friendlies," or coalition forces; another door gunner, Specialist Paul Eshom, who grew up south of Jackson Hole in Pinedale, Wyoming; and Major Smalley, the brigade flight surgeon whom I considered a friend, and hoped would remain an ally despite my screw-up.

Once we landed at Udairi, we waited to see if the weather would clear and the mission could proceed. There needed to be sufficient time to carry scores of infantrymen into the fight in Iraq and to get the pilots and birds back to Kuwait before dark. Forrester's helicopter, Tail Number 9326493, was parked behind a row of Black Hawks that were facing north toward Iraq and stretching as far as the eye could see. The colonel left the aircraft at once, theoretically freeing me to go up and down the line of helicopters in search of Ruiz and other pals. Not wanting to incur Forrester's wrath, I kept myself on a short leash; I couldn't chance being AWOL in case he and the others suddenly flew out.

While we were waiting to see what developed, Geraldo Rivera showed up on the airfield, making for what Ruiz and I called one of Operation Iraqi Freedom's "Fellini moments," since odd characters were always unexpectedly darting in and out of your war. Rivera, from Fox News, was the 101st Airborne's newest embed. He strutted from helicopter to helicopter, glad-handing soldiers and obligingly posing for snapshots. He was smaller than I had imagined and so trim that his waistline seemed girlish. He wore desert camo pants with a crisp white shirt, a black neckerchief, leather jacket, black cowboy hat, and raspberry-colored sunglasses. I wondered where his gas mask was; everybody was supposed to carry one at all times. When he neared Forrester's bird, those of us who had stayed behind with the aircraft turned in the other direction and spoke amongst ourselves, acting as if we had no clue who he was.

Lieutenant Colonel Sabb, though, wandered over and hammed it up so much with Geraldo that you'd think the battalion commander had been summoned to central casting. "I can have the infantry out here like this," he said, snapping his fingers theatrically to indicate the mission could be under way at a moment's notice.

By now I'd privately declared a cold war against Sabb, and seeing him give Geraldo the equivalent of a big, sloppy French kiss—since he'd treated me like dirt when I arrived—confirmed my impression that the Fourth Battalion commander was a blowhard. You had to hand it to Sabb, though, for being able to judge character; Rivera later was booted out of the 101st after drawing a map of Iraq in the sand and broadcasting where the division was and where it was heading, a clear violation of the ground rules.

Eventually somebody in a small truck came to ferry those of us from Forrester's bird to Udairi's flight operations office, a command and control facility for the aviation brigades. There, soldiers did what the Army is expert at: multitasking. They drew up passenger manifests, kept flight records, monitored the movement of aircraft, and maintained radio contact with the pilots nearby. That was all well and good, but what mattered most was this: the modern offices occupied by "flight ops" featured flush toilets, porcelain sinks, and air-conditioning—each one of them a wonder to a sun-baked, sand-coated desert rat like me. It sure beat the portable toilet I'd used that morning at Udairi; while doing my business, I'd looked up and detected dried feces on the ceiling, the result, I suspected, of the latrine being turned upside down during the week's high winds.

With the mission on hold, I interviewed Brigadier General E. J. Sinclair, the 101st's assistant division commander for support, who had an office in the flight ops building. A forty-eight-year-old West Point graduate who hailed from Glendive, Montana, he had spent twenty-seven years around the world with the Army in tank, attack helicopter, and air cavalry units (the latter of which are combat maneuver forces trained to locate the enemy and delay their attack on friendly forces). Sinclair seemed like a jolly good fellow—I told him, in fact, that he seemed too jolly to be a general. Maybe it was his down-to-earth Montana upbringing. He'd left for the academy just a few days after graduating from high school; he'd planned to put in five years with the Army and return to Big Sky country, which happened to be one of my favorite places. Instead, Sinclair got hooked on the Army, mostly because of the soldiers and the camaraderie, and by the time I met him had served stints all over the world.

The high-spirited Sinclair described the mood of his soldiers as "hungry" and previewed the mission for me. He said that more than 216 aircraft from the 101st were poised to travel about 240 miles into Iraq, making it the deepest single-day helicopter air assault in the history of military warfare. The Marines had come up with the notion of moving troops by helicopter, and they had tested the idea in 1948 along the North Carolina coast; but helicopters first were used as medevac aircraft during the Korean War to carry wounded soldiers to MASH units. During the 1960s, the Army began trials using helicopters to move infantry troops forward—no matter that rivers, rough terrain, and other impediments lay below. During the Vietnam War, then, the UH-1H "Huey"—officially called the Iroquois, named for a Native American tribe, like its successors—would alter the way troops were transported into battle, by breaking the friction with the ground and moving soldiers deep into enemy territory. For a time the Huey was the most recognizable aircraft on the planet.

According to Sinclair, more than one hundred Black Hawk UH-60 utility helicopters were poised to take part in the present mission, along with seventy-two AH-64 Apache attack helicopters, twenty-four CH-47 Chinook heavy-lift helicopters, and twenty OH-58 Kiowa observation helicopters.

The mission stood to test the 101st Airborne's air-assault capabilities to the maximum. With no significant coalition forces ahead of their destination, just south of Karbala, it was not entirely certain what threats might be looming there. Helicopters gobble up gasoline, and the refueling stations already in place were thought to be vulnerable to attack. The timing and sequencing of the aircraft were challenges; maintaining communications with the birds over extended distances also posed logistical headaches.

Sinclair characterized Iraqi resistance in the war to date as light, except for the paramilitaries trying to harass coalition forces and halt the movement forward. Should his fliers take fire, "they're prepared to react to it," he said. "They'll do good. They know what to do—shoot back with a helluva lot more. We'll teach 'em that they shouldn't shoot at us."

He said his troops were well-trained—some steeled from Afghanistan, some from rehearsals in California's Mojave Desert—and prepared for contingencies, including urban combat and chemical warfare. Finally, Sinclair hinted that more was ahead for the 101st. "There will be several key things that we do, along with other forces in theatre, in ridding weapons of mass destruction and removing Saddam Hussein. We'll be part of that team that makes it happen."

When word came down that the mission was formally put off for another day, I continued my slow crawl toward getting back into everybody's good graces by volunteering to make a trip to Udairi's post exchange. The lines outside this general store—where you could pick up everything from CDs to soap to sports bras—were tremendous, but as a rare woman in civilian clothing I could skip the wait by pretending that I worked there and striding right in. I rationalized my bad behavior by recalling that the 159th's camps never merited a PX. That day, whatever anybody on Forrester's aircraft asked for—a six-pack of Mountain Dew, a carton of generic cigarettes, extra batteries—I picked up.

Forrester spent the night in his bird, which struck me as so hard-core that my lips just about curled. He was beginning to seem bionic. The rest of us from his aircraft joined others from the 159th Brigade and filed into a large, sparsely populated tent littered with discarded food wrappers and sneeze-inducing dust balls. There was so much coming and going by military units at Udairi that one didn't sense much pride in ownership, hence the mess. I took a hot shower—another of the camp's luxuries—then tidied up my sleeping area, setting up an empty cardboard box as a nightstand and throwing essentials, like eyeglasses, inside my upturned helmet so I knew where to find them in case a missile alert disrupted the night.

Kitch was in the cot next to me, and we spoke for a bit before lights out. He wasn't going to call it a day before needling me about oversleeping and signaling that I was fortunate to be along. "You know, I would have left without you," he told me.

"I would have left without me, too," I answered him.

The next morning I was up like a shot at four-thirty, knowing that on-time performance was critical and not wishing to board a helicopter again feeling like I'd washed ashore after a shipwreck. The fliers and crew were champing at the bit to go; several minutes before the prearranged departure time, they were left to study me as I crammed a down-filled sleeping bag into a duffle bag and, glancing at them with worried eyes, collected the rest of my gear.

I scrambled in the dark, lugging my belongings over the camp's up-and-down terrain, trailing the others on the way to the airfield as a navy-colored, starlit firmament was dissolving into pastel blue skies and a fat golden sun was creeping over the horizon. The skies were clear, with light winds, and the temperature was in the sixties. The weather conditions made it plain that the small army of dark-hued helicopters, neatly lined up nose to tail on the tarmac, would be in business.

Forrester was alone on the airfield, soaking up the scene, so I tiptoed up to him and asked to have a word. Shaking his hand, I remarked, "Thank you, Sir, for a second chance for a 'Rendezvous with Destiny.'" He looked at me with a poker face, but at least I'd acknowledged my mistake again.

Next Ruiz showed up and, judging from his grin, was happy that I'd had a change of heart about going forward into Iraq. After I spilled the details of my boo-boo, he let out an "O-o-o-o-o-h, no-o-o-o-o," and burst out laughing.

Despite the early hour, General Sinclair turned out, as did Colonel Ken Brown, the 101st division's sturdy-looking chaplain, and others keen to see off the historic mission.

Before boarding, those of us bound for Iraq put on our nuclear, biological, and chemical gear overgarments, which were mandatory for the mission. While hoisting on the cumbersome pants, I talked with Specialist Paul Eshom, who had never flown in combat and admitted to being "a little bit nervous, a little bit excited."

"I think that a world without Saddam Hussein and his regime is a better world," he judged, "and we're the only people who actually realize that and are willing to do something about it."

Once we were on board, a stone-faced Kitch knelt on the floor in front of the window seat behind Forrester, the copilot, and swiveled his machine gun back and forth; Eshom manned the gun on Driggers's side. To my right, Hernandez, who had a Mighty Mouse sticker on his helmet, began singing "Roxanne" ("It's my good luck song") until Driggers told him, in so many words, to put a sock in it. "Sing it to yourself," is how he put it. Smalley wordlessly took his place on the other side of Hernandez.

At once the morning's quiet was shattered by the collective roar of the helicopter engines, the ear-splitting, high-pitched whistle of the auxiliary power units, and the signature "whop-whop-whop" of the rotors. Now at the point of no return, I didn't feel a lick of fear, not in the company of these six men. I might have been flying to Salt Lake City or St. Maarten. Beneath my steady-nerved exterior, though, it all seemed electrifying: enemy territory, combat flying, the prospect of danger, and—courtesy of the Black Hawk—the thrill of vertical lift.

So at 6:40 a.m., Friday, March 28, 2003, the ninth day of the war, Driggers and Forrester took off and brought up the rear in a serial of seven helicopters flying as a group. Through the windshield it looked like a military recruiting poster had sprung to life; the only thing that seemed missing was Wagner's "Ride of the Valkyries."

About fifty feet below was the desert—a vast, treeless continent of sand bearing the skittering shadows of the menacing army of helicopters cutting through the skies.

Kitch and Eshom, in turn, let off fifteen rounds, test firing their machine guns whose loud, sharp, rat-a-tat-tats commanded attention.

The monotony of the landscape was broken up by herds of camels, flocks of sheep, sage-colored shrubs, and, many miles into the flight, an old, degraded fortress that looked like a huge sand castle after a few gulps of high tide. Sometimes I'd catch a mother camel leading a pair of young; other times, I'd notice a few of the long-necked, hump-backed desert dwellers break away from the pack in a jaunty trot.

Animal behavior was not on anybody else's agenda. Driggers and Forrester scanned the horizon and examined their dark-hued instrument panel and its green digital readings. Kitch studied every truck and every Bedouin tent—and anything else big enough to conceal a bad guy and a gun—while poised to fire. Hernandez pecked at the laptop and reviewed a printed handout, some of its data classified.

After fifty minutes, the bird came down with a thud in a blaze of sand and dust so thick it was like sinking into a giant vat of brown sugar. We'd landed in Iraq. The first stop was a refueling station known as "Exxon," a name that seemed to connote toilets, truck-stop coffee, and a cherry pie under a plastic bonnet—but that was a mirage. Safety procedures dictated that everybody except the pilots leave the aircraft as it was being gassed up, since the engine was left running. This meant getting out and walking away from the helicopter bent at the waist to avoid being decapitated by the rotor blades, nearly fifty-four feet in diameter.

Kitch seemed pleased with the safe passage across the border, saying, "I hope the infantry is up north, doing the killing for me."

After two hours of flying, we reached the final destination, "Shell," which, like Exxon, was a forward arming and refueling point. There the "Rakkasans," the Third Brigade of the 101st Airborne Division, were dropped off to do battle.

The place looked like a moonscape, not least because of the solitary American flag fluttering in the wind amid bleak terrain. I noticed antitank missile launchers, defensive trenches, and other security features, as well as fuel trucks and lines and a hodgepodge of vinyl tents for housing, but little else. The only place to pee was next to one of the fuel truck's oversized tires, but inhibitions vanish at such times.

Afterward I rejoined Eshom, and the two of us waited several feet from the aircraft. He broke the tension by regaling me with jokes. "Why does it suck to be an egg?" He was dark-haired, lanky, good-natured, and young; he'd turned twenty-one the day before the war began.

"I don't know," I replied. "Why does it suck to be an egg?"

"Because you only get laid once. You only get eaten once. When somebody sits on your face, it's your mother. And when you come, you're in a box with eleven other guys."

I howled, not least because my being warehoused in a tent with about five dozen guys and a dozen or so women meant that I had less privacy than even an egg enjoyed. I didn't get all the double entendres, unfortunately, although later, as I recited the joke again and again, nobody suggested that I'd crossed the line.

On the return trip, Chief Warrant Officer Driggers and Colonel Forrester followed a similar flight path, stopping at Exxon before making it back to Kuwait less than eight hours after it all began. Afterward the colonel exuded satisfaction, noting that in a half-day's time, he'd deposited troops into Iraq at a distance that would have taken forty-eight hours over land, and none of the aircraft had taken fire—everybody had made it back safely.

"Now that the weather has lifted," he said, "the 101st can go about doing what we were brought here to do: projecting forces at operational distances. We'll keep doing the same thing: moving soldiers forward and establishing strong points to continue to move forward."

Driggers's assessment of the day's work? "Super," he offered. "Peachy. It don't get any better than this."

I bumped into Sinclair, the general, and told him Churchill had it wrong: nothing in life was more exhilarating than not to be shot at at all.

Eshom's only comment was that I needed a suntan.

"What?"

"We all saw you at Shell, and we think you need a suntan."

Finally I got it; he was referring to my behind.

After the mission, I undertook one of my own, something I was becoming expert at: begging, borrowing, or stealing a relatively sand-free place to work. Back at the flight operations office, the commander of Udairi's airfield, Lieutenant Colonel John Newcomer, surrendered a portion of his desk in his private office. The forty-year-old Newcomer was a full-time reservist from Fort Sheridan, in Highwood, Illinois, outside Chicago, so was from my old neck of the woods.

The only aggravation? As I was getting close to wrapping up my story, soldiers kept banging on the door and demanding to know when I would be done. "It's movie night!" they clamored, hoping to evict me as soon as possible and commandeer Newcomer's office.

By then I was in a bizarre physical state—beyond exhausted, but too cranked up to sleep. Compared to the military, my work didn't seem like heavy lifting; I just asked questions, tried to make sense of what I saw, and assembled a beginning, a middle, and an end. It's not like I knew the sorcery that made an aluminum-coated whirlybird fly or had the machismo to operate an automatic weapon. Still, the up and down and back and forth from my first combat mission left me feeling like I'd spent time in a washing machine on the agitator cycle. Once my story was sent, I was bedraggled, hungry, and lonely.

I needed to find Ruiz.

Udairi was a huge outpost with hundreds of tents, but I tracked down the shelter that Fourth Battalion had been assigned and searched for him out there. Most of its pilots had figuratively crashed and were huddled under sleeping bags—and I couldn't blame them, since they would move more troops forward tomorrow. I was relieved to find that my friend the flight surgeon hadn't turned in, and we left for a vacant tent nearby—a dust bowl, really—where we chewed over the mission and all else that had taken place in the days we'd been apart.

I offered to let him read my story off the laptop and munched some crackers from an MRE. Then we talked some more. The war seemed to magnify the strangers-on-a-train syndrome, especially since the scenery was bleak, the creature comforts few, and safety never guaranteed.

Ruiz and I had a few things in common. Both of us were born on the edge of big cities with a stainless-steel spoon in our mouths. We'd done our share of odd jobs while growing up; once at Thunder Road we polished off MREs for lunch in between revealing the ways we'd earned money for college. I couldn't imagine him in the men's department at Montgomery Ward's; he couldn't picture me delivering mail for the U.S. Postal Service or selling women's clothes at Evan's Furs. We were both Catholics, schooled by the Jesuits, familiar with a few corners of the world where writers for travel magazines haven't left footprints—and anchored by loved ones back home.

"I love the way you write," he said, breezing through my story. The military never censored my copy, but Ruiz's imprimatur meant I hadn't committed malpractice in translating things military for a mass audience.

"I like you because you're a healer and not a killer," I told him.

I got along with most of the soldiers, though a few were impossible to stomach, too obnoxious even to qualify as "trailer trash." Others had such low-watt bulbs in their brains they couldn't switch their sports watches to Greenwich Mean Time as ordered. Some infuriated me, like the guy in the motor pool whose boom box blasted bad rap music near my cot; the only lyric that registered was "Bitch, ho. Bitch, ho. Bitch, ho." Others, inadvertently, scared me half to death with their video games whose battle sounds were so real that I was ready to duck and take cover.

Ruiz, pure and simple, was a mensch. He was smart, experienced, witty—and a man of integrity. He began calling me Kate, saying I reminded him of Katharine Hepburn. I was with him so regularly that I'm sure that some people thought something was up. But with spouses we cherished back home, ours was a pretend flirtation. Once he eyeballed one of my Diana Krall CDs, showing her with long, windswept blond hair, a short, sexy black dress, and stiletto heels. "I wish I had a woman who looked like that," he mused. I looked up at him from my cot, wearing a dirty T-shirt, camouflage pants, and heavy boots, with my sandy hair pulled back in a ponytail. Chances are I smelled like a pair of dirty socks.

"You do," I said, looking him in the eye and cracking up.

After our talk that night, I set up a cot near Forrester's crew—it was late, so I'm sure they didn't appreciate the racket—and collapsed into a deep sleep. Not many hours later, they were up and at 'em in the dark, trudging off for another air assault into Bad Guy Land. I declined the invitation to boomerang back into Iraq, since I couldn't reprise the same story, and returned to a dreamless sleep.

After I made my way by helicopter back to the brigade's home base, Thunder Road, I was heralded by some of the young soldiers as if I were a returning warrior. Most, like the cooks and mechanics, had not yet set foot inside Iraq; they seemed to hold me in new esteem and were eager to hear what enemy territory was like. "It was no big deal," I said.

Theirs wasn't idle curiosity; there were major security concerns about the marathon trip they were due to make in the ground convoy into Iraq. One officer had taken me aside privately, indicating that some of his soldiers might be killed during the long haul—in his words, "We're probably going to lose some people." While I appreciated the heads-up—and made a mental note to stick to flying and avoid the road trip—it made my heart sink, since I felt anguish for my friends, and wondered why they'd drawn the short stick.

A day later Major Alex Covert, the brigade's executive officer, offered on short notice to send me back to Iraq with a Chinook crew heading to Shell. The installation, south of Najaf, was a forward arming and refueling point as well as a gathering site for attacks deeper into Iraq. The pilots were taking in much-needed aircraft fuel and supplies, such as ammunition, concertina wire, and lumber, plus food, water, and mail. Shell now was home to the 101st Aviation Brigade, a sister unit comprised mostly of Apache attack helicopters, and Covert suggested I seek out its commander, Colonel Gregory Gass.

This would be my first trip in a ten-ton Chinook, and I can't say I left without any qualms. I'd examined one of these big birds at Camp Udairi after it had been hit by small-arms fire and mortar rounds. The words of Lieutenant Colonel Sando, from media boot camp, echoed in my mind: "You'll have your 'pucker moments,' " he'd said, though it took me a while to figure out he was not referring to lips, but to another part of the anatomy. "You just keep going."

So I grabbed a day bag and left to catch up with the Chinook guys of the Seventh Battalion. "Our motto is 'You call, we haul,' " pilot Jon Nowaczyk said. "We fly anything, any time, anywhere," He invited me to sit in the cockpit in the jump seat between himself and the other pilot and gave me a headset so we could speak en route.

The desert was old news to Nowaczyk, who, with three machine gunners, a flight engineer, and two crew chiefs, had traveled over what he called "the vast nothingness" for several days running. Early in the flight, as we were cruising over the sands of southern Iraq at about 140 miles per hour, he had a question for me: "Are you a Green Bay Packers fan?"

My husband's mania for the Packers had rubbed off; together we owned a single share of the NFL's only publicly held team. "I own Green Bay Packers stock," I told Nowaczyk.

"That's a very good answer," he responded. "I would hate to drop you off right here."

Nowaczyk, a chief warrant officer 2, was an Army brat. He was born in Japan at Camp Zama, a U.S. installation about twenty-five miles outside of central Tokyo. His father, Dick, was a helicopter pilot who cut his teeth in Vietnam flying an AH-1 HueyCobra, an attack helicopter. After leaving Asia, the elder Nowaczyk was posted with his family in Alabama, Kentucky, Germany, and Alaska. After retirement, he and his family put down roots in Michigan's Upper Peninsula, which borders Wisconsin. Jon Nowaczyk came to revere the Packers so much that he named his yellow Labrador "Lambeau," after Curly Lambeau, the legendary coach for whom the team's playing field is named. And he never left for a deployment without his green-and-gold team blanket.

Most recently he'd served in Afghanistan. "Sucked," he remarked. "It was a different experience. Lotta mountains. My first time in a Third World country."

Thirty-two years old, Nowaczyk was a big, plump-faced guy—six foot one, 220 pounds—with brown hair, light eyes, Oakley shades, and chewed-up nails. Like most of the men on board, he had a working man's hands, with traces of the aircraft's grime and grease. His heritage was Polish and Czech, hence his nickname, "the Polack." He seemed colorful and quotable—perfect for a story.

After the Chinook landed at Shell, I showed up at the 101st Brigade's tactical operations center, where somebody, after sizing up who I was and where I'd come from, couldn't resist thumping his chest, announcing, "Welcome to the varsity."

The 101st Brigade had more than sixty Apaches, more than twenty Black Hawks, and more than twenty Kiowa Warriors, which are lightly armed scout helicopters, at work. That day the Apaches had seen action in Najaf, south of Baghdad, and eight helicopters were reported to have taken fire. The aircraft, which can fire at targets from as little as ten feet off the ground, is armed with thirty-millimeter guns and Hellfire and Hydra 70 rockets. It was being used primarily against Iraqi tanks, artillery, and air-defense systems.

Colonel Gass was occupied when I arrived, but I had all the time in the world, since we'd flown in late in the day and planned to bunk out in the Chinook at Shell before heading back to Camp Thunder Road.

Maybe my lukewarm reception had something to do with the bad news involving the eight damaged aircraft; maybe it was because the outpost had so few comforts. "Good star-gazing" is all it had, in the words of a pilot from the 159th Brigade who previewed the place for me. His was a more generous appraisal than I heard at Shell, where a warrant officer in his fifties remarked: "You live the dream and embrace the suck. And this place is nothing but a suck."

While waiting for Gass, I chewed the fat with the brigade's personnel and took in the unit's satellite television, which was tuned to Fox News. Except for the war's opening salvos, I hadn't watched television in more than a month, so I was transfixed by the scenes from all over Iraq showing the advance of U.S. and British troops.

But before long it became clear that I was an outsider at best, and a problem to solve at worst. After the sun went down, Major Joseph Crocitto, the brigade's media liaison, worried that he'd have to find some tent space for me to stay the night.

"You don't have an extraction plan," he scolded.

Extraction plan? That was a new one. "But I'm sleeping in the Chinook," I protested.

"But you don't know where it's parked," he said acidly.

He had a point there. I didn't have an inkling, not that I was alarmed. How hard could it be to track down a helicopter big enough to transport a small herd of elephants?

Crocitto agreed to an interview and told me to follow him from the tactical operations center to his tent. Immediately after leaving the TOC, I tripped in the dark on some tent ropes, landing hard, smack on a kneecap. It hurt like hell, but I got up and kept going. Once we got to his quarters, the blubbery, barrel-chested Crocitto took off his shirt and proceeded to give himself a sponge bath and shave while answering my questions. It wasn't a pretty sight.

Crocitto said the brigade's aircraft were being hit by rocket-propelled grenades; ammunition from small arms, including rifles and machine guns; and S-60s, which are long-barreled, high-velocity 57-millimeter antiaircraft guns. He called the resistance "sporadic in frequency but well coordinated" and noted that an Iraqi had to hit the right part of the aircraft to take it out and "be brave enough to shoot at them."

Talking about the combat in Najaf, he said, "As far as actual operations, it's risky, but we're doing well."

Crocitto allowed that while the Iraqi Republican Guard was a formal division "with nothing unconventional about it," more worrisome were paramilitaries loyal to Saddam Hussein who he said were compelled to shoot at Americans or risk the punishment of having their own families slaughtered.

Afterward we returned to the TOC, and when Gass was free, he showed himself to be a genial commander and was generous with his time. He said he expected that he and his fliers would be shot at and that, so far, no aircraft had been lost. The damage ranged from small bullet holes in a tail blade to a whole tail boom being "pretty much shot out." Some pilots had suffered bumps and bruises from so-called hard landings, but Gass said he worried more about accidents at Shell, which was like a big industrial plant. He noted that the $30 million Apache, loaded with the latest computer technology, would be worthless without pilots, crew chiefs, refuelers, and support personnel.

"America's sons and daughters are out there every day—in the heat, in the sandstorms—and they keep driving on," Gass told me. "They want to get right on it and get home."

As if on cue, two guys from the Chinook I'd come in on showed up to lead me back to the aircraft, which was parked in the desert about a half mile away. Still stinging from Crocitto's grumbling and the implication that the 159th Brigade was the junior varsity, I was pleased to extract myself. Before I left, somebody gave me an address to invite readers to send mail to "Any Soldier" in the 101st Brigade; I copied it down dutifully, knowing full well that I'd deep-six it—my way of saying thanks for the mixed reception.

The lesson learned, as the Army would put it? I told myself that I'd be smart to stay with the 159th Brigade for the duration and not leapfrog into another unit. More than a month with the Screaming Eagles didn't seem to count for much with people like Crocitto.

Meantime, the Chinook crew from the 159th Brigade was so accommodating you'd think I was Amelia Earhart. Maybe these fellas were hungry for publicity—or company—but they couldn't have been more hospitable once I returned to the "Boeing Hilton," as the aircraft is nicknamed when it doubles as sleeping quarters.

These were spacious digs compared to what I'd had; and improbably, the pull-down mesh seats running along the sides of the cabin were a cozy place to climb into a sleeping bag. I was in enemy territory, sleeping in the vicinity of five guys, most of whose names I'd forgotten; but with a breeze billowing into the open rear door and some R&B from Luther Vandross on my headphones, I was a happy camper.

The next morning the crew must have gauged my contentedness—there's nothing like a good night's sleep and some instant coffee from water fired up with JP-8 jet fuel—because one of them volunteered, "You must like to camp."

I found that so hysterically funny, I almost spit my coffee out. "Don't tell my husband that" is all I could say.

Nowaczyk, wearing a visor from Bass Pro Shops, the purveyor of hunting and fishing equipment, set a folding chair out in the sun and sat for an interview, which was interrupted when he spied an energetic black scorpion coming his way on the desert floor. All of us took a gander at it before he squished it with his right boot, observing, "That was a pretty good-sized one."

Like pilot Russ Toeller, Nowaczyk had come to flying after several years in the military. He'd graduated from high school in Gwinn, Michigan, joined the Army a year later in 1990, and knocked around the service as an administrative clerk and legal specialist before getting into flight school nine years later. "I knew my dad flew, and I thought he was cool. I always wanted to fly. It just took me a while before I got my act together."

When his father got his wings in 1974, he was the distinguished honor graduate of his class. Twenty-seven years later, when he pinned the same wings on his son, he wept, saying, "You're my distinguished honor graduate."

"It was pretty emotional," the son remembered. "I was elated. It was the best day of my life."

Nowaczyk was enamored with his aircraft, describing it as big, fast, and able to carry more than it weighed. "Typical man thing," he shrugged. "It's the biggest, baddest thing there is."

Talking about the sensation of flight, Nowaczyk called it "better than walking . . . just awesome. You have all this power underneath you, and at any minute you could crash or something unforeseen could happen. You have to be paying attention to everything around you. People say flying a helicopter is easy, but in this environment, it isn't. And we have precious cargo on board: people."

His breakfast? Skoal Mint chew. He said he'd have the same thing for lunch and break into one of the vacuum-sealed MREs only for supper; he only liked MRE Menu 12, the bean and rice burrito. Besides, he hoped to drop forty pounds during the war. Meantime he was expecting a care package from home, hoping for tortillas, refried beans, jalapeño cheese, and smoked oysters.

Nowaczyk told me that his hobbies were wine-making, hunting, and "hanging out with the kids"; the thing he most regretted was missing his boy's Little League games. Back home was his thirty-year-old wife, Melissa; daughter Chelsea, nine; and son Jon, eight. "I married a very good woman," he told me, boasting that his spouse was renting an auger and installing a chain-link fence at home; while he was in Afghanistan, she'd poured a cement walkway.

"Nobody wants to leave their family, but you have to look at the bigger picture: the greater good for the U.S.," he said. "The U.S. being over here, it makes America safer for my family, for my kids' family, and generations on down."

"There's an inherent risk in what I do, but once again, it's for the greater good. You have to deal with the risk in order to get the job done."

The risks announced themselves that morning in short order. Out of nowhere, two U.S. Patriot guided missiles screamed through the skies, signaling the prospect of an incoming enemy missile. In double-time we packed up the aircraft and made haste for Kuwait. It was April 1, but nobody was laughing.

Back at Thunder Road, few could resist having some April Fools' Day fun. According to Ruiz, Nelda Scenie, a sergeant, slipped a note to Sabb at a Fourth Battalion meeting saying that she, too, would be leaving the field since she'd become pregnant. Scenie was forty-seven years old. According to Ruiz, people could barely contain their laughter, and when Sabb finally got the joke, he muttered something about payback being sweet.

Scenie struck me as a quiet, unassuming, and efficient woman—the last person you'd see wearing a lampshade at a party. I knew her casually; she'd loan me her mirror every so often or hold up a poncho in the corner of the tent so I could change clothes, never asking for anything in return. When I heard about her prank, I took her aside and congratulated her, saying, "I didn't know you had it in you."

"I didn't know I had it in me, either," she answered.

The same day I got back to camp, the Chinook fliers wanted me to return to Iraq, saying, "Hey, come with us. We're sling-loading today." It meant they would be hauling cargo from the underbelly of the aircraft from a sling made of ropes and chains. But I had stories and photos to file, so I declined.

A few days later, the chance to go into Iraq with the Fourth Battalion's Alpha Company presented itself, and I was game. I knew they'd thundered into combat and taken enemy fire in the dangerous skies over Afghanistan, dumping infantry into that war's largest ground battle, Operation Anaconda. Naturally, I was presented with another one of their business cards—World's Greatest Pilot, War Monger, International Playboy, Social Outcast, Ladies Man, Renowned Booze Hound.

"The Alpha Males," I christened them privately. It was Friday, April 4, a blistering ninety-seven-degree day.

"What are you writing about today?" one of the fliers asked as I sat in the rear of the helicopter, awaiting liftoff.

This was war, I thought: kill or be killed. "I'm writing about Alpha Company, *allegedly* the best pilots," I told them. My sarcasm was apparent, and now they seemed to be wincing, just as I had been when I'd seen their calling cards for the first time.

Flying by now was getting to be routine; and if I wasn't scrawling out a story, I had time to kill, since the crew was busy and the rotors and engines were too loud to conduct much of an interview. Besides, I already had the scenery down pat: camels, sheep, Bedouin shepherds, sage-colored shrubbery. So during an idle moment that day, I scribbled in my notebook, creating a business card for myself. I wrote:

> Babe
> Blond
> Ex-cheerleader
> Chanteuse
> Ballet, modern, and dirty dancer

Newly incarnated as an Alpha female, I mulled letting a pilot take a peek at what I'd written, but instantly thought better of it. When you're staring at fifty, you can say a lot about yourself, but I wasn't planning much self-disclosure in front of these dogs of war, even if they were the purported leaders of the pack.

Still, writing out my Alpha card made me feel young and wild and free-spirited and sexual—like Dennis Rodman, basketball's bad boy, I was in touch with my inner freak. The war seemed to be transforming me into the woman I knew only on occasion: bold and brave and even cunning. Maybe the Stockholm Syndrome had kicked in and the prisoner was beginning to resemble her captors, as brimming with derring-do as they were. I was reminded of what Robert E. Lee once said: "It is well that war is so terrible, or we should get too fond of it."

From then on, I wore my "Action Girl Reporter" face, discreetly keeping from my supercharged, testosterone-fueled companions my duller, grayer alter ego, the Suburban Virginia Housewife.

I was, after all, an ocean away from Arlington, Virginia, my azalea bushes, and Felco pruner, from my floral-patterned recipe box, grocery-store coupons, and stash of Control Top pantyhose. Some of the pilots gave off the aroma of sex-deprived flyboys; more than a few seemed to regard me as an exotic hothouse flower, so just to be on the safe side, I took to chirping, "My husband works for *USA Today*."

Meantime I informed those who inquired of my life that I hiked mountains, had traveled wide and far, spoke a bit of several languages, owned a chocolate Labrador named Princess, rode in Virginia's horse country, and had belted out a song in front of a two-star general at the closing dinner of the reporters' boot camp. All of this was true.

But on my Alpha card, I did not write:

> Bottle blond
> Married eight and three-quarters years
> I brake for outlet malls
> Mountain bike gathering dust
> Average at tennis

Meanwhile I jazzed up my repartee with some French, Spanish, German, Russian, and Polish, even Latin, maybe a "Ciao" or a "Prego" thrown in, although once I uttered a word in Arabic—"Salaam"—and a major shot me a dirty look. Clearly, I was not among peaceniks.

In no language known to man did I breathe a word of my bunion surgery or my big butt. Actually, I did joke once about my butt, calling it a potential target for the Iraqis. We were just so desperate for a laugh.

Some guys started calling me "Blondie." Wood, the chief warrant officer with whom I'd shared a foxhole on the war's opening day, once deemed me a "dizzy blond." At first I found that offensive, but maybe he had a point. What civilian woman would march into war—voluntarily and unarmed—if she wasn't mildly insane?

Move over, Amanpour. I was standing tall in a war zone, armed with nothing more than ambition. The time I caught the raven-haired Amanpour at the anchor's perch, I had only one dark thought: *That woman is wearing eye liner!* I went the entire war without so much as mascara. It didn't matter. Under an unforgiving sun I was getting tanned and toned, flitting across desert sand and asphalt airfields as I chased one story after another. The only thing that mattered was survival—staying healthy enough to report and shoot pictures, catching some sleep, eating something from time to time, downing bottled water, and heigh-hoing my forty-six-year-old tail into the foxhole at every unnerving alert.

So what if I was going through more cigarettes than I ever had; plenty of others were, too.

I told Eshom's joke—"Why does it suck to be an egg?"—to anyone and everyone; I also repeated a gag I'd gotten from Sergeant Ashworth: "What's the difference between kinky and perverted? Kinky is a feather; perverted is the whole chicken."

I was enjoying such smooth sailing that I stopped telephoning home every day; the same for calling my office. Once Tom reluctantly reported that after working the late shift, he'd accidentally backed his SUV into my Honda Civic, leaving its rear end badly dented. "It doesn't matter," I assured him. "I'm still alive. Don't worry about my car. We'll take care of it later."

The convoy had finally, bravely, chugged out of Thunder, but not before Captain Goveo approached me one morning and asked to speak to me privately, giving me the knot-in-the-gut sense that I was being summoned to the principal's office.

Once we left the crowded tent, he played highway cop. "Do you know what we're going to talk about?" he asked me. Shit, I was clueless. Given the abundance of arcane military laws, rules, regulations, lessons learned, orders, doctrines, manuals, and handbooks, there was any number of possibilities. I felt a headache coming on. Still, I wasn't going to fall for his trap. I'd been stopped for speeding enough times to know better than to volunteer anything. "No, I haven't any idea," I lied.

Then he told me. During a time when water was running low, somebody had ratted me out: I'd been seen using Al-Rawdatain to shave my legs.

Having seen some top-shelf criminal lawyers in action, I sprang to my own defense. I hadn't been briefed on the shortage; and the "water buffalo," a large tank that held nonpotable water for washing up and doing laundry, was empty. Furthermore, I was a member of the media and had to talk to everybody from the colonel on down, so I had to look presentable. Besides, I added, as I understood it, people were supposed to pay attention to hygiene and grooming, which struck me as a bit difficult when the showers weren't working, and the buffalo was bone-dry.

And you know what else, Captain, I continued, my travel orders indicate that I'm supposed to be billeted like a major, and instead I'm thrown in a seventy-man tent with the motor pool guys, and did you hear me complain once? He knew I hadn't.

I promised not to waste bottled water again, but, for good measure, I reminded him that I don't read minds.

Goveo, the gorgeous Goveo, nodded his head at almost everything I said. And he didn't seem ready to rip into me, so I could breathe more easily. I knew he had a heart of gold; he hadn't protested when I'd borrowed his CD player and used it until all the life was sucked out of it. It had taken a lot of persuasion for me to get him to accept $50 for a replacement.

The captain then asked if there was anything I wanted to bring to his attention, and in fact there was. I suspected that the jerk who fingered me was the same guy behind the offensive rap music. Not mentioning names, I told Goveo that I didn't like hearing the words "bitch" and "whore" over and over and over.

Guess what? I never heard that music again.

On the mission with Alpha, the lead pilot was John Butora, the company commander, an earnest thirty-two-year-old who held the rank of captain. The other pilot was Chief Warrant Officer 3 Ralph Ferrell, who, at forty, was flying in his third war. Earlier he'd served in the first Persian Gulf War and in Afghanistan, where he won the Air Medal with a "V" for valor after his aircraft was struck by a rocket-propelled grenade while he was depositing a brigade command team into a fighting position in the Shahi Kot Valley during Operation Anaconda.

The aim now was to pick up infantrymen who had been providing security at Exxon, the "gas station" for military aircraft that the Army had set up in southern Iraq, and ferry these soldiers north to the front lines. But the mission was a bust; by the time the birds landed in blazing heat at Exxon, the infantrymen had hitched a ride with someone else. No story there.

So the pilots flew to Camp Udairi to await further instructions. When nothing developed that day, it meant I would have to do something that once inspired dread but now was merely unnerving: I'd have to sleep in the Black Hawk.

Compared to the Boeing Hilton, the Sikorsky Hotel was tiny. There were six of us that night in the Chinook, which was built to carry up to forty-four

troops. Five of us needed to share the Hawk, which I'd seen carry sixteen soldiers, but only in college-student-stuffed-in-a-telephone-booth style. Char-
acterizing the aircraft as a "hotel" seemed as plausible as calling its alu-
minum exterior a precious metal.

Discreetly I changed into shorts and T-shirt and spread out my sleeping
bag in the rear of the cabin, thinking it would be better to call it a night between one relative stranger and a wall rather than between two people I
hardly knew. Once inside my goose-down sack, I plastered my limbs to my
frame to avoid reaching out and touching someone or hogging too much
space. But trying to shrink, if not disappear, wasn't necessary after all; these
stand-up guys just crashed out in sleeping bags strewn on the tarmac.

The temperature dipped after sunset, and the winds splashing through the
two open cargo doors were as refreshing as being attended to by hired help
waving palm fronds. The bird's flooring was another matter; it felt like reclin-
ing on an automotive chassis. While working the kinks out of my back the next
morning, I learned that I'd slept on a Kevlar blanket lined with steel, which is
installed to protect fliers from small-arms fire. Officially known as the "ballistic
armor subsystem," it's a wonderful thing, providing vertebrae don't get a vote.

Fortunately, I kept my mouth shut, acting as if I'd spent eight hours on
a Sealy Posturpedic. Sergeant John B. Tengel, part of the crew, soon made it
clear that asphalt wasn't conducive to sweet dreams, either. "From dark to
sunrise, every time I rolled over, I woke up," he complained.

While waiting for word on the day's mission, the experience seemed as
good a feature story as any, so I asked the guys the pros and cons.

"Lotta cons," said Ferrell, who hailed from Bangor, Maine, and had retired in his Black Hawk virtually every night during a three-month stretch
during the first Gulf War. "There's limited space, and you're very close to
your other crew for an extended period, which does get on your nerves.
When it's 120 degrees outside, a slight snorer becomes your worst enemy,
even if it's your best friend."

"Anything comfortable is a luxury," Tengel interrupted.

"And if it's comfortable, it's not provided by the Army," Ferrell observed.

I was starting to like Ferrell, a short, agile flier with a boyish face and
receding hairline. Like a lot of warrant officers, he seemed willing to speak
his mind, not just parrot the company line.

Privacy, needless to say, was the first casualty when camping in the Hawk,
Ferrell and the other frequent fliers told me. Few details were spared as they
unloaded memories of foul-smelling feet, flyaway comb-overs, and fellow
soldiers suffering a "windy" night.

"It would be like living in your news agency," Tengel said. "You're fixing
the bird, cleaning it, working in it. You miss little things, like the drive home

from work. You don't get that personal time, that alone time, when you vent, when you get to—for lack of better words—bitch about things that piss you off."

"It can always be worse—that's one thing you have to remember," added Specialist Scott Kaeding, a twenty-seven-year-old on the flight crew who had a $1 bet on being out of Iraq by August 2, 2003.

How did they cope? Ferrell's much-ridiculed vice was gulping down freeze-dried Taster's Choice coffee and washing it down with water. Meantime he learned to appreciate little things, like the once-in-a-blue-moon occurrence of an MRE with all the fixings for PB&J; generally you got either peanut butter or jelly, not both.

He didn't mention the off-color jokes and magazines like *Maxim* and *Stuff*—those I could hear and see for myself. One crew member, paging through a men's magazine, pointed out that he'd be reading *Playboy* if I wasn't part of the entourage.

From Ferrell: "This is your extended family when you're away from home. You yell at 'em and bitch at 'em, but you worry about 'em when something happens."

He told me only later that when he was seven, his father, Army Captain Charles Ferrell, died in a Huey crash in Vietnam. He hadn't immediately followed in his dad's footsteps; for five years he was a research diver off the coast of Maine, and later he joined the military, learned to fly, and was pinned with his father's wings. "People always ask me why I'm doing this," he said. "It's in my blood, Army aviation. But my mother's not too happy about it."

That day the mission called for the Black Hawk pilots to carry staff from the 101st Division's rear echelon, including legal, administrative, and support personnel, from Kuwait to Tallil Air Base, which was located near Nasiriyah. Tallil had been an Iraqi installation, but had recently fallen to coalition forces. The mission, though, was aborted in midflight, reportedly because there was bad weather ahead, so Ferrell and Butora tooled back to Udairi and disgorged the passengers. By then the sun was brutal; the thermometer on somebody's watch showed a reading of 105 degrees. Still, returning to Udairi meant a shower and hot chow; and after dark, somebody in Chief Warrant Officer Michael Patton's crew managed to get their hands on some no-alcohol Budweiser. With external speakers wired to a CD player, we listened to the Dixie Chicks and enjoyed what generously could be called a party.

It was Saturday night, when all seemed right with the world and the war and, parenthetically, nobody knew the Chicks were in hot water for their anti-Bush statements in London.

Then word of mouth brought some ominous news: the Fourth Battalion had lost a Black Hawk in a fiery crash at Shell. The fate of the pilots and crew, who were from Bravo Company, was not known. All that was reported was that a helicopter flying them out for medical treatment was given "urgent" status, suggesting grave injuries.

"Who were the pilots?" I asked instinctively. It was getting late, and I wouldn't be writing a story based on such slim facts; I was inquiring more as a worried friend than a journalist.

The pilots' names weren't known, but my question set off a debate among the no-alcohol Bud crowd about whether I could or should write about something that would be devastating to the "Black Hawk community" of relatives and friends in the States.

No one seemed to get that I cared about the victims; nor did some seem to know that the embedded journalists had been told they could write about the good, the bad, and the ugly. One pilot in particular didn't seem to appreciate both that the crash was going to make the news, regardless of whether it was I or someone else who reported, and that I had a job to do. He seemed to think I should blow off the story and let the military notify the victims' families, reasoning that nobody back home would be left to agonize needlessly that way.

"Maybe I should just write about how *valiant* you all are," I said, practically spitting the words out. "The *valiant* Army aviators."

Perhaps to separate the warring parties, Patton suggested that he and I go off and have a cigarette. I wasn't sure where he stood. Firing up a Camel Light, he asked, "Do you know what a Spitfire is?"

"Yes, I do," I answered. "It's a British plane from World War II." It's not that I'm an expert at flying machines; it's just that one hung prominently in Chicago's Museum of Science and Industry, a favorite childhood haunt of mine.

"You're just like a little plane," he told me. "You keep going and going and going."

I took it as a compliment. At least somebody was on my side.

The next day Alpha got a green light to take the division support personnel to Tallil. By now I was so hand-in-glove with these guys that they let me test-fire one of the machine guns over the desert. I felt it best not to be greedy, so I pulled the trigger until six shots pumped out, giving everyone on board a laugh, even one of the 101st's top lawyers. Amusements were in such scant supply that nobody cared that I'd bent the rules.

Returning to Camp Udairi after the mission, I learned that a number of officers, including Ruiz, had been at the crash site and were willing to be interviewed. Ruiz and others told me that two Bravo pilots and the crew of three had been sling-loading cargo into Iraq and stopped about 220 miles into the trip to refuel at Shell. It was a couple of hours before dark. First they dropped off their load, a sixty-cubic-foot storage container, in a remote location; then they had their fuel tank topped off. The mishap took place when the pilots returned to retrieve the load. Brown-out conditions were believed to have led them to lose their bearings, and the aircraft, while in descent, tipped to one side, causing the rotor blades to strike the sling ropes. "The blades just beat themselves off and broke off, flying about seventy yards away," Ruiz said.

The pilots were Dave Napier, a flier from the 101st posted at Fort Campbell, and Johnny Sims, who'd come from a Maryland National Guard unit. Two specialists and a private also suffered minor injuries, including burns and bruises. Napier was Bravo's standardization pilot, which means he was one of the senior aviators, charged with ensuring the proficiency and qualifications of other fliers. I'd seen him around, but I didn't know the others; in any case, under the ground rules, none of their names could be reported, even though I understood that their next of kin had gotten the word.

The crew members who were not badly hurt were able to wrest the seriously injured pilots from the Hawk just minutes before it burst into flames. Smoke was seen rising an estimated 800 to 900 feet in the air.

According to Ruiz, who flew in after the accident, both pilots suffered moderate to severe head trauma from the impact and were lucky to be alive, since both the aircraft and the cargo they had been hauling became completely engulfed by fire. "The aircraft was burning and the [machine gun] ammo was cooking. It pops as it burns," Ruiz told me.

"We're grateful that they are all alive, we're proud of our crew chiefs, and we're heartbroken that it happened," said Chief Warrant Officer 4 Kenneth Ballard, one of the Bravo pilots I'd quoted on the first day of the war.

I was struck that Ballard used the word "heartbroken," but not surprised. By then I'd learned that these men lusted for the skies; a number had made it clear that getting their wings was their life's greatest achievement; Ferrell even chased the dream although it had killed the father he barely knew.

Ballard had recovered Napier's helmet from the scene of the accident and remarked: "He might want to have it bronzed and put it in his attic." I took from that remark that Napier's flying days were over.

Weeks into being embedded with the fliers, I continued to take their measure. And I envied them. Flying, despite its perils, seemed seductive, powerful, and liberating to them; it was their pride, passion, and paycheck.

That afternoon, after six flights in three days, I went back to Camp Thunder Road, where I was hammered by the same heartache and grief that Ballard described. It was Sunday, April 6.

Maybe it was predictable that an embedded journalist would not make it out of Bad Guy Land. But some of us, who for some untold glory were making the big gamble—going for the gusto, as the old Schlitz ad used to say—just swept that idea out of our minds with a broom labeled cognitive dissonance, until it actually happened.

That afternoon, in a call to my office, I learned that Michael Kelly, editor-at-large for the *Atlantic Monthly,* had been killed three days earlier. Attached to the Army's Third Infantry Division, he was traveling near Baghdad in a Humvee that came under enemy fire and crashed into an irrigation canal.

I didn't know Kelly, but had heard about his great reputation covering the first Gulf War; and I had interviewed his mother, Marguerite, a syndicated columnist in Washington who writes about children, when doing some feature stories. I was the same age as her son, forty-six. My heart ached for Kelly's wise and kind-hearted mother, and a little part of me died that day, too. Then I gave myself some motherly advice: don't take any silly chances.

8
Watching Baghdad Fall

Camp Thunder Road was practically a ghost town, since most of the brigade had left permanently for Iraq. The next encampment for the 159th Brigade was just outside Najaf, a major city along the Euphrates about 100 miles south of Baghdad. Officially the new camp was named Thunder II, but Patton told me that it was so dreary that people were calling it Thunder Deux, and I don't think he was speaking French.

For the couple hundred of us left to bring up the rear, outwardly—and briefly—the mood was like when the boss went on vacation before the invention of the fax machine and e-mail. While we waited for space on aircraft bound for the new camp, I had a number of stories to write, but the pace around me slowed down; some soldiers even took to wearing shorts, generally with light-colored, high-top boots, since the scorpions remained a nuisance.

The news of late was welcome: the U.S. momentum in the war was picking up and the Iraqi forces were being ground down. Missile alerts became a thing of the past. Meantime soldiers breathed a sigh of relief at word that the overland convoy from the 159th had made the twenty-six-hour trip to Thunder II, over paved roads, dirt, and sand, without a casualty or major screwup. Several vehicles were lost, though, because there were orders not to stop if they became disabled. The soldiers were to strip the vehicle of "sensitive items"—weapons, ammunition, night-vision goggles, and classified information—and hitch a ride in another truck.

With coalition troops still dying, Iraq remained as ominous as a blind alley. I went to bed at night with a favorite song, part English, part Italian, from *Prelude: The Best of Charlotte Church*, a CD I'd selected from a picked-over bin at Udairi's post exchange. It began:

> I pray you'll be our eyes,
> and watch us where we go,
> and help us to be wise
> in times when we don't know.

Let this be our prayer,
when we lose our way.
Lead us to a place,
guide us with your grace
to a place where we'll be safe.

I didn't know it then, but the song is called "The Prayer."

When I finally pulled out of Thunder Road, I was assigned a spot on a Chinook jam-packed with soldiers and gear, and once I got a whiff of the female soldier next to me, had to wonder if she'd been swimming in sour milk. More annoying was the mildewy, five-foot pile of soldiers' rucks monopolizing the entire length of the cabin and giving us precious little space to breathe.

No longer did I have VIP treatment. Nowaczyk wasn't offering me the jump seat, Ferrell wasn't giving away Tootsie Rolls left over from his MREs, and Eshom wasn't firing off ribald jokes. Nobody was inviting me to fire one of the aircraft's machine guns, either.

I took my circumstances in stride, but the mundane flight presaged a grim place. We'd left the golden deserts of Kuwait for a dry, barren, wind-blown part of the world that brought to mind the colors of a grimy old basement shag rug. The skies were ashen, the heavily rutted soil was dun, and the vast tangle of Army tents and mud-splattered trucks was the usual dull green.

The sun hid behind hazy skies at the new home to roughly 2,300 soldiers living cheek-by-jowl in vinyl tents of various sizes intended to sleep four or ten or twenty.

According to Major Shenk, the battalion's operations officer, the area was thought to have been a recent staging ground for the Iraqi Hammurabi Division, an armored unit that was part of the elite Republican Guard, the country's best-trained and best-equipped forces.

I found myself assigned to a tent away from many friends and next to the one housing my least favorite person, Lieutenant Colonel Sabb. While blessedly my shelter slept only four—instead of seventy—it was what a scientist would call an experiment and a poet might entitle "An Ode to Mold."

My hypothesis: If you leave gunk behind in a vinyl tent, fold up the tent, shove it God-knows-where, ask the United States Navy to transport it across the Atlantic, then, voilà, the gunk will multiply, spread, fester, turn black and green—and lead me to practically cough my lungs out.

Why, I wondered, hadn't somebody disinfected this lame excuse for lodging with a scrub brush, hot water, and bleach? When I complained to Patton, he reminded me that sunlight alone would have done the trick.

Now I confess, I was a relapsed smoker devouring more cigarettes than I had in years, but inside the tent my lungs barked and rattled and hacked and heaved and shook and stammered at the allergens invading my space. During one paroxysm in this Army-issued petri dish, I pondered whether a person could cough to death.

Next, the real shocker: while I was prepared to sacrifice sinks and showers, I learned that the unit had ditched the portable toilets in Kuwait.

It was the dawn of the twenty-first century and, in the company of troops flying the flag of the wealthiest nation in the world, I had flown into the cradle of civilization in a multimillion-dollar helicopter only to discover that some atavistic military genius had me relieving myself on a fifty-five-gallon metal drum cut in half and topped with plywood. With no doors! And, as a final insult, these jerry-rigged thrones were crowded together, closer than long necks in a six-pack. Trust me: cave men and women had more privacy.

By that point, I had been in Uncle Sam's tender, loving care for seven weeks and had met many, many people—from each of the fifty states, from Puerto Rico, Guam, and American Samoa, plus Jamaicans and Africans and others making a living the immigrant way, risking their lives for a lousy paycheck. I did not wish to drop trou' in front of any of them—especially the men.

During the war, I know now, there were prayer circles from Maine to California whose members clasped hands and begged God to keep me safe. I thank them, one and all, but, looking back, what I also needed was for Him to grant me one almighty shit. I learned, though, that I could survive a long time without going Number Two; humiliation simply prevented it.

So call me a wimp or a whiner. I was a road warrior, not a real one. Up until now my idea of roughing it had been at the Hotel Sofitel in Bloomington, Minnesota, when the electricity went out.

My idea of roughing it had been at the Hilton in Crystal City, Virginia, when, having just blown in from the reporting trip to Kosovo, I ordered dinner from room service but, it being after bar time, couldn't get a drink.

My idea of roughing it had been, while at Le Merigot in Santa Monica, California, I overheard that Bruce Willis, early in his marital woes with Demi Moore, had shown up at the bar with a very trashed woman, and I wasn't there to gawk.

Le Merigot had a concierge desk; the Army does not.

Soon into my stay at this camp—Thunder Doo to me—I declared it the worst place I'd ever spent a night. I felt I was crisscrossing the birthplace of Medusa—she of staring eyes, protruding fangs, and writhing snakes for hair—because new vexations kept popping up. A major, for laughs, showed me a digital photo of a bat living inside his helicopter. Then a voice squawked over the camp radio advising that the wind had knocked over some of the latrines; pity the private assigned to clean up that mess. Later I caught a glimpse of a glum-faced friend of mine saddled with an even worse chore: once the drums were filled with Doo's doo, soldiers were ordered to burn it and stand by to ensure the fire didn't spread. At first I felt badly for my buddy, but then I realized, better he than I.

All that said, in the grand scheme of things, maybe none of that mattered. Probably I was down in the dumps because I'd been Bob-less for some time. With Ruiz off on missions someplace, I had no shoulder to cry on, no thigh upon which to lay my war-weary head, no confessor, no confidante, no partner in crime, and no chow line date—which was irrelevant, since Doo had no chow line.

After sundown, even hanging out alone in my tent—and reading by flashlight, or something—was virtually impossible; one of my cohabitants had pulled the midnight shift and invariably was trying to sleep.

How in God's name, I wondered, do soldiers cope? I launched a quest, planning to kill two birds with one stone. I would interview the troops about their survival techniques, insert them into a story about these bleak environs, and then steal their ideas so as not to be such an unhappy camper.

Captain Alicia Chivers, who'd graduated from West Point, told me that she tried to keep a sense of humor. Twenty-seven years old, she'd grown up in Kalispel, Montana, near Glacier National Park, and had taken several rugged trips to the Bitterroot Mountain Range. "I've camped in equivalent places, but the difference is you had a lake, a bonfire, and a case of beer," she said, laughing.

One soldier suggested keeping your focus and turning to faith. "I try not to think so much about missing home and family," said Specialist Manuel Holmes, a thirty-year-old native of Charleston, South Carolina, who is married with two sons, aged seven and two.

He said the high point of his deployment had come that very day, when he left camp to travel about ten miles away to pick up necessities from a central supply area. He'd been cautioned beforehand that the locals may or may not be friendly, but he saw no one armed or hostile. Instead Holmes was bombarded with thank you's smothered with hugs. Some people seemed so happy they were crying. A few spoke broken English, including a man who gave him a thumbs-up and said, "I no enemy. I friend."

"It made me feel that I had a higher purpose being here: in addition to conquering a regime, it was liberating a people," Holmes said. "They were just ecstatic and eternally thankful."

He told me that he spent his quiet time reading his Bible and meditating—what he called "quality time" with God. "Not a day goes by without it," he enthused. "It's support for the day that carries me through the next day."

Then he recited the opening of Psalm Ninety-One: "He who dwells in the secret place of the Most High shall abide in the shadow of the Almighty. I will say of the Lord, 'He is my refuge and my fortress; My God, in Him I will trust.' "

I walked a good distance across camp and found the three trail bosses from my old quarters at Thunder Road: Captain Goveo, 1st Sergeant Kolesar, and Staff Sergeant William Tipton, the last an affable guy from Detroit whom I'd nicknamed "Sergeant Tiptop." The three had eased themselves into canvas chairs in their new quarters, where within reach were nine M-4 rifles hanging from a gun rack and a trove of creature comforts. The men had a coffee maker, a mini-refrigerator chock full of A&W root beer, a stand-up electric fan, Deep Woods Off, and other possessions I coveted.

When I began interviewing him, Goveo conceded that the 119 soldiers in his company missed "home, family, junk food, mail, privacy, and real toilets."

"But we don't complain; we're soldiers," he said. "We adjust and overcome. There are logistical problems, but we make do with what we have."

"Home," the thirty-three-year-old Tipton observed, "is where I lay my helmet." He picked up a K-pot to illustrate his point, then chuckled, observing, "This ain't mine."

"It's only as bad as you make it," said Kolesar, who hailed from west central Pennsylvania's Ellwood City. "If you sit and dwell on what you don't like, it just makes you more miserable. You just drive on."

Next I went over to see my buddy, Private Krystal Carter, who was no longer my tentmate, since she and the other cooks were segregated in their own shelter. Their normal duties—"We bake, cook, fry, skilletize, grill, and boil"—were supplanted by other tasks now, like collecting trash, since without a steady supply of water, they didn't expect their "mobile kitchen trailer" to be operating for weeks.

Carter was not buying into the concept for my story. "You really don't want to hear my honest opinion of this place," she began. "It sucks. I hate it. I want to go home. I want to go into the Air Force." Hers was a typical escape plan, since nearly everybody in the Army regards the Air Force as a bunch of mollycoddles.

The other cooks began bantering about the good and the bad. "I'm glad everyone here is safe," said Heather Denham, who endured the all-day, all-night, 425-mile trip in the heavily-armed convoy. Officials said that many of the early military caravans on the same routes had been ambushed or thrown off course by civilians or suspicious vehicles, so her point was taken.

"And I'm glad everyone at home knows we're fighting to keep them safe," she added. "We're protecting them."

Denham, who was married but had no children, continued: "I'm glad I'll be able to look at my kids' history books someday and say, 'Mommy did that.' And this isn't going to last forever. For real."

Sergeant 1st Class Teresa English, who grew up in Front Royal, Virginia, said the toughest part was being away from her husband and eight-year-old son, Nathan. He was five when she was on a six-month deployment in Kosovo, "but that was peacekeeping," she said. "This is more real."

The twenty-eight-year-old English groused about not having gotten a single piece of mail from home; and it had been two weeks since she'd been given a cell phone and allowed to make a five-minute "morale call" to her family. She also complained about "jumping," the term the military uses to describe packing up and moving out to a new location. "We're constantly jumping, jumping, and jumping," English said.

"When you train," Denham interjected, "you know in a few weeks you're going home."

"Here," English said, "you don't know how long you're going to be deployed. You hear bits and pieces, and you know that some people know more than you do. I've been in the Army for ten years, and it's my job, but I would not have pictured myself being in a war. But I'm here, and I'm going to do what I got to do, and just take it one day at a time."

Thirty-three-year-old Sergeant Kendra Myers said he reminded himself that some people had it worse, lacking even food and water. Soldiers from the convoy reported seeing barefoot Iraqi children, out in the streets under a broiling sun, begging for something to eat and drink. "Light, water, shelter, something to eat, and I'm fine," said Myers, who grew up in Jackson, Mississippi. "We gotta get Saddam and go home. Those are our top priorities."

Denham and Carter were heading out in a two-and-a-half-ton truck to pick up garbage from the other companies and invited me along. I hopped on board, hungry for a change of scenery, and the trip proved instructive as well: as Denham drove, she pointed out the bright-orange warning symbols marking unexploded ordnance found on the fringes of the outpost.

"You get used to being taken away from home and family," she said. "I call these deployments 'my little camping adventures,' even though they're a little more dangerous." She noted that she'd beaten the heat, and stolen some solitude, by sleeping outdoors on cardboard boxes filled with MREs the night before.

Carter started reminiscing about her family—five sisters, two stepbrothers—and why she and three of her sisters joined the Army the same day. "We wanted to get away from home and have our own life," she said.

With a milestone coming up, she would be celebrating not with the Carters in Miami but with the Headquarters Company of the Fourth Battalion of the 159th Aviation Brigade. "I never thought I'd be spending my twenty-first birthday in the desert," she told us.

Soon she and Denham began having a high time of it, laughing and joking and trading stories as the truck bounced up and down over the uneven dirt roads. Their high spirits were contagious.

"At least," Carter blurted out, "we have each other."

Of all the advice I'd been given—it's historic, temporary, best not to complain, you can always turn to God—it was Kolesar, the guy who had told me to unfuck my shit, who had zeroed in on why I was threatening to lose my marbles: I was dwelling on the glass being half-empty, missing Ruiz and moaning over everything, from my uncontrollable cough to my newly broken camera.

And it was Carter, the young woman who called me "Momma," who was now teaching me the facts of Army life: At least we had each other.

After I finished the piece, the sun mercifully reappeared, and there was enough daylight left for me to toss around a football with Denham and Carter and some of the other enlisted soldiers. We weren't the only ones recreating; off in the distance some guys who had shed their uniforms and seemed to be wearing little or nothing were driving around camp, roaring wildly and girding for a talking-to from their chain of command.

All of a sudden I spotted Ruiz coming my way—a heartening sight: my friend had returned to the camp. Later, over an MRE, I gave him an earful about my unhappiness until we were both cracking up about our latest encampment.

Thunder II was under "light discipline" at night, which meant that outdoor lighting was prohibited in order to keep the camp's location hidden from the Iraqis. All that was allowed were tiny, red-colored "micro lights" with bulbs about as big as the pupils of your eyeballs.

The illumination was barely sufficient to set up my satellite phone, but I needed to call my office to see if my story had passed muster. Kent Lowry, my deputy editor, had something else on his mind: he informed me that Saddam Hussein's regime had collapsed, there was euphoria in the streets of Baghdad, and he wanted me to produce a story—ASAP.

I muttered a long list of reasons why this was not doable. It was late. It was dark. I was tired. I was a hundred miles away from the Iraqi capital. I had heard on my shortwave that these were sporadic celebrations and hadn't drawn big crowds. I couldn't possibly write that story tonight; why not wait and see what happened?

And so I begged off the assignment. The instant I hung up, I regretted it and tracked down Ruiz for a second opinion. He gave me a figurative kick in the rear, urging, "Do it."

Fumbling in the dark with the sat phone, I tried to reach my office again. The call took two or three attempts. "I'll do it," I told Kent. "You'll have the story as soon as possible."

For all of Thunder II's deficiencies, the Fourth Battalion had just installed a large-screen television in a lighted tent that had dusty plastic sheeting for flooring and was big enough to sleep twenty, but instead doubled as the battalion meeting room. Three weeks into the war, it gave the troops a window to the world just in time to catch the cataclysm so near and yet so far away.

I found a half-dozen soldiers inside catching Fox News—everybody seemed to have work to do, so people breezed in and out—trying to digest the reckless jubilance in the Iraqi capital and the measured responses that top Pentagon bosses wanted telegraphed to the four corners of the Earth.

In the most powerful image of the day, Iraqis wielding a sledgehammer whacked at a twenty-foot statue of a proud Saddam Hussein portrayed with one arm uplifted in the style of Soviet dictator Joseph Stalin. Less clear at the time, at least to me, was that the U.S. Marines hastened the telegenic demolition with the help of an armored M-88, a full-tracked vehicle so durable it normally is used to recover tanks disabled in battle.

The television broadcast Hussein's likeness toppling to the pavement, where the fallen icon was pelted with stones and beaten with chains. As a coup de grâce, some Iraqis confiscated the statue's head and dragged it through the city in celebration. With the Iraqi dictator's whereabouts unknown, his former subjects proceeded to deface the murals of him and ripped poster-sized portraits into pieces, as if to exorcise his tyrannical, murderous legacy. Other footage showed U.S. troops welcomed with flowers, American flags, candy, and kisses.

At Thunder II, the soldiers' eyes passively absorbed the street scenes, but they said little to each other.

At the Pentagon, Defense Secretary Donald Rumsfeld and General Richard Myers, the chairman of the Joint Chiefs of Staff, attempted to put the momentous events in Baghdad in perspective. Myers was the VIP to whom I had written, asking for a spot in the media boot camp.

"This is a good day for the Iraqi people," Rumsfeld began. "There is no question that there are difficult and very dangerous days ahead and that the fighting will continue for some period. But certainly anyone seeing the faces of the liberated Iraqis—the free Iraqis—has to say that this is a very good day.

"Tomorrow will mark three weeks since Operation Iraqi Freedom began and the progress of the men and women in uniform who make up the coalition forces has been nothing short of spectacular. They drove through the south up, braving dust storms and death squads to reach Baghdad in record time. They secured Iraq's southern oil fields for the Iraqi people, took out terrorist camps in the north and the south, secured large sections of western Iraq, preventing the regime from attacking its neighbors with Scud missiles. They've liberated cities and towns and are now in the Iraqi capital removing the regime from its seat of power and center of gravity. . . .

"The scenes of free Iraqis celebrating in the streets, riding American tanks, tearing down the statues of Saddam Hussein in the center of Baghdad are breathtaking. Watching them, one cannot help but think of the fall of the Berlin Wall and the collapse of the Iron Curtain. We are seeing history unfold, events that will shape the course of a country, the fate of a people, and potentially the future of the region. Saddam Hussein is now taking his rightful place alongside Hitler, Stalin, Lenin, Ceauşescu in the pantheon of failed, brutal dictators, and the Iraqi people are well on their way to freedom."

Myers, for his part, said that although Iraqis were beginning to celebrate in parts of Baghdad and other areas, portions of the country still were in the grip of fear. He said that death squads in the west were still harassing citizens and travelers, forces from Saddam Hussein's regime continued to hold parts of the north, and there were pockets of resistance in other areas.

"More must be done in Baghdad as well," the general said. "Fighting inside the capital presents a substantial risk to coalition forces, and we cannot and must not become overconfident."

Not a single person in the TV lounge turned down the chance to be interviewed about the collapse of Hussein's regime. But on the distant fringes of the front lines, their applause was muted, tempered by the fact that they were warriors and their war was still going on. It was welcome news that a bloodbath some had feared would take place in Baghdad had been averted, but there were no high-fives or handstands: these soldiers knew they wouldn't be homeward bound anytime soon. I might have been asking a pro football team its prospects with a lead after the first quarter.

Sergeant Paul Valencia, a thirty-three-year-old from Bravo Company, said he felt like he was witnessing a "turning point in history" and compared it to "seeing the wall come down after the end of the Cold War."

"Every time I see the Iraqis tear down a symbol of the regime and wave an American flag, I feel there's one less terrorist act that may occur in the United States," he said. "These kinds of images speak volumes. The Iraqis are truly grateful and glad that we're here."

Valencia, a native of Los Angeles, noted that the footage would be broadcast to the Arab world and would likely change the face of the U.S. soldier in Iraq from one of an aggressor to one of a liberator. "I don't think there's anything more than that that we would want. And I'm glad I was able to witness this part of history. From what we can see on TV, what we've achieved here is going to outshine any bad things down the road."

Part of a Black Hawk flight crew, Valencia specialized in training heli-copter door gunners. He said he believed that members of Hussein's Baath Party and other loyalists had lost out, but did not rule out one "last stand" against the U.S.-led coalition forces.

Ruiz said he was both happy and cautiously optimistic.

"I think it's the beginning of the end, but it's not over," he judged. "There's a lot of work ahead: reorganizing this country and helping install a national command authority and rebuilding Iraq and undoing the evil of Saddam Hussein."

"We're definitely a big step closer to peace," he said. "I think there'll still be fighting, but it's one day closer to finishing the fight."

He expected that the 101st Airborne Division would remain in Iraq for many months, noting, "There's going to be a role for us in the postwar nation-building for a long time. I'm anticipating about a year."

Chief Warrant Officer 4 Gregory Wood picked up on what Myers had signaled from the Pentagon. "Just because we have a show of force in the city, like the general said, by no means have we secured the city," he said. "We have a strong presence, but we haven't secured it."

"The good thing that I'm feeling," Wood continued, "is the sooner we take down Baghdad, the earlier we can get to the outlying areas, and the sooner we can go home. It's a good thing that we've come here and been able to—and I don't want to use the word 'conquer'—liberate the Iraqis. And I'm thankful that we haven't lost more lives, like we did during World War II, Korea, and Vietnam."

Wood observed that cities such as Tikrit, Saddam Hussein's birthplace and a stronghold for his followers, still was up for grabs; the same was true for Kirkuk and Mosul in the north. And he reminded that close-in fighting in populous areas is risky business, since the enemy has the advantage of being on home turf.

He predicted that the day's developments would result in more, not less, work for the 159th Brigade, saying, "I think we'll get more involved work-ing with our brothers in the infantry, maybe doing air assaults, support mis-sions, and resupply missions."

Some soldiers were not persuaded that the drama unfolding in the streets of Baghdad meant that the specter of weapons of mass destruction had lifted. "There's still a threat out there of Hussein using chemical weapons when more people are gathered in Baghdad from U.S. and coalition forces," said Specialist Robert Jenkins, twenty-five, who grew up in Omaha, Nebraska. "But things look good. I hope we continue at this rate of success with little or no resistance. I think it's a good thing that the Iraqis are finally getting a new beginning for something they've wanted for some time, and the whole world wanted. Hopefully we'll finish taking control of the cities Hussein controls and install a new government."

Specialist Brian Quick, a thirty-year-old who repairs Black Hawks, pronounced it good that Saddam had been ousted. He said his long trip into Iraq, in the convoy in a ten-ton cargo truck, opened his eyes to the disparities between Iraq and its southern neighbor. "I didn't see a whole lot of Kuwait, but from what I could see, the people were wealthier and more stable and took better care of their appearance. In Iraq, the little kids were walking around barefoot on hot pavement, sweating, begging for food and water—just waiting for someone to throw them a cracker."

For security reasons, the convoy was under orders not to stop or hand out food, but Quick said the troops couldn't help but give away some of their MREs—as he put it, "maybe a few just fell out of the windows or something."

Quick, who grew up in Rockingham, North Carolina, estimated that he'd seen two or three hundred Iraqis en route, and that many of them were delighted to see U.S. soldiers. About ten or so waved American flags; many more flashed a thumbs-up.

While he appreciated the reception, he wasn't letting his guard down. "As a soldier, I'm always worried till it's over, and I don't think it's completely over yet. There's always the threat of chemicals. Our troops went in Baghdad pretty easy, and maybe there's a reason for that. Maybe the Iraqis will wait till we all get there and use chemicals. Nobody knows anything until it happens."

Captain Kerry Greene, the battalion chaplain, was more buoyant than the others, greeting the developments with the words, "Prayers have been answered."

A native of Holly Springs, Mississippi, Greene, as a member of the clergy, was forbidden from carrying a weapon; he had an armed soldier assigned to him for protection. He thought the exuberance in Baghdad and the demise of Saddam Hussein's regime portended only less bloodshed.

"I think we'll see less U.S. deaths and less Iraqi civilian deaths as a result of this," he said. "I really believe that God has been merciful to the Americans and to the Iraqi people because it went so fast, and we took control so fast. I believe the really heavy fighting is over with. It makes me feel good because this is the main city, and once you get that, it's pretty much over. There are other small towns, but we've proven we can take smaller towns."

I dashed off the soldiers' remarks from the small tent that housed the battalion's administrative and logistics operations center. Afterward, at my editor's request, I put in a call to our sister television station, WTMJ-TV. Reading from my laptop, I told viewers in Wisconsin what the reaction was from Thunder II and quoted Ruiz by name, trying to make clear his view that there was more work ahead—"reorganizing this country, helping install a national command authority, rebuilding Iraq, and undoing the evil of Saddam Hussein."

I signed off by saying that living conditions here were tough and the troops appreciated the public's support.

Engrossed in my work, I didn't realize that I had a small audience behind me as I spoke to the television interviewer. But as I was packing up my things, Sergeant Nelda Scenie looked up from her seat and said, "That was very nice. Thank you." Her words startled me. No one had thanked me for anything in weeks.

As I crawled into my sleeping bag that night, I congratulated myself for snapping out of my funk and managing to produce two stories and fit in a TV interview. I promised to reward myself by sleeping in the next morning. I should have known better; wishing for something like that in the Army means putting a hex on it.

Bright and early the next day, I received instructions to pack up my things as soon as possible. We were jumping again. Whatever I couldn't carry needed to be ready ASAP for a convoy to transport it. I stuffed many of my belongings into cardboard boxes, the tent came down in short order—and then nothing and nobody went anywhere for hours. When it was clear that plans were on hold, I took the time to fetch some nonpotable water and wash some of my clothing; having freshly laundered clothing in the field was a rare and instant form of gratification. The heat was searing that day, as it had been for days on end. With the tents broken down, there were no ropes or otherwise obvious places to hang out laundry, but I wasn't deterred. I'd seen soldiers do much with so little: make a festive veranda at the entryway to their tent with spare fabric and tent poles; build a desk out of plywood from packing crates; one day they'd even erected an elaborate work station for me with stacks of MRE boxes.

I realized I could stand up my cot perpendicular to the ground, stabilize it at the base with duffel bags, and string up some utility cord for a makeshift clothesline. It was homely, but functional. Afterward I saw Major Shenk walking by and inspecting my handiwork from a distance. "Is that field craft?" he called out.

"I'm not sure if it's field craft or witchcraft," I answered.

In due time I got back to work, borrowing Captain Alicia Chivers's digital camera and doing a short profile, one of the "Postcards," featuring the invariably cheery Sergeant Sherre Maxson, the noncommissioned officer in charge of logistics for the battalion. She was responsible for securing everything from a new Black Hawk helicopter to replace the one lost in the fiery crash five days earlier, to the fifty-five-gallon drums used for the camp latrines.

Halfway through my interview with Maxson, a military truck roared in and dropped off mail for the troops. "Mail call" always reminded me of a scene from an old war movie. The brigade had gone without mail for a long stretch, so a gaggle of soldiers stood by with outsized anticipation as a young corporal leafed through a stack of letters, sorted parcels beaten up in transit, and called out the names of the lucky recipients. When your name wasn't called—and I speak from experience—you felt like an empty-handed orphan forgotten on Christmas morning, just as soldiers around you were squealing over fresh socks, disposable cameras, baby wipes, homemade chocolate chip cookies, Fig Newtons, and Hershey bars, the last of which the heat usually rendered into chocolate soup.

For me, mail call at Thunder II that day was a bonanza: my editor's wife, Barbara, had put together such a bountiful box of toiletries and treats that I started giving stuff away to people whose names weren't called. My Aunt Mary in Arizona sent me a tiny medal of St. Jude, who is widely known as the patron saint of hopeless cases but also, more appropriate to my surroundings, of things despaired of. I took it as a good sign; finally I had a replacement for my lost St. Catherine medal. Finally, the *Milwaukee Journal Sentinel*'s top editor, Marty Kaiser, sent me a handwritten letter.

Kathy—

You are doing outstanding work. Your stories have been wonderful. Everyone in the newsroom is incredibly proud of you and what you are doing for the newspaper. Your TV appearances have also been great. When you are on TV, the whole newsroom gathers around the TV and cheers.

You and your work are never far from my thoughts. My prayers are with you.

—Marty

"That's class," Ruiz said, when I showed it to him. "You're lucky to work for someone like that."

Gobbling down a Rice Krispies treat, I took stock of the fresh bottle of shampoo, my new saint, and major kudos from my editor in chief, pleased, too, that my text and photo had gotten to the States without a glitch. But the good feelings didn't last long. Baghdad may have fallen, but at Doo, things always conspired to send my mood up and down like the fine, squiggly lines of an electrocardiogram.

The latest downer came just as the day's light began to fade. While I was waiting around on my cot and with my pared-down possessions, one of the battalion bosses asked me if I was planning to move forward with the others.

Was I planning to move forward? What kind of question was that? Did he imagine me living out my days in this remote and desolate slice of hell? Or did he expect that I would take a buck knife to the umbilical cord attaching me to the United States Army, saunter down a dirt road, coax from a shepherd the telephone number of a taxicab company, and be on my merry way?

I felt like such an afterthought. And while this officer was threatening to take his place in my hand-picked pantheon of Greatest Assholes I've Ever Known, I had no alternative but to hold my tongue.

"I assumed when I was told to pack my things for the convoy that arrangements were being made for me," I told him.

Shenk, overhearing all of this, walked past me, shook his head, and observed drily, "You are writing comedy now."

Eventually a place was found for me with a Black Hawk from Bravo Company, which would leave at daybreak with the other birds. The convoy had left that afternoon, and the tents had gone with it. It was decided, then, that I should immediately go over to where the aircraft was parked and bunk down with its pilots and crew. Lucky Mertes, the flier who'd been such a help to me at Thunder Road, bailed me out again, helping me tote my cot and other belongings over to the flight line and locate my ride.

Introductions were made in the dark to the four men who were preparing to call it a night on cots arranged willy-nilly outside the helicopter. By then I knew the ins and outs of changing inconspicuously into nightwear, concealing my hocus-pocus with a sleeping bag to the extent I could, and hoping my companions practiced what had been explained to me several weeks ago about co-ed life in close quarters: if you're not supposed to see it, don't look.

At least my former tent, the mold factory, was out of sight. Soon everything else unnerving during my two-and-a-half days at Doo, not least the wise guy who asked me if I was moving forward, floated away. Inching toward Baghdad, I was drifting off to sleep in a five-thousand-star hotel, studying the big sky and its gleaming half moon one last time, and slipping in ear plugs to drown out the evening serenade of noisy frogs.

9
Unbedding

We left Camp Thunder II at a minute past seven on Friday, April 11, lumbering through the skies for the first real look at Iraq outside of what pilot Jon Nowaczyk called the "vast nothingness" of the desert.

The signature feature of Najaf, the most sacred of cities to the Shiite Muslims, was the towering Iman Ali mosque, named for the Prophet Muhammad's son-in-law, the first leader of the Shiites. Rising on the outskirts of the city was a massive, sun-bleached, rocky plateau, home now to a battery of U.S. Patriot missiles.

Herds of camels and livestock—either cattle or water buffalo, I couldn't tell—came into view while veiled women dressed in red and turquoise clothing hung laundry out to dry and laborers, swathed from neck to toe in loose-fitting garments, tended emerald green fields. The Iraqis looked to the skies, observing the procession of Black Hawks above them, while sheep and cows scampered nervously away from the roar of the aircraft. Some people merely eyeballed the helicopters, but others waved enthusiastically. One young boy jumped up and down, shaking both of his hands above his head as if he was trying to hail a ride.

"The little kids are dancing," observed Sergeant Paul Valencia, who was operating one of the two door guns. He speculated that some of the grown-ups were wary because they probably had noticed that on each side of the helicopter were pods that resembled bombs, though they were just used for carrying extra fuel. I myself had wondered if they were explosives the first time I saw them.

The sparsely populated farmland, alive with spring, yielded to residential enclaves featuring handsome, sand-colored homes, some with graceful arches and set amid vast groves of towering palm trees.

Our destination was Iskandariyah, an old Iraqi Air Force base built in the sand twenty-five miles south of Baghdad—far enough for the new camp to be out of the range of Iraqi artillery fire from the capital. The facility was nicknamed "Skandy Airfield," but its official name was Tactical Assembly Area Thunder III. I was instructed to tell readers only that the 159th Brigade now was "more than ten and fewer than fifty miles" from the Iraqi capital.

After landing in a huge stretch of sand, I was anxious to settle into the camp, find my tent, and get to work, but instead came the Army's common directive: Wait. At first I found this frustrating, but after a while I surrendered to the idea and set up a cot, catching up on my sleep while soaking up the sun's restorative powers. I was resting outside for so long that a pilot, worried that I'd get a killer sunburn, suggested that I take cover in the shade alongside the aircraft, which I did.

When we finally moved into the camp, soldiers from the Fourth Battalion were still carving out space for the companies and setting up tents. Finally I got my wish: an all-women tent, which I shared with Chivers, the can-do captain from Montana; Scenie, the sergeant who'd pulled the April Fools' joke on Sabb; Carron, the young lieutenant working in intelligence; and 1st Lieutenant Veleka Douglas, the soft-spoken woman who was the battalion's chemical officer. I helped them set up the tent, and once some turf issues were settled—one of my tentmates warned me emphatically that my belongings had better not spill into her domain—it was a harmonious, albeit sandy, home.

I was content to be back in the sand, although the aviators preferred Thunder II's hard, crusty soil, since it made for easier landings. Scoping out the new outpost, I located a plywood latrine with an actual front door that you could shut from the inside by wrapping utility cord around a nail. Then I spotted something I'd never seen before: an inflatable plastic shower stall, which might be considered a distant cousin of the blow-up rafts you take to the beach. The device didn't feature plumbing—it was BYOW, bring your own water—but at least it afforded privacy. Next, happily, I discovered that my buddy Ruiz was a hop, skip, and jump away from my tent, sharing quarters with three young medics. Eventually a spacious TV lounge went up in camp. And since the folks in the administrative and logistics operations center, or ALOC, were agreeable to giving me desk space when I had to write, I had everything I needed.

The next day I accompanied a mission transporting infantrymen to the Baghdad city limits, part of a big push to move soldiers from the 101st, more than a thousand troops in all, by air north into the capital. It was a goal of mine to get to Baghdad, and except for that one time early on, when I was weak-kneed about heading into Bad Guy Land, I'd never turned down a chance to fly.

As the Black Hawk was being loaded and preflight checks were under way, I interviewed the pilots and crew, some of whom were putting on the dog, as if wanting to be included in whatever I ended up writing. When the intelligence update was passed down, indicating it was deemed safe to fly into southwestern Baghdad, Specialist John D. Brown cracked: "I think intel uses an eight-ball from Wal-Mart." A twenty-two-year-old from Beaumont, Texas, he seemed like a card, laughing as he recalled that he'd joined the Army to earn money for college, travel, and be on his own. With his studies on hold, the Army had taken him to Afghanistan, Kuwait, and Iraq in circumstances we all knew meant precious little independence.

First Lieutenant Walter G. Green III, a twenty-four-year-old pilot from Augusta, Georgia, and an ROTC graduate of Vanderbilt University in 2001, intrigued me because he had been an American history major; I hadn't met any of those since I'd embedded.

Ultimately I gravitated to the other pilot, thirty-three-year-old Gene Goetzke, a chief warrant officer 2 from Boise, Idaho. Not only was his story compelling, it didn't hurt that his grandfather and great-grandfather were from Wisconsin and his wife was born in Milwaukee.

Goetzke kept with him a pocket-sized New Testament, shielding it in a Ziploc bag just as he had when he'd deployed to Afghanistan. He'd graduated in 1992 from Bethany College, a school operated by the Assemblies of God in Scotts Valley, California, and afterward worked as a youth pastor. He joined the military in 1995, following a path that was becoming quite familiar to me: his father, just like Nowaczyk's and Ferrell's, had flown helicopters in combat in Vietnam.

Goetzke's father, Loren, had died just a year earlier in a commercial helicopter crash. Fifty-eight years old, he was flying for a logging company when his chopper mysteriously went down near Mount Shasta, California.

Gene Goetzke, along with his Bible, never flew without a copy of "High Flight," a poem that was recited at his father's funeral. It reads:

> Oh! I have slipped the surly bonds of Earth
> And danced the skies on laughter-silvered wings;
> Sunward I've climbed, and joined the tumbling mirth
> Of sun-split clouds,—and done a hundred things
> You have not dreamed of—wheeled and soared and swung
> High in the sunlit silence. Hov'ring there,
> I've chased the shouting wind along, and flung
> My eager craft through footless halls of air. . . .
>
> Up, up the long, delirious, burning blue
> I've topped the wind-swept heights with easy grace
> Where never lark, or even eagle flew—
> And, while with silent, lifting mind I've trod

> The high untrespassed sanctity of space,
> Put out my hand, and touched the face of God.

Although I was neither a pilot nor a poet, the words came alive for me. It seemed to me that the author had captured the best of what I'd experienced during the past several weeks: dancing the skies, chasing the shouting wind, and doing a hundred things. Copying the poem in my notebook, I planned to weave it into a story.

Later I learned that the poem was written by John Gillespie Magee, Jr., an American who served in the Royal Canadian Air Force, went to England during World War II, and perished when his Spitfire collided with another aircraft. He'd penned the poem just months before his death.

Soon the other passengers on this mission showed up, the so-called Widow Makers from the Third Battalion, Second Brigade of the 101st. Thirty-two of them were being carried forward in four helicopters, so eight of the soldiers crowded into the aircraft I was in. The flight crew had set up a seat for me; behind me the cabin was a mishmash of men and assault rifles, light machine guns and AT-4s, which are antitank guided missile systems— "tank killers" for short.

Sergeant 1st Class Mitchell Foley, a thirty-two-year-old platoon sergeant, was the highest-ranking soldier in the group. He and I spoke as we stole glances at the Euphrates River Valley, lush with palms, below us and, in the distance, the outskirts of Baghdad. From the capital you could see three narrow columns of smoke rising diagonally in the wind; they were so far away that no one could tell what was on fire.

One of Foley's twenty-something charges was snapping pictures with a disposable Kodak as I asked questions and took notes. This struck me as curious. Hadn't these guys seen any embeds? Was a woman in a flak jacket and helmet that unusual?

I went back to the interview, capturing Foley's responses and half-listening to the background chatter, including when twenty-four-year-old Staff Sergeant Michael Fletcher asked the guy behind him, "Is that your foot in my butt?"

Foley told me that he'd grown up outside Cincinnati in Covington, Kentucky, and was a fourteen-year Army veteran. He'd spent the first Gulf War as a sniper in northern Iraq and had arrived in Kuwait this time in early March. After U.S. forces took over Iraq's Tallil Air Base, he and his men were posted there to conduct "personnel recovery" missions in case a Chinook helicopter went down. It didn't happen, leaving him with mixed feelings. "It's good because none of our guys got hurt," he said. "It's bad because I wanted to go into action."

Six foot three and 225 pounds—he guessed he'd already lost ten pounds—Foley was fired up about getting down to business, even if it meant operating in the mean streets of Baghdad. "I've been waiting for thirty-five days to get there, because the sooner we get there, the sooner we get this over."

Would it be risky?

"Very," he answered. "You don't know who the good guys and bad guys are. You don't know if they're your enemy or they're your friend. And there's a lot of looting going on. But the infantry is the Army, period," he said matter-of-factly. "Everybody else supports us."

He said that he'd joined the military to serve his country, just as several generations of Foleys had before him. The toughest part? Just as for everyone else, it was "not being able to go out and see your family."

So far not only had Foley and his men had to contend with the sand and heat; they even had to carefully allocate food and water to avoid being caught short. "We had to ration for seven or eight days," he told me. "We were down to one to two MREs a day and two bottles of water; on a good day, three bottles."

It astonished me that these men were being asked to do so much with so little. Although I felt like a glutton for having used bottled water to shave my legs, I was mainly incensed that the U.S. government seemed to be nickel and diming the war effort. Every time somebody mentioned a shortage—like toilet paper or water—my mind flashed to the U.S. Capitol and our well-tended federal lawmakers and their power of the purse.

Foley expected to be in Baghdad until the end of April while a government was put into place and humanitarian efforts got under way. "We'll help feed 'em and install a democratic-style government," he said, making it sound so simple.

Then someone from the crew announced, "Two minutes," a signal for the infantrymen to get ready to disembark. Once the aircraft touched the ground and the sliding metal doors rumbled open, the soldiers were out in a flash, dropped off near a bland, low-slung building where others from their brigade were based. Within a minute, Goetzke and Green arced the helicopter back toward Thunder III, leaving me to study the neatly cultivated fields, the tight knots of thick-coated sheep, and the black-and-white splotched cows that I took for Holsteins, their tails swaying. It seemed like any farm town in America's heartland—if you overlooked the palm trees and mud-roofed homes—and it looked nothing like a war, except for the U.S. military convoy motoring north on the six-lane highway leading to Baghdad.

The air move was over in less than a half hour, prompting Goetzke to remark: "It went well, without a hitch. I wish every mission was this straightforward."

I caught a ride in a Humvee heading back to the tents, and found myself seated next to Chief Warrant Officer 3 Ralph Ferrell, who took the occasion to examine my helmet, palming it to judge its weight and inspecting the internal suspension system that kept it from hammering my noggin. He handed it back to me as the truck approached his tent, instructing, "When you leave, you're giving this to me."

We all sensed that the war was dying down—one pilot even complained about it, until I told him to shut up and be grateful that he was still standing—but Ferrell's edict struck me as asking a cop to hand in his badge or a cowboy to hang up his spurs. Someday, somewhere, I might need a helmet; in any case, I couldn't imagine spending the rest of my career covering congressional hearings. "You can't have it," I snapped at him. "You're an asshole."

Once he left the truck, I regretted what I'd said. I could have named two or three assholes in the battalion; Ferrell was such a good-natured guy that he never would have qualified. In truth, he was among my favorite people. So I yelled in his direction, saying, "I take it back. You're only an asshole some of the time."

Later I caught up with Major Michael Shenk, the Fourth Battalion's military operations boss, to get some basics about Thunder III, where the 101st Aviation Brigade, with its attack helicopters, had joined the 159th to be in position for air missions farther north in Iraq. With brass from the 101st Airborne Division and support personnel, the number of officers and enlisted personnel at Iskandariyah reached about 6,000.

According to Shenk, most of the division's infantry had, by then, been ferried into Baghdad, where their role would include going house to house and questioning people about potential sites housing weapons of mass destruction. "We're still interested in talking to the locals, who might have been oppressed and afraid to talk before," he said. "We'll do a thorough search. And you really can't do that without going door to door."

Meantime, Shenk said, the Apache pilots from 101st Brigade were "still out shooting at stuff," chiefly military targets, and the 159th Brigade's birds stood to transport personnel and conduct resupply and logistics missions. He noted that the missions remained dangerous for the aviators because helicopter flying had inherent risks, particularly with an "undetermined amount of resistance out there."

"It doesn't take a large, formidable army to make us think twice about going into harm's way," Shenk explained. "Danger is relative, and for helicopters, two guys with rifles can be as dangerous as a tank. And when we take people from Point A to Point B, sometimes B is secure and safe, and sometimes it isn't."

Down the road for the 159th Brigade, he said, there might be humanitarian missions, such as distributing food, water, and blankets.

After filing my copy, I began picking up scuttlebutt about what lay ahead. The next stop was believed to be Mosul, the largest city in northern Iraq. Greg Wood, the chief warrant officer 4, told me that stop was expected to last two to four weeks, but that it might stretch into "two to four months."

I wasn't convinced that I could sell that prospect to my editors. After all, how long would handing out blankets be newsworthy? More to the point, I knew I couldn't sell Tom on the idea.

"Sunward I've climbed . . . and done a hundred things," I told myself, recalling the poem and beginning to think about bowing out.

*   *   *

I was frittering away the next morning, organizing my gear and fiddling with my broken camera, when someone outside hollered, "Gas, gas, gas." This was the first alert I'd heard in Iraq, and since so many days had gone by without any warnings, it got my attention. I put on my gas mask, grabbed my duffel with the nuclear, biological, and chemical protective garments, and scampered into one of the just-dug survival trenches. But I found myself all alone there. The camp was like a ghost town; there wasn't another person in sight.

Feeling forlorn, I returned to my tent, which was empty. Afraid to be alone, I searched out a group of soldiers huddled in a shelter near mine. There I learned that I'd gotten it all wrong. "Lightning, lightning, lightning" meant head to the foxhole because a missile might be coming at us; "Gas, gas, gas" meant take cover within a tent, because the vinyl sides and canopy would offer a layer of protection against a chemical or biological agent. But nothing was headed our way, as we learned after fourteen frightful minutes, when an all-clear went out.

Afterward, I took a broom to the floor of my tent; I felt I owed it to the other women, since the day before, while I was out flying, they'd taken the trouble to remove the cots and gear and install plastic sheeting for ground cover. While I was sweeping I heard a big, dull boom in the distance, then seven more big booms in succession. Soldiers tried to assure me that it was just unexploded ordnance being detonated to make the compound safer; but still, we were on the outskirts of Baghdad, so it made you wonder, and the booms punctuated the rest of an uneasy Sunday morning.

I got around to hand washing some clothing, and later tried to figure out what was wrong with my Nikkon. I discovered that the door to the battery compartment had broken open, so the camera wasn't getting any juice, but after seeing soldiers in action, and remembering that the Army didn't have problems, it only had "issues," I decided that I could engineer a solution. But attempts at repair with duct tape, rubber bands, and elastic hair bands left me no closer to conquering my issue.

Next I unzipped my nylon SportSac grip—looking for what, I don't remember—and saw a pale, rope-like thing glisten and slither. At once I shrieked and dropped the bag, then instantly scolded myself. "You're at a military installation," I thought. "You shouldn't alarm people unnecessarily."

I needn't have worried, because nobody heard me—or responded to my distress signal—and the long, legless reptile and I remained the only living creatures in the tent. I marched outside and mustered the closest soldiers I could find, paying no heed to name, rank, or age. Corralling two guys, the latent drill instructor inside me emerged. "I need your help," I barked. "There's a snake in my bag."

Private 1st Class Steven Cruz was in the middle of getting a haircut, but that was inconsequential to me. "I hate snakes," I whimpered, distorting my face to make plain my distress.

He and Private Zachary Bridgeford followed me back into my tent. After I pointed out my bag, they hauled it outside. Then I scurried behind a truck and turned in the other direction, since whatever was going to happen, I thought it best not to look. Back in February, when the embeds were briefed at Fort Campbell, we were given a seventy-four-page, pocket-sized booklet called *A Soldier's Guide to the Republic of Iraq.* I'd read the whole damn thing, including the section titled "Dangerous Animals."

"There are forty-six species of poisonous snakes in the region," it advised. "Their habitats range from the mountainous areas to the desert. Avoiding a snakebite is easier than treating one. Do not panic if faced with or bitten by a snake."

For good measure, I'd even forced myself to examine the color photographs of the snakes in the handout—one showed a hooded cobra with beady eyes preparing to strike—and tried to convince myself that I was tough and could handle anything. Yeah, right.

With my lips quivering, every so often I glanced back at Bridgeford and Cruz; it seemed to be taking them forever to fish the elusive reptile from my bag. "Maybe I'm losing my mind," I told myself. "Maybe it was just the cord to my blow dryer."

Finally they turned the bag upside down and the reptile tumbled out. Cruz grabbed a sledgehammer to immobilize it, while Bridgeford delivered the coup de grâce, using a wooden tent stake to grind off its head just below the neck.

The nineteen-year-old Cruz was from Farmingdale, New York, on Long Island, and had for the first time in his life seen and captured a snake earlier that Sunday in the "commo shop," the tent where the soldiers in communications lived and worked.

"I wasn't scared," he told me. "It was like, 'Cool.' "

"If somebody needs help, I'll help," he added. "Plus I'm used to helping my little sister, who's afraid of spiders. I'll go into her room and get them out." His sister was all of sixteen years old, making me feel less like a village elder and more like an overgrown baby. Cruz didn't want me to feel bad, though; he told me he thought that some female soldiers might have been "crying their eyes out" had it happened to them. (In fairness to the women, I have to admit, I'd never seen any one of them in tears.)

Bridgeford, who'd grown up in Auburn, California, echoed what Cruz had said. "If somebody needs help, I'm there," he told me.

I thanked the two profusely, then sought out Ruiz to unload my troubles. That's when things got really scary. He told me that Thunder III had no antivenin and said that had someone been bitten, he or she would have had to have been flown out in a medevac with "urgent" status, taken to the closest field hospital for treatment, and then airlifted out in a fixed-wing aircraft to another country for the cure.

Ruiz lifted the cover of his laptop and installed a Defense Department CD-ROM entitled "Medical, Environmental, and Disease Intelligence and Countermeasures," or MEDIC. We read through the descriptions of the various snakes to try to identify the one that had invaded my tent. Don Gregg, the battalion command sergeant major, helped us along by loaning us a fat paperback on outdoor survival, a book that depicted all manner of snakes. Ruiz and I concluded it must have been either a sand viper or a saw-scaled viper, both of which were potentially deadly.

Ruiz said the antivenin for a bite from these snakes was available in Germany, France, Pakistan, India, and Iran, then laughed, saying, "Nah, you don't want to go to Iran."

The episode gave me license to go from tent to tent like the town crier, telling my tale of woe to anyone who would listen, though I found myself facing tough crowds.

"There's no antidote to a helicopter crash, either," a pilot reminded.

"If you want sympathy, get a dictionary. It's in there between *shit* and *syphilis*," someone else suggested.

"S-w-e-e-e-e-t" was one of the kinder reactions.

Only when one of the men confessed that he, too, had a phobia about snakes, did I feel vindicated—though since I still was spooked, I decided a few calls home were warranted.

"That sounds exotic," said Tom, who launched an Internet search while he had me on the line and proceeded to educate me about the two species.

Everything he told me was very creepy. The sand viper, for example, "has a short temper and will strike several times," and the saw-scaled viper is "ill-tempered [and] will attack any intruder."

"Oh, that's awful!" my mother remarked, seeing it my way.

My sister Nancy talked past my misfortune, observing, "On television, the soldiers look really handsome."

"Some of them are," I assured her.

Afterward I gave myself permission to blow off work for the rest of the day, content to spend my time hanging up my gear with hooks, which Chivers and Scenie supplied, to keep it off the ground. At least my tentmates were sympathetic. Dread pervaded the tent; it was as if all of us had been riding in a car that suddenly slammed on its brakes and narrowly averted a collision.

Over dinner, Ruiz told me that he'd shared my news at that afternoon's battalion meeting (the "BUB," for battle update brief) and told people that I was "freaked." I was a little miffed, preferring to masquerade as the embodiment of the 1972 Helen Reddy hit: "I am strong. I am invincible. I am woman." But I knew that Ruiz was right on the money.

Colonel Forrester, for his part, was a hard-ass about the whole thing, looking me in the eye when we next met and asking, "Did you have food in your tent?" I wanted to say something smart, like, "Yeah, I had a big chocolate birthday cake. I'm sorry you didn't get a slice," but of course I didn't.

The next morning I made a point to go to Mass to thank God for my avoiding a snake bite. Ruiz agreed to tag along. A pattern was emerging: I was the spiritual equivalent of a foul-weather fan. When I didn't get hit by the Iraqi missile, I went to Mass; when I survived the snake's visit, I went to Mass for the second time.

Father George led an inspiring service and afterward greeted me with his trademark exuberance. Never for a moment did I doubt that he was in my court. After Mass, either I'd calmed down sufficiently or run out of shoulders to cry on, so I offered a story about the snakes to my editor, Carl. He liked the idea, so Cruz and Bridgeford provided the blow-by-blow in interviews.

"If it would have been me, I would have been terrified, too," Cruz confessed. "It's not so much the fear of the snake, it's the fear of the encounter."

By the time I got down to writing I could even poke fun at myself, admitting my phobia and spoofing my dumb luck while spotlighting the two young privates who helped without a moment's hesitation.

But while I could be self-deprecating in print, the episode left me with a chill. Discovering the snake in the SportSac didn't drive me out of Iraq, but it helped point me in that direction, along with a few other things that happened that week.

With the satellite TV up and running, I had stopped relying on my short-wave radio and could now hear—and see—more of what was happening in Iraq, just as I took in what the retired generals "embedded" with the television networks were saying, and what the Pentagon and White House were telling the American people and the world.

After Basra, Nasiriyah, Najaf, Kut, Karbala, Kirkuk, Irbil, Mosul, and Baghdad had fallen, Tikrit, which was thought to be the last stronghold for Saddam Hussein's loyalists, was taken by coalition forces on Monday, April 14. The Marines had seized control of Hussein's ancestral home without much resistance, and afterward, at a Pentagon briefing, Major General Stanley McChrystal announced, "I would anticipate that the major combat engagements are over."

President Bush spoke from the White House Rose Garden a day later, intoning, "In Iraq, the regime of Saddam Hussein is no more . . . Our victory in Iraq is certain, but it is not complete . . . We have waged this war with clarity and purpose. And we will see it through until the job is done."

Once that week while catching the news out of the White House, I found myself not only watching the correspondent, but studying what was in the background. Whenever broadcasters did stand-ups from the North Lawn, the men were favoring shirtsleeves, and I could see that the grass had sprung back to life and the tulips were in bloom. "Look at that! It's spring in Washington," I said out loud to no one in particular in the tent crowded with soldiers who were taking a load off.

Yes, it was spring, back at home and here in the desert, and meanwhile Chaplain Kerry Greene had been trying to get me to join a new choir he was forming for a sunrise service on Easter that coming Sunday. With very little in the way of recreation, I thought it would be an outlet and a chance to be proactive with God, so I agreed. In the beginning, though, everybody was so out of practice and Greene's CD player so creaky, probably from ingesting so much sand, that it was less a choir and more a cacophony; but we did get better.

Tom had fewer worries about my well-being as the U.S.-led forces made steady progress, so he began boasting that his wife was "as tough as a two-dollar steak." He was always supportive, lifting me up when I was low and reading my work closely, always citing portions he liked. He's a gifted writer, so his praise meant a lot.

After I'd left home to join the 101st in late February, neighbors and friends had been inviting him for meals, and our relatives had been checking in on him by phone. But as time went by, I sensed that it was mostly him and the dog, who refused to leave his side, as if she worried he might up and leave, too.

My husband never complained or told me to come home, but one day that week he took a deep breath and said wearily, "This is getting old." From a strong, silent type like Tom, those four little words, tinged with loneliness, spoke volumes.

As Fox News made evident, Iraq remained a volatile country, and U.S. soldiers were getting picked off with regularity. When I'd arrived at Thunder III on April 11, one soldier was killed elsewhere in Iraq; on April 12, two; on April 13, one; and on April 14, six.

Now that the Pentagon brass had announced that major combat operations were over, I could unbed in good conscience. In my head, the calculation came down to this: I'd had a couple of brushes with danger—seeing Patriot missiles launch twice, and finding a deadly snake in my luggage—and I knew I didn't have nine lives. My heart could only agree with the idea of leaving, since after one of Chaplain Greene's choir practices, I weighed the prospect of welcoming Easter at dawn in the desert or going home to mark the day with my spouse. "You should be home for Easter," I said to myself.

My inclination made its way onto the rumor mill in no time. Once word spread that I would not be staying much longer, I sensed some genuine regret within the brigade. I figured that a few of the troops considered me a poor excuse for a soldier, a prima donna, a pain in the butt, or a laughingstock—but whatever detractors thought, at least I was getting out the story of the 159th Brigade.

Around that time there was grumbling in the television lounge, since Fox halted its wall-to-wall coverage of the war in Iraq and was featuring long segments on the news out of northern California. A woman's badly decomposed remains had washed up on a beach in San Francisco Bay, one day after a dead infant boy was discovered on a trail not far away. The woman was believed to be twenty-seven-year-old Laci Peterson, an attractive brunette who'd disappeared on Christmas Eve when she was eight months pregnant—and whose husband was not off the hook for the murders.

You could read the disappointment in the faces of the troops. The Peterson story was a sensational one, told over and over—but it was so irrelevant to the war and its risks. Some of them took to asking me, the resident journalist, "Aren't we news anymore?"

Later one of the Alpha guys, addressing me in front of a handful of colleagues, protested, "You can't leave, you're our favorite reporter."

"I'm not your favorite reporter," I corrected him, laughing. "I'm your *only* reporter."

They knew it and I knew it: I was free to leave at any time. In some ways, checking out was a no-brainer, since every other day something new would seriously annoy me. There was the woman who claimed my neon-orange

Leatherman pocket knife as her own after I'd left it behind in her tent, and wouldn't fess up when I asked her about it later. There was the officer who berated me for using too much of the battalion's copy paper to print out and pass around my stories. At the time I thought, "I've paid taxes for more than thirty years! I bought that paper for you!" I thought about mailing him a ream when I got home and inviting him to shove it up his you-know-what. And I'd noticed a disturbing trend developing at my favorite latrine: guys started filling empty water bottles with urine and depositing them there. Seriously, there were twelve bottles of urine in there one day; I took the trouble to count because I was brainstorming a way to insert that detail into a story; although after I talked it over with Ruiz, the bottles somehow disappeared.

But just as the hassles in this hot, sand-drenched, snake-infested outpost grew out of proportion, the pleasures did, too: a shower with a plastic bag of water heated in the sun; a frosted, freshly baked sheet cake that showed up magically one day in the ALOC; a hand-out from somebody else's care package; or a quip about our mundane universe, like the time Specialist Jon Jenkins, a Black Hawk crew chief from tiny Adairville, Kentucky, saw an Army truck with the identification number 69 stenciled on its doors, and hollered, "Hey, there's the party Humvee," and busted his gut laughing.

Even when the going got tough, there were consolations. I wasn't writing the mortgage check, washing dishes, waiting in traffic, figuring out my taxes, or calculating the tip on a bill from a Washington hair stylist that rivaled the price of an airline ticket. And I was learning the ropes on how to survive in a different culture, albeit an American one; when I'd arrived, I couldn't so much as assemble a cot or, without scalding my hands, heat an MRE. Plus it didn't hurt that I was slimming down and getting a tan.

Tom, much later, said that he thought I'd gone native. He never said as much at the time, but four words from my husband—"This is getting old"—made the point that it was time to boomerang back to where I'd come from.

Once I inquired about catching a helicopter for Kuwait, there were no more verbal brickbats, only bouquets.

Greene took me aside, put his hands on mine, and said warmly, "You were great, Katherine. You didn't complain once." At first I was flabbergasted by the chaplain's remark, since I'd had any number of complaints about Army life, but then I was just relieved. Maybe I'd managed to keep most of my tribulations to myself; I knew Ruiz had had an earful, and now I knew that he'd kept my confidences.

When I relayed my plans by telephone to the 101st Airborne's public affairs shop in Iraq, I heard more praise. "We've been tracking your stories," Staff Sergeant Mark Swart said. "You've done a wonderful job for the 101st."

I was so stunned to hear that that I wrote it down in a notebook.

There was more. Ever since arriving at Thunder III, I was periodically allowed to use a military computer to check my e-mail. My cousin, Betty Wroblewski, wrote to let me know that the embeds were being applauded. "Congratulations to the journalists," she wrote. "There is so much tribute being paid to all of you covering the war."

It was truly news to me.

One afternoon I settled in the sand with my satellite phone a good distance from the tents—I couldn't bear to arrange for an airline ticket within earshot of the troops—and quietly made a few calls to my newspaper's travel agency. I was told I could travel on Kuwait Airways from Kuwait City to London, then connect on British Airways for a flight to Washington Dulles. The one-way fare was $1,545. There were seats available on Friday, April 18, but nothing sooner than that. Now I'd learned that helicopters from Thunder III were going back and forth to Camp Udairi in Kuwait regularly, so if I left on April 17, I could finagle a ride from Udairi to the capital and make the flight the next day.

As much as I relished the thought of going home to my husband, and being out of harm's way, my final days with the soldiers were bittersweet. I'd been with them for fifty days, forty-five of them in a war zone. I knew these men and women faced a tough, uncertain future. Now part of me felt giddy and part of me was weighted down with guilt. I imagined myself racing out of a burning house and not bothering to look back, even though I knew that friends were trapped inside amid the flames. I started drafting a letter of farewell to Colonel Forrester and the 159th Brigade, but couldn't find the right words. So I moved on to another item on my checklist, splitting up my gear.

I jettisoned soap, shampoo, tampons, the plastic tub I'd used for "bird baths," some extra cigarettes, and a favorite CD. I gave Sergeant Nelda Scenie my desert camouflage shirt—the same one the soldiers had, but I hadn't worn it once. I gave Command Sergeant Major Gregg my back-up pair of reading glasses. I gave Private Carter some minipads and, because her twenty-first birthday was the next day, I threw some cash in an envelope, telling her that once she got to a PX she should buy something on me.

In return, soldiers gave me the e-mail addresses of their wives and kids and asked me to get in touch with them. Some asked me to send the photographs I had taken of them to their families. Ruiz asked me to call his wife, Phyllis, and he wrote down a message for her in my notebook so I'd get it right. He and I said good-bye more than once. "I'm so glad you stayed with the Fourth Battalion," he told me. "I don't know how I would have survived without you," I would reply.

Later, Ruiz asked if I could leave my sat phone with him. Although he was scheduled to return to the States in mid-June (he was one of the few in the brigade to have a tentative departure date), I couldn't let him have the phone, because my newspaper had leased it. I knew where he was coming from, though, since everyone was suffocating emotionally and wanted a lifeline back to the real world.

For my last story, I did a short feature—a "little saga, but a tiny footnote to Operation Iraqi Freedom," is how I put it—on the Harley flag having made it into Iraq. After it had been ordered down in Kuwait, twenty-nine-year-old Brian Buol had unfurled it during a stop on his first mission into Iraq on March 23, and had some digital snapshots to prove it.

As a result of my first story on the Harley colors, a company official, George Petropoulos, had e-mailed Buol and invited him and his buddies to the motorcycle company's upcoming 100th anniversary celebration in August. He'd even offered Buol help in finding a place to stay.

A native of Columbia, Missouri, Buol, like so many of the others, earlier had deployed to Afghanistan, so he knew better than to hazard a guess on whether he and the brigade would be back in time for the Harley blowout. "I don't accept we're going home until I'm sitting on a plane," he said bluntly.

I'd had in mind a much different swan song. Once I got to Kuwait City, I was hoping to get on board the U.S.S. *Comfort,* the Navy hospital ship that had left Baltimore with much fanfare to treat war casualties from the Persian Gulf. I figured I'd spend a few days on the ship and finish with a story that some soldiers had paid a high price in Operation Iraqi Freedom. But after squatting in the sand with my sat phone and dialing one military contact after another, I seemed to be spinning my wheels. I thought it would be simple to leap out of the Army as an embed and into the Navy, but in the end I decided it was not worth the trouble. I was getting out for good.

I went back to my letter to Forrester, and finished it.

April 16, 2003
Colonel William Forrester
Commander, 159th Aviation Brigade
101st Airborne Division
Camp Thunder III, Iraq

To Colonel Forrester and the Soldiers of the 159th:

I'm most grateful for all the assistance and care shown to me as an "embedded" journalist during my time with your unit during Operation Iraqi Freedom.

Needless to say, this has been a once-in-a-lifetime experience for me professionally and personally. Leaving is a bittersweet experience. I'm delighted to return to the U.S.A., but I know my many friends here will be working diligently under difficult conditions to secure the peace.

I wish you and your troops the very best in all you do. I will keep all of you in my prayers asking that you be safe here and that soon, you, too, will be back in the warm embrace of family and friends.

It was a great honor to take part in the historic effort to place journalists in close contact with military units. As I promised my family, I was in the best of hands with the Screaming Eagles—through sandstorms, a thwarted missile attack, combat missions, multiple trips to the foxhole and finally, the sand viper's visit.

I depart tremendously impressed by your unit's bravery, dedication, team work, can-do attitude, field craft, agility, adaptability, and prowess in flight.

America is truly blessed, just as I was during these past seven-plus weeks.

The day before I left, I went to see Forrester, but he was tied up, so I just dropped off the letter and figured that was that. I made copies of the written good-bye letter and addressed them to the commanders of the companies I knew best: Captain John Butora and the Alpha males; Captain Jeff Beierlein and the boys from Bravo; and Captain Carlos Goveo and his charges from Headquarters Company, my former tentmates: the signal corps, cooks, medics, refuelers, and motor-vehicle repairmen.

Darkness always seemed to fall early, but on the eve of my departure, as I wrapped things up and glad-handed the soldiers, the curtain seemed to drop with a thud. The sky was navy blue and starlit, and I took a long look around Thunder III, swallowing hard and realizing I hadn't left enough time to make my good-byes. Now my back was up against the wall. So much had changed, but one thing hadn't changed: I'd waited once again until the eleventh hour to pack up my things, just as I had on the day I left for Fort Campbell. If I wasn't leaving at four o'clock the next morning, I might have procrastinated even longer, but I had four tentmates who deserved a decent night's sleep.

Out of the blue, Sergeant Willie Jacobs showed up, fetching me to the heavily fortified tactical operations center to say good-bye to Forrester. When I got there, the colonel thanked me for my letter, said he would read it to his staff, and presented me with a plastic mug with the brigade's insignia. Then I made more farewells at the operations center—to Alex Covert, Sean Connolly, Bill Allen, Brent Driggers, and others—telling them to be safe and hoping they'd be home soon.

I should have known that I couldn't get out without one last Army insult: two staffers, apparently overseeing some secret mumbo-jumbo, spotted me walking out of the center and broke into a sweat, muttering, "She's in here! Cover up the maps!"

As if I were a spy? As if I hadn't already checked out? As if I gave a shit about their classified maps? But I reacted in the manner to which I had become accustomed: I bit my tongue.

On the way out, I bumped into Father George. I gave him a big hug and promised to e-mail him. Curiously, he was handing out government-issue lip balm, so I took one, figuring I'd palm it off to a friend.

Before too long Ruiz popped in my tent, wondering if I could shave his mustache for him before I left, since there'd been a crackdown on personal grooming; soldiers whose haircuts or mustaches were deemed unruly were in trouble. I made quick work of it—his seemed an intimate request, but then field mirrors were scarce—and said good-bye to him again. Then some pilots came to see me off, and—in the nick of time—a clerk dropped off cards and packages that had arrived for me from the States. There were Easter cards from my parents and sister and a letter from Tom, who'd sent some of my favorite toiletries. Then, with great precision, I organized my things and put out what I would wear the next morning—loathing the idea of getting up at three, but knowing soon I'd be bedding down in a Hilton.

The alarm on my wristwatch went off at three—after I'd slept two hours at best. For good measure, a female soldier pulling an overnight shift delivered a wake-up call in person—"Miss Katherine," she said in a dulcet voice—to make sure that I made the flight.

I forced myself up and traipsed outside in flip-flops, feeling the cool sand caress my feet and marveling at the camp's stillness. Lately there'd been booms and bangs and blasts in the direction of Baghdad, plus flares and whatnot streaking through the evening skies; one night the racket was so intense that a sergeant stormed out of his tent with his rifle at the ready, investigating whether we'd come under attack. It was so tranquil now, with nearly everybody asleep—even, apparently, the pack of feral dogs, which, after dark, raced about the far reaches of the compound, yelping and barking and whipping up the sand.

After making a pit stop at the latrines, I knelt in the desert to wash the sand out of my hair and then quietly dressed in the tent, using only my tiny red light so as not to awaken my tentmates, Scenie, Chivers, Douglas, and Carron.

I'd given several things away, tossed out a bunch of stuff, and turned in my NBC overgarments; I'd been asked to hand in my gas mask, but requested and received permission to keep it until I was safely out of Kuwait. Still, my gear amounted to six bags and a fanny pack, so it was a chore to carry it in one trip over to Bravo Company, whose pilots were flying me out.

Though the camp was shrouded in darkness, the company's command post was brightly lit, though only a few souls were stirring inside. I'd been told to show up a couple of hours before departure, and with nothing much to do, I paged through somebody's *Maxim,* helped myself to a nearly empty bag of Chips Ahoy cookies, and made small talk with the few soldiers who were awake.

Just before dawn, a truck was readied to drive the pilots and crew and a few odd passengers out to the airfield. After we loaded up and pulled out, I took a long look at the drab-olive tent city housing the soldiers I'd come to know—the brass and the grunts, the West Pointers and the high school dropouts, the true believers and the searchers, the muscle men and the rare pipsqueaks, the uptight and the comedians, the grizzled old-timers and the smooth-skinned teenagers, the brownnoses and the rebels you could always count on for a rousing "Fuck the Army!" They were white and black and brown and tawny, men and women, some of them brand-new soldiers, some in midcareer, and some counting the minutes until retirement. A number had reenlisted right there in the sands of Iraq, which was unfathomable to me, since I couldn't comprehend, amid so many hardships, what glue bound them to Uncle Sam.

As the truck pulled away, the compound grew smaller and smaller, and whatever guilt I'd harbored lifted away like a helium balloon climbing merrily toward the clouds. By the time the sun came up, I was silently singing a song of glee, privately hooting and hollering as the soldiers did when their aircraft was wheels-up back at Campbell.

I loaded my things onto a Black Hawk and buckled myself in—I knew the drill so well now—but then was given new instructions. I was being reassigned to another aircraft. Asking no questions, I transferred my bags to the other helicopter. As I did so, I noticed somebody off in the distance waving at me excitedly. Someone was bidding me an enthusiastic good-bye, but I couldn't make out who it was—maybe the brigade's command sergeant major, Bill Allen.

As I stepped into the new bird, I spotted Ruiz inside the cabin. I had no idea that he was "going south" that day; when I learned he needed to check on patients who were convalescing in Kuwait City, it seemed too good a coincidence. Plus, this helicopter was going directly to the capital, not the more distant Udairi—another boon. I took a seat next to my buddy, smiling broadly, wondering to myself how I'd gotten so lucky, and asking him greedily whether he had any spare time in Kuwait, since I'd have twenty-four hours there to kill. He didn't; so all that was left for the Army of Two, me and my best friend, was three hours.

The engine began to bellow, while the rotor blades spun faster and faster and the auxiliary power unit let out its familiar high-pitched scream. In a blaze of sand, we were up and out and tearing through the pale blue skies, past the compound of trucks and tents encircled in concertina wire and neat rows of helicopters lined up in the sand. As we ascended, the flying machines appeared to be no bigger than crickets.

For the first time in seven and a half weeks, I was off the clock, not taking notes, not noodling what material I had and what I needed, not finagling a chair and table space, not flipping hurriedly through a notebook, not struggling to ignore the background chatter and commentary ("You're so disorganized," a soldier once observed as I was paging through my notes, offering me a metal binder clip, as if that held some mojo), and not fretting over whether the satellites in the heavens would smile upon me and whisk my text and pictures to Milwaukee.

Punch drunk from so little sleep, I was practically beside myself with emotion. I was finished with the assignment. I was leaving a dangerous place, heading home, and thankful—overwhelmingly, eternally, and six ways to Sunday grateful—to be alive. By then, I had a rough idea of the death toll— 130 American troops and 14 journalists from the United States and abroad, including four embedded journalists—and I felt fortunate to be getting out with barely a scratch.

It was difficult to carry on a conversation with Ruiz over the roar of the helicopter, so I took out a notebook, number 17 (I'd begun numbering them at Fort Campbell). Ruiz and I began jotting down smart-aleck remarks about people in the brigade, passing the notebook back and forth and cracking up like schoolkids. I would say something snide, he would pile on, I'd take it the next step, and then after a while we'd move on to somebody else who'd gotten on my nerves.

Then I remembered that my photos were stored on my laptop, so I pulled it out and tapped at the keyboard to see a retrospective of the journey: the first major sandstorm (there's Ruiz, pointing to a rhinoceros-sized hole in the tent's canopy), the chemical-attack drills in the oppressive heat (there's Carlos Goveo, his good looks hidden by enough protection to ward off Ebola), the trips to the foxhole (when we were sweating bullets, so the camera came out only after the all-clear), the time Geraldo Rivera showed up at Udairi (photographed from behind, since I'd refused to acknowledge him), and the mission into Iraq (with me first as a nervous onlooker, then as a good-to-go participant).

After the slide show, the notebook seemed too low-tech, so Ruiz and I started banging away at the laptop, saying outrageous things like "Maybe we'll crash and be taken P.O.W. and the Navy SEALS will come and rescue us."

At one point I typed out that I was worried that all this nonsense would be preserved on my hard drive, but Ruiz typed back, "I don't think anyone will do an autopsy on your C: drive," so we kept going, like kids fiddling around with an Etch A Sketch.

Not far from Kuwait City, Ruiz typed: "Tell me about your sex life." At first I looked at him like he was out of his mind, then he added: "It'll be the most sex I'll have in two months."

Everything had been on the up and up between us; from the very beginning we had forged a deep connection, but for both of us "Carpe diem" was never in the cards. Ruiz was my sounding board, my saving grace, and, on some days, guarantor of my sanity. We were two strangers who had long ago left the figurative train and boarded a lifeboat. He brightened the good days and helped me exorcise my troubles on the bad ones.

"It's Platonic love, the highest form," I once said to him about our friendship, summoning the only thing I remembered from a Greek philosophy course I'd taken in college.

Now he was heading to a field hospital, and I was checking into a resort hotel with a beach along the Persian Gulf. I was drawn to Ruiz, although what I did next was motivated as much out of charity as the desire to leave a last impression that I was certifiably hot stuff. On the computer I dashed off a few zingers from long ago and far away, grinning like a Cheshire cat and handing the laptop back to Ruiz. He let out a howl—not really knowing whether to believe me—and that was that.

It was midmorning when the Black Hawk touched down at the portion of Kuwait's international airport reserved for coalition forces. I thanked the pilots and wished them well; then I walked over to Ruiz, who, now that he was out of Iraq, had traded his helmet for a soft, floppy boonie cap.

"Is this good-bye?" I asked theatrically. I kissed him on the right cheek, told him to take care of himself, and thanked him for being such a good friend. We hugged, promised to get together when he got back to the States, and then he strode to some medical tents on the edge of the tarmac.

Although I wasn't supposed to be leaving until the next morning, Friday, April 18, I was determined to have a plane ticket in my hands, not wanting to leave this detail to chance. I hitched a ride to the distant perimeter of the airfield and caught an Al-Quds taxi. The driver was likable and seemed trustworthy, so I asked him to wait outside the Kuwait Airways terminal with my belongings in his cab while I bought the ticket. Inside the terminal half the people were in Western clothing, the others in flowing Arab tunics and head scarves—much like the capital itself.

The driver, Romani Hashash, an Egyptian, was waiting when I returned, and on the way to the Hilton Kuwait Resort, I studied the city's architecture while getting a short course in Arabic, writing down what I might need on the back of a notebook. It was simpler than trying to dig out my phrasebook, and I figured I could survive for a day with "Hello" (*ah*-lan), "Thank you" (*shuk*-ran), "Yes" (*ay*-wa), "No" (la), "Good-bye" (*ma*-a s-sa-*leh*-ma), "Please" (min *faD*-lak), "Please help me" (min *faD*-lak, sa-*id*-nee), "Sorry" (*as*-fa), and "How much?" (bi *kam?*).

Hashash gave me his business card in case I wanted to go anywhere else; I figured I'd at least call him to take me to the airport the next day.

As I walked into the hotel lobby I was struck by how immense, immaculate, and plush everything seemed. It was the same place I'd visited for the meeting before the war—and where I'd taken a tumble into the pool of water while hanging out with Matt Cox—but after weeks in primitive conditions, it was like a palace, and for one glorious day, it would be mine.

My room wasn't ready, but I didn't care. I could have collapsed outside under the palm trees and been content. I was invited to use the health club and spa while I waited, and when I learned that all the spa appointments were booked, that didn't faze me, either. At this point a shower would have been more than fine. I'm sure I was quite a sight in the locker room: a bedraggled woman who, except for having the tan lines of a farmer, might have recently been marooned on a desert island.

After reveling in a hot shower, I headed outside for the turquoise pool and its wooden chaises and plush royal-blue towels and inviting lunch menu and fawning waiters.

Except for the hotel staff, I had nothing to say to anybody: nothing to the British reporters I spied in an animated story discussion to my right at the pool; nothing to the men and women in uniform who I imagined were attached to the Coalition Forces Land Component Command public affairs office, which was housed at the hotel; and nothing to the small parade of journalists who were checking in after checking out of Iraq, with the telltale bellman's cart loaded with powdery luggage, helmet, boots, and bullet-resistant vest.

Normally I'm an outgoing person, but now I craved privacy, anonymity, relaxation, and sun. I ordered a salad, an iced tea, and a no-alcohol Budweiser. After eating, I took a dip in the Persian Gulf and picked up seashells. After that, I swam some laps in the pool, and when a woman swimming nearby accidentally brushed her arm against my calf, I righted myself in the water and let out a scream worthy of my finding a scorpion crawling up my leg. I wasn't sure why I'd done that, and I scanned the chaises around the pool, hoping people didn't think I was a kook.

After my swim, I showered again, then took a sauna until my room was ready. It was a huge space, with a view of the Gulf, stylish furnishings, and a massive bathroom with a shower, tub, and vanity with two sinks.

My first order of business was making phone calls to tell everyone I was winging my way home: to Tom in Virginia, to Carl in Wisconsin, and to my parents in Florida. When my mother's voice broke as she told me, "You'll never know how much I worried about you," I found myself wiping away tears.

A sensible person might at this point have collapsed on the 300-thread-count sheets, but I was too wound up, and the bathroom was too inviting. Out of habit I began hand-washing a bunch of laundry, hellbent on having some clean clothing.

Next I ordered room-service coffee and called Mr. Hashash, the cab driver. I wanted to shop. He ferried me to the Al-Sharq mall, and while he confirmed my suspicions—this was the place narrowly missed by an Iraqi missile—I was too battle-hardened to let that stop me. What happened was not so much power shopping as it was a spending jag: I bought a pricey watch, Portuguese shoes, ties and socks for Tom, electric-yellow hand towels, lotion and other toiletries, plus Starbucks Kuwait coffee mugs for my friends. God knows why, but I even bought a shower curtain.

Back at the hotel, I packed up ninety percent of my belongings and arranged for FedEx to get them home.

The next day I dropped some more money, hitting the duty-free shops at the airport in Kuwait and later at Heathrow. On the way to London I put my papers in order and spent most of the flight, when I wasn't sleeping, compulsively using baby wipes to rid the few possessions I had left to carry of sand. Cleanliness wasn't next to godliness; it seemed perfectly divine.

In London I came out of my shell and spoke to somebody who was not standing behind a cash register. I made the acquaintance of a British police officer because what I really wanted was to pet his black Labradors, Henry and Thomas, who were making the rounds in the airport to sniff for bombs. They were gentle beasts and it had been weeks since I'd seen a domesticated animal.

It had been ages, too, since I'd had a drink. After dinner, and two Tanqueray and tonics, on the flight home, I was out like a light for the rest of the trip across the Atlantic. Though I was surrounded by strangers, in my mind I was flying solo—away from the Army, out of the war zone, and expecting no turbulence.

10

Hard Landing

It was around midnight on Good Friday, April 18, when I arrived at Washington's Dulles International Airport. The lights in the Immigration and Customs section of the terminal struck me as harsh; I'd been so knocked out on the flight from London that I was like a grizzly bear roused out of hibernation in the dead of winter.

There was a long line at Immigration Service, something that in another time might have seen me peeved. Not now. I was so relieved to be home, and so steeled to waiting, and by the Army's hurry-up-and-wait standards, the line seemed to move at supersonic speed. I looked nothing like the woman in my nine-year-old passport photo, which showed an amiable, fair-skinned, blow-dried brunette in business attire. My new coloration borrowed from the periodic table of elements—copper skin, golden hair, and annoyingly long silver roots, since I hadn't been near a bottle of L'Oreal for ages. Still, I was waved through after only a few cursory questions.

Customs didn't bother to inspect my belongings, which suited me fine, not that I had anything to hide. Some reporters brought back looted art and artifacts, but I found the idea of collecting war booty vulgar. All I had was a 250 dinar note, an oversized bill whose colors—pastel green, pink, and lilac—reminded me of saltwater taffy. It showed a self-satisfied Saddam Hussein in a coat and tie; it was the only souvenir I needed. By and large I'd followed the camper's ethos, leaving only footprints and taking only photographs, if you overlooked the fistful of sand and stone I felt compelled to filch from the desert—not to mention the granules of sand adhering to every shred of clothing I'd had over there.

Though the hour was late, beyond customs I could see a throng of people waiting for overseas passengers. Because of the crowd it took me a while to spot Tom, but there he was—broad-shouldered and fit, with his blue eyes and salt-and-pepper hair, wearing his gentle smile. I buried my head in his shoulder as we hugged. The two of us held each other for a good, long while, tuning out the helium balloon bouquets and women in saris and men in turbans and Town Car drivers in dark, rumpled suits holding placards bearing names like "M/M Ammerman" and "Barbieri." When I pulled away from him I studied his face, then planted kisses on his mouth and neck.

Compared to when Tom had last set eyes on me, I was long-haired, tanned, and shrunken, and sporting all sorts of goodies from my splurges—a new watch, shoes, pashmina, you name it. I wasn't wearing a lick of anything Army.

I clung to his side like his Siamese twin all the way to his SUV, where he opened the rear door and surprised me. Tom hardly ever took the dog on car trips, but there she was, seventy-five startled pounds of disbelief, nervous energy, and wet kisses: Princess, our Labrador.

It was a balmy spring night and, though I was groggy from the journey, my eyes were hungry for the familiar sights along State Highway 267: the sleek corporate palaces, dense foliage, and—by God—grass that, despite the dark, I knew was green. I cradled Princess in my arms and kissed her head, reassuring her in baby talk, "Momma home. Momma home."

When I crossed the threshold of our home, the place seemed so monstrously large that I might have been stepping into a nineteenth-century mansion in Newport, Rhode Island, or a studio mogul's spread in Bel Air. I went from room to room in our house, checking things out like the way the dog does after a week at the sitter. Tom and I had so many rooms and so much space. The "home" I just left was no bigger than an Army cot, and you could have lined up three of them end to end in one of our hallways. Just as the roominess seemed uncanny to me, the refrigerator, faucets, and toilets seemed nothing short of remarkable.

Once I figured it out—yes, you've left the moonscape and landed back in the place where you live—I took a deep breath. Every cell in my weary body seemed to be muttering, "Thank God I'm alive." It was as though a brain tumor had been removed and I'd been given a clean bill of health. I had my old life back—my real life, my civilian life—and I could pretty much do as I pleased.

Tom and I wasted no time making love—and then I sank into a deep sleep.

When morning dawned, the curtain rose to reveal the Washington area's springtime finery at its peak. Hot pink tulips and yellow daffodils—I'd forgotten I'd planted them in the fall—sprouted in front of our home, and the area's delicate white dogwoods and soft pink cherry blossoms swayed to the season's gentle breezes. It seemed like Mother Nature had laid out a petal-strewn welcome mat just for me.

When the FedEx man came to the door with the belongings I'd shipped from Kuwait, I noticed that the top of my backpack had come undone and some of my things were spilling out onto the walkway. "Don't worry about it," I told him, not really caring what had been lost en route. I was alive, and everything I'd carried into war seemed inconsequential, although I was grateful when he went back to his truck and retrieved my cell phone, which apparently had fallen out in transit.

Every time the doorbell rang for the rest of the day there seemed to be another delivery of flowers. Another pleasure: I tried on blue jeans that long ago had been banished to the back of a closet—and every single pair fit. Another: I couldn't step out the door without a neighbor rushing over for a robust "Welcome home!" and a curious "How was it?" I was the hero of my cul-de-sac. Reentry, in the beginning, was so triumphal and heady that the last thing I predicted was a hard landing.

Any number of friends asked me to lunch; people wanted me for speeches and media interviews; and, both here and abroad, my reflections were sought for university research papers. I wasn't expecting such a fuss. Hadn't lots of self-respecting journalists done the very same thing? I wondered. Besides, I knew full well that the real heroes were stuck in an increasingly precarious Iraq.

With my body clock still attuned to the rhythms of the Persian Gulf, I'd get up with a jolt at three or four in the morning, ignore the coffeemaker, and go straight for the bottled water. Then I'd head for the deck and light a cigarette. Invariably I'd look up at the tall trees in our wooded backyard, fiddle with my St. Catherine's medal—I had a couple of spares at home, and now wore one constantly—and ask God why it was me who had won the lottery. "Why did Michael Kelly die and not me?" I'd ask. "He was forty-six, too. Why him, and not me?"

I was imbibing heavily—bottled water. Chilled Evian was a favorite, but for good measure, I'd loaded up at Sutton Place Gourmet on San Pellegrino from Italy, Apollinaris from Germany, and Vittel from France. I could buy what I wanted, waste what I wanted, and nobody was going to tell me otherwise.

When I hit Smith & Hawken and found potted daffodils on sale—once $15 apiece, now $1.50—I snatched up as many as I could carry. They were a bargain, it was springtime, and I'd gone for so long without fresh flowers . . . I seemed never to run out of reasons for this and other buying binges.

Once I stopped at a drugstore, needing nothing in particular; still, I went from aisle to aisle, examining the lotions and batteries and first-aid supplies, wondering if I needed something, or maybe a friend did. The soldiers were my phantom companions now; I couldn't seem to shake them. One hundred twenty-five dollars later, I left the store with, among other things, a Wiffle® ball and plastic bat.

I e-mailed Ruiz a lot, and was excited when he replied and forked over tidbits on the Fourth Battalion. If the news was bleak—if the latest encampment was abysmal, or Lieutenant Colonel Sabb was up to his old tricks—I did my best to be a friend, cheering him on and assuring him it wouldn't be long before he too was home.

I was also burning up the phone lines with my parents, in-laws, brothers, sister, and friends, sharing highlights and low points and thanking them for their support. Tom, not unexpectedly, quickly tired of hearing this chatter: the blow-by-blow of the sandstorms, the missile, the Black Hawk crash, and the snake that spooked me. To him, I was a broken record playing at 78 rpm.

As I spoke on the phone to my family, I realized how worried they'd been. Every bit of bad news about the 101st Airborne—which had a huge presence with 14,500 division soldiers in the theater joined by several thousand from other units—had given my loved ones a fright. They were seeing the worst of the fighting on television, but missing the camaraderie that kept me going and the laughter that kept me from becoming unhinged.

Not that my siblings hadn't resorted to some gallows humor themselves. My sister, Nancy, had been e-mailing my stories to our family—to her in-laws and friends, too—and sometimes they'd answer with commentary. "Why didn't the snake bite Kathy?" my brother John, the policeman, asked the group. "Professional courtesy" was his punch line.

To the outside world, I held my head high, happy to appear the strong, determined, and daring woman many people made me out to be. But I was living in two worlds and, once home, didn't seem to fit in my old skin. I was exhausted, short-fused, and profane. I missed my old buddies—and worried about them. Early one morning I was stunned to see the paramedics race into the home of my elderly neighbors, so I hurried over to see if I could help. My neighbor, who'd gotten out of bed and collapsed, was pale and dazed, sitting in her Lanz nightgown in the kitchen as her concerned husband looked on. Once it was clear that she was going to be all right, I studied the paramedics: strong, unflinching, take-charge guys who worked as a team and seemed primed for action, 24–7. These were creatures who did not take to life behind a desk.

"They're like soldiers," I thought, glad for the flashback, but then feeling a bit bereft.

When I resumed the Washington journalist's morning ritual, reading a stack of newspapers, there were times I felt like a skinned cat. The *Washington Post* featured long, searing stories and large color photos depicting burials at Arlington National Cemetery and amputees being treated at Walter Reed Army Medical Center. I didn't like the idea of my former companions being in such grave danger, possibly even the next casualty. And there always was a next. I was on a Department of Defense e-mail list that announced to the press every fallen soldier, sailor, and airman, and if the subject field read "DOD Announces Army Casualty"—rather than Navy or Air Force—I cringed.

"Army," by osmosis, had become my official language. I thought nothing of uttering nouns and verbs and stringing them together with "shit," "bullshit," "fuck," "fucking," "freaking," and "flipping."

Tom had been told to expect this new twist. "When your wife comes home, she'll probably say, 'Pass the fucking mashed potatoes,'" Bill Nicholson, the top night editor at *USA Today,* had teased.

But though no prude, Tom was increasingly annoyed by my tirades. "Lose the potty mouth," he urged.

Tom had so wanted his wife back, and he'd gotten her—except that she'd morphed into something of a monster. One morning the two of us were in my home office when the phone rang and I practically mowed Tom down to answer it, hollering, "Out of my way!"

I still don't know why I did that. Maybe it was because I wasn't used to a phone ringing, or because I'd seen and heard so many orders being issued, or because "hurry up" was second nature now. Afterward I was ashamed that I'd ridden roughshod on my husband—over a stupid phone call.

I was channeling Miss Uncongeniality with regularity after my homecoming. One day I went to the city for a haircut, driving a car for the first time in seven weeks, and running late. Near Lafayette Park, where there's usually a traffic jam, I castigated a pedestrian for moving too slowly in a crosswalk by shouting, "Out of my way, lard-ass!" I had the air-conditioning on, and the car windows were closed, so my ire boomeranged directly from my mouth into my ears.

On the way out of the salon, I examined some plump strangers—men in pinstripes and women in St. John's suits on the sidewalk along F Street and felt only contempt for them. "Look at these Washingtonians," I thought to myself. "They're pale, pampered, well dressed, and well fed. They're fat! And they're clueless about the sacrifice Americans are making halfway around the world."

Hold on, a voice inside me said. Wasn't it your job to tell people that story?

Over lunch my friend Melinda Cooke told me to give myself some time to readjust. "The desert," she said, "is with you, in you, and on you. That'll change."

Her advice made sense, but whatever it was I had—battle fatigue, maybe?—persisted. Once I got up in the middle of the night to answer nature's call and, like a confused six-year-old, started to pee on the hardwood floor outside the master bathroom. Tom jumped out of bed at the strange sight and calmly inquired, "What are you doing, honey?" while leading me by the elbow to the toilet. I don't really know why I made the navigational error, except that I had relieved myself in strange ways during the war, crouching underneath a poncho adjacent to a helicopter or squatting next to a truck tire.

I had nightmares, but just a few. During the war it seemed like I was either too tired to dream or too preoccupied to remember doing so. I didn't put too much stock in my night terrors now, thinking that my subconscious was wrestling with something deep in my psyche and surely it was better to banish the demons than invite them to make themselves at home and stay awhile.

More unnerving was the habit of jumping out of my skin at next to nothing. If I reached into a pocket and felt something strange—once it was a waterlogged book of matches that had gone through the washing machine—I'd let out a shriek, half expecting to discover a scorpion. Another time, I felt something odd while putting on a sweater and screamed, though it was only a rhinestone bracelet trapped inside a sleeve.

I went back to the office for a few days and went through the motions, until I realized I was too worn out to take on any new assignments, so I scheduled a long stretch of time off.

One day outside the mall ("retail therapy" I enjoyed, especially after shedding twenty-seven pounds) my cell phone rang. It was Matt Cox, my old buddy from the *Army Times*. He'd come home several days earlier to be there for his wife's unexpected heart surgery. He and I talked for about half an hour, discussing how our wars went, putting the best face on things, until I finally blurted out what a hothead I'd become, especially with my husband.

Cox, who had been on other deployments, knew what coming home was like and didn't seem surprised that I was hell on rollerblades. He had two pieces of advice: take a vacation; and be nice to your husband. I knew that Tom and I were overdue for a getaway, but I appreciated the kick in the pants. It was Cox's second suggestion—"Be nice to your husband"—that seemed so dead-on that I scribbled it in my reporter's notebook. I hadn't heard "Be nice" in many weeks. Once I got home after my talk with Cox, I started phoning for reservations in North Carolina's Outer Banks.

A few days later, Cox and I met for lunch. I barely recognized him. Once he had a full head of hair; now he had a soldier's buzz cut. Once he was clean-shaven; now he was sporting a beard. He'd lost weight, too. We ate a little, talked a lot, and read some of each other's work. Then we got around to talking about a long story we'd seen in the *Washington Post* that day by Howard Kurtz, the *Post*'s media critic, who had interviewed me back in

Kuwait. It was a look-back at the embedding program—a balanced story, really—but the second-guessing in the article from some journalism professors who were so far from the fray infuriated me. Cox asked me what I thought.

"What do I have to say to people in the ivory tower casting judgment about what I did when they weren't there to judge for themselves, and who were too afraid to go in the first place?" I replied. "Eat my shit."

We dissolved into laughter at the voice of my inner soldier.

Before Tom and I headed for the beach, I wanted to go through the e-mail messages I'd received from readers and from friends and family members of the 101st Airborne. Buried within an avalanche of spam were more than a hundred messages responding to my work. There were so many, and they were so touching, that I broke down and wept. Having had scant access to the Internet during the war, I knew that some soldiers' families had written me, but I had no idea how large and far-flung this following was. I heard from mothers and fathers, wives and daughters, brothers and sisters, godmothers, aunts, cousins, and brothers-in-law, in addition to people who didn't know any soldiers—a Brownie troop leader, a schoolteacher, a police chief—who had reached out, expressed their support, and asked how they might help.

Many of the messages came from the Fort Campbell community and from readers in Wisconsin. But I also heard from places where the *Milwaukee Journal Sentinel* is hardly known—Greenwich, Connecticut; Manning, South Carolina; Sarasota, Florida; Birmingham, Alabama; Little Rock, Arkansas; Houston, Texas; Livermore, California; Boonville, Missouri; Forest Lake, Minnesota; Naperville, Illinois; Cincinnati, Ohio; Slippery Rock, Pennsylvania; and other places big and small.

Nothing I'd ever done professionally had generated such a response.

"I am the mom of a soldier who is attached to the 4th Battalion," Robin Moreau wrote. "Thank you for your wonderful writing. I can picture in my mind what you describe and what my son is seeing: the landscape, the weather, the environment. I know there are many, many soldiers and at some point they must all start to look alike. But, should you come across Private Damian Moreau, door gunner on one of the many Black Hawks, please tell him that I love him and am very, very proud of what he is doing.

"Thanks again for your reports. It does bring me closer to my son."

From Frances Romero, whose brother is a crew chief on a Chinook, in an e-mail message to my editors: "Just getting a sense of the troops in that region and how they are doing helps. Please thank Ms. Skiba for her courage in going over there and giving family members here a link to our loved one. And please pass along our support for our loved ones, our troops, our defenders of freedom."

From Joy Stout, the mother of Joshua, a Chinook mechanic: "Reading your articles is the second best thing to getting a letter from him. It is difficult for us (eight-year-old sister Hannah, fourteen-year-old sister, Amanda, seventeen-year-old brother Robert, and retired United States Marine Corps father, Cecil) not to have information, and the letters take their time getting to us. Keep up the good work, be safe and know that you have an avid following in Clarksville, Tennessee."

Reading their words took my breath away. I'd been residing on the equivalent of a small, faraway, and isolated planet; I'd been able to make phone calls out, but I'd not received much in the way of incoming messages.

From Teresa Parks, a sister of Brian Buol, the Bravo Company flier with the Harley flag: "I am so glad I found your Web articles. Believe it or not, it made me feel closer to my brother just reading his name. I realize what you are doing is a tremendously dangerous job. I will be following you from now on because you are with him when his family cannot be."

From Jill Beierlein, sister of Captain Jeff Beierlein, one of the other conspirators behind hoisting the Harley colors: "The story you wrote brought a huge smile to my father's face. You could not have painted a more realistic picture of how Jeff thinks and works. While it seems next to impossible to communicate with Jeff and the other soldiers outside of the letters and packages our family sends, it is great to hear the stories about him and his company through the media."

From Nicole Camejo, the wife of Corporal Ian Camejo, also assigned to the Fourth Battalion: "You are a very brave woman and I commend you for your reporting of this war. Though it is very hard for me and our four-month-old son, I know he is with a great unit and I am so proud of what he is doing. He is a wonderful father and husband. Thank you for profiling the lives of our soldiers away from home."

From Mary Alaimo, whose son, Sam Agostine, was a private within the 101st Aviation Regiment's Seventh Battalion: "Hooah for your coverage of the 159th! It is a wonderful blessing to hear where the soldiers are, what they are doing, thinking, how they sleep, what they eat, how the Iraqis respond. Should you cross paths with Sam, tell him many towns in New York, Massachusetts, Virginia, California and Ohio are anxiously waiting to hear that he has received our letters and packages."

From Carianne Brown Stinson, a sister of Corporal Matthew Brown, a twenty-nine-year-old from Ozark, Alabama, working in operations for the Fourth Battalion: "What a wonderful job you are doing. If you see Matthew, please give him our love. I will also pray for you as you are over there risking your life to keep America informed of how our troops are doing. May God bless you and keep you safe!"

That strangers had been praying for me, encouraging me, and sending me heartfelt thanks was an overwhelming revelation. It seemed like more than the wind beneath my wings. It made me wonder whether their support, and the power of their prayers, though unknown to me at the time, had helped keep me safe and carried me home.

Some people asked for copies of photos I had taken, or wanted to adopt a soldier, or send on Harley memorabilia. I tried as best I could to respond, but found I was unable to reply to every message, so I crafted a letter that I sent to almost everyone who had written.

May 1, 2003

Dear Families and Friends of the 101st Airborne,

Please accept my heartfelt thanks for encouraging and supporting my work as a journalist traveling in Kuwait and Iraq with the 159th Aviation Brigade.

I apologize for not answering your e-mails sooner. I had e-mail access for a scant two hours during seven weeks overseas and recently returned home.

I'm afraid I am unable to reply individually to many of your specific inquiries. But in light of common questions, here are a few personal observations:

- The teamwork I saw was like none I'd witnessed. We shared gear, food, words of encouragement, letters from home—and often recycled jokes for morale. My media boot camp, at Fort Benning, Georgia, last year, ran only five and a half days, but gave me the skills to stay safe and healthy. Many of your soldiers gave me assists while in theater.
- Care-package desires vary by the individual. I had access to a PX a handful of times. A small point: chocolate candy doesn't travel well in the heat. I personally appreciated packages from home with gum and travel-sized toiletries and current articles off the Internet on subjects I enjoy. Many soldiers asked me for sports news, by the way.
- Many of you asked me to contact your soldier in the 159th Brigade or other units within the 101st Airborne and only in some cases was I able to say hello on your behalf. I hope you can appreciate that reporting, taking photos, and speaking by phone to the *Milwaukee Journal Sentinel*'s sister TV and radio stations—not to mention moving forward, hand-washing clothing, and so on—put constraints on my free time.

Please know your encouragement and prayers were unexpected kindnesses that I shall never forget. Whenever I spoke to our broadcast outlets, I told them the Screaming Eagles appreciate the public's support. Our troops have my thanks, prayers, and hopes for a safe and timely return.

All good wishes.

Sincerely,

Katherine

There were two e-mail writers I left out of the mass mailing—because both of them made me furious (which, looking back, didn't take much at the time). One was from Terrance Larinto, a "close friend" to Lucky Mertes, the pilot who'd hastened me into the foxhole on the first day of the war when the brigade was threatened by one of the earliest Iraqi missiles. "I don't mean to pry into any of your business," he wrote. "I was only curious as to whether or not you are insinuating that something happened between the two of you. There does seem to be a gap in that part of the story that leaves much to the imagination."

His evidence? Larinto cited the words I had written: "Mertes, from Arlington, Washington, led me into the nearest canvas tent, where the light was low . . . Mertes calmly helped me strap on my gas mask. Then we raced together into a foxhole."

Clueless, I thought. There I was, preparing for the worst and making my peace with God, and this guy imagines I got it on with his friend. Anybody who had been in such a tight spot would have known better. But I had to reply to this one, telling Larinto that Mertes was a great soldier who'd gone out of his way to help—and left it at that. Larinto's insinuation was too absurd—and crass—to dignify with a formal denial.

Then there was Eric Larsen of Stevens Point, Wisconsin, who responded "with considerable disgust" to my story about finding the viper in my luggage. "Equally possible," he wrote, "the snake may have been the Iraqi desert equivalent of a common garter snake. Irregardless [sic], snakes play a vital role in desert ecosystems and I am saddened that their wanton destruction is sadistically described as 'cool' in your column. If you have nothing better to write about than killing the local wildlife I would suggest it is time to come back to the USA so the Iraqi snake population, at least, can live in peace."

I was incensed that someone could be fixated on snakes dying, when soldiers were being killed.

A couple of days later, after I had replied to the soldiers' families and friends, Tom and I were off to the Outer Banks. Six days on the Carolina shore went a long way to negotiating a truce with my demons and evening out my moods. It was early May, so the crowds were sparse, the beaches uncrowded, and the pace even gentler than usual. The Atlantic's waters were too cold for swimming; but sunbathing, watching the waves crash along the shoreline, power-walking on the beach, and unwinding in a hot tub proved just the tonic, along with gym workouts, massages, and bountiful meals. We were a couple again, too, although the marital skirmishes hadn't ended completely. I was still obsessing about the war, it seemed to Tom—talking about it, writing to Ruiz, and returning phone calls from friends and regaling them with tales from "the front."

Gradually, Tom and I began to understand that the difficulties of the separation had taken a toll on both of us. He'd had his pain and I'd had mine—but neither of us had seen the other's suffering. We had to take it on faith, respect it, and go forward.

Our retreat proved so restorative that we stayed a day longer than planned. But my postvacation high ended as we approached Arlington, Virginia. Just as we drove past the Pentagon, there was bad news from National Public Radio. A Black Hawk had gone down in Iraq, hitting a power line over the Tigris and crashing into the river. One soldier had survived; three were dead.

I had flown in a Hawk dozens of times, so I felt both grief and survivor's guilt as I worried that friends of mine had been killed. Why them, God, and not me?

The radio report didn't name the military unit, but I was on pins and needles, afraid that it could be Ruiz, Beierlein, Ferrell, Wood, Mertes, Ballard, or Shenk—these or any of the other guys I'd liked and admired. They'd watched my back, toughened me up, and taken me along for the ride of my life in an alien, austere, and hostile place.

On the day after the helicopter hit the power line, I got on my knees and prayed that the dead would rest in peace and rise in glory, then begged God, "Please, please, please, don't let them be from the 1-0-1."

The next day, a Saturday, I found the suspense was so unbearable that I finally called the duty officer in the Pentagon press office. I told him I'd just embedded with a helicopter unit and needed to know if the fatalities involved the 159th Brigade. He said they didn't. The three victims were from the 571st Air Medical Company in Fort Carson, Colorado. They had been on a mission to rescue an Iraqi child who suffered serious head injuries after unexploded ordnance ignited near Samarra.

After I got the news, I was relieved; then I hated myself for rejoicing for my friends while other soldiers had died.

"Comrades in arms forever"—that's what Major General Larry Gottardi, the Army's chief of public affairs, called the embedded journalists when a number of us gathered at Fort Myer in tribute to David Bloom and Michael Kelly, the two U.S. journalists who died while embedded with the Third Infantry Division. There I had the chance to express my condolences to the Kellys in person, after having sent a letter to Kelly's mother a few weeks earlier.

It wasn't just a dead helicopter crew that got to me. About this time Elizabeth Neuffer, a veteran foreign correspondent for the *Boston Globe*, was killed in a car accident in Iraq. I hadn't known her, but she, like both Kelly and me, was forty-six years old, and I saw from her obituary that she and I had reported from some of the same countries when they were hot spots. "Why her, God, and not me?" I wondered.

I never got a clear answer when I looked up at the trees and toward the heavens in my backyard sanctuary. The answer doesn't lie there or anywhere else on Earth, I imagine. It's unknowable, and I had to accept that. But the little voice inside me reminded me that I had two hands, and one beating heart—enough to make the world a better place. And I can demonstrate my gratitude for the gift of every day by being a better person.

Some days, I succeed.

In the aftermath of the invasion of Iraq, another question gnawed at me. When would the 159th Brigade come home?

In May, a Pentagon official told me that depending on how things were on the ground, it looked like June. It didn't happen. Ruiz managed to get out then—and so did a select few, including Colonel Forrester, who moved to a new command. But nearly everybody else stayed behind. Then I got an e-mail message from Iraq from Sergeant Nelda Scenie, asking if I could check out a rumor that they'd be back at Fort Campbell on the Fourth of July and welcomed by President Bush. It wasn't true. Then came word from an officer in the 159th's rear detachment at Campbell that at the earliest, it would be September. It wasn't to be.

The postponements stung, and even though I make my living bombarding people with questions, eventually I just stopped asking.

11
Reminiscing

I landed in Nashville on May 13, 2004. Stubborn clouds had drenched the music-loving capital of Tennessee, but the emerald green of spring was bursting out in every direction, suggesting hope and promise and portending rebirth.

Almost four hundred days had gone by since I'd left the Screaming Eagles, and I was delighted at the prospect of seeing them again, particularly since this time I would be skipping the off-to-war chapters, the raison d'être of my last visit.

While driving to Fort Campbell, I stepped on the gas, since I remembered the high esteem in which the military holds punctuality. Not wishing to deprive myself of one drop of local color during the drive, I punched the radio's buttons until I found a country station, then cranked up the volume.

Thanks to my addiction to coupons, I'd scored a double upgrade from the rental car company, which gave me a full-sized Chevrolet Impala with an automatic transmission. At home I drive a five-speed compact with a stick shift, so the rental felt like a battleship, but it might as well have been a birchbark canoe heading north along the Niagara toward certain doom.

Tooling along the Briley Parkway, a six-lane divided highway that skirts the Grand Ole Opry, I was parroting the singer on the radio, checking my notebook for directions, and doing god-knows-what-else. While rounding a curve, I sensed the Chevy veering dangerously toward the median barrier and tried to steer the car back on course. But I must have overcorrected, because the car swerved right and then skidded left, striking the divider and ricocheting across all three lanes of traffic. All the while, my brain silently telegraphed a single sentence: "This is not happening to me."

In the blink of an eye, I had hurtled, bounced, and banged across the slick asphalt in a 3,500-pound pinball. The Impala screeched to a halt in the far right lane, pointing in the wrong direction—which is to say, facing whatever oncoming vehicles loomed around a bend.

I steered the car around, pulled onto a meager shoulder and used my cell phone to dial 911. The space at the edge of the parkway was tight, and the traffic was too brisk for me to step out and inspect the damage. As I fingered a grape-sized lump on the top of my head, it occurred to me how lucky I was not to have hit another vehicle or been hurt worse. Semis thundered past, big and loud and in a hurry, like rogue elephants stampeding toward distilleries in West Bengal, India—you know, the ones you read about in briefs moved by Associated Press.

I was stunned, yes, but embarrassment rained down, too, and then guilt, naturally, over the devil-may-care driving that had landed me in such a fix. I managed to cut short the self-abuse upon remembering the voice of Captain Carlos Goveo, speaking from the desolate landscape of "Thunder Doo." He told me that a soldier doesn't complain; he adjusts and overcomes.

Goveo, who I'd heard was no longer with the 101st Airborne, had given my morning a mantra. There were no two ways about it: I would adjust and overcome.

It turned out the car's front bumper was a total loss, and the rear bumper sported dents on both the driver's and passenger's sides. Within a couple of hours, I had traded in the sedan for an identical model after assists from a take-charge insurance agent in McLean, Virginia, a strapping policeman from Nashville ("Possible hydroplane," he judged), and a certifiable redneck who looked like he'd lived in any number of places. He was the one who'd shown up in a tow truck that dull, soggy morning to return me and the bruised rental to the airport.

The tow truck driver remarked that I seemed like a woman who traveled a lot, and asked me if I was married, which made me smirk. Such banter virtually guaranteed that he would let me bum one of his Marlboro Reds, so I wound up smirking and smoking—inhaling deeply, in fact, after weeks of being tobacco-free. My companion was outgoing, at least, so I began to yak about the irony of having gone in and out of Iraq with the soldiers of the 101st and experiencing a close call on the outskirts of Opryland. He palmed me another cigarette for whatever lay ahead.

My trip was timed so I could see Major General David H. Petraeus turn over command of the 101st to Major General Thomas R. Turner, who formerly led the U.S. Army's 173rd Airborne, based in Italy. Petraeus, who was heralded for his work in helping restore elements of civil society in northern Iraq, had been nominated by President Bush for a promotion to three-star general, and was waiting for the U.S. Senate to make it official.

General Petraeus, like most of his soldiers, had come home from the war in February 2004 after a full year's deployment. According to the grapevine, he took just one day off and immediately jumped back into the job. Soon thereafter he was back in Iraq with a new, more challenging responsibility. He was being named the chief of the Office of Security Transition, which was charged with rebuilding Iraq's security forces. Petraeus was taking the reins from General Paul Eaton, the "CG," or commanding general, whom I'd admired at Benning when I'd trained there with other journalists.

When members of my old unit, the 159th Aviation Brigade, came home in various increments in February 2004, a lieutenant colonel retired from the 101st suggested that it would be fitting for me to show up; he'd heard that other embeds were traveling to the homecomings of their former units. Privately, though, I was relieved that I was otherwise occupied that month, covering the 2004 presidential primary election in Virginia, where it fell on February 10, and Wisconsin, where it fell on February 17. The stories had me on the road for a good stretch.

I had two reasons, actually, for not wanting to wait in a chilly hangar at an odd hour for an airliner to disgorge my weary, war-torn friends. First, I remembered how frazzled I was when I arrived home; second, and more to the point, I knew that the troops would have better things to do than waste their new freedom talking to me. They belonged in the arms of rejoicing family members and friends. With that in mind, I kept my distance, hoping they would have time and space to decompress.

The soldiers never really left me, though, not with the war being Topic A in Washington, across the country, and in capitals around the world. I'd kept up with some of them through e-mail to Tall Afar in northern Iraq, where the Fourth Battalion ended up for many months, and visited with a few others who'd already made it back to the States. After Bob Ruiz came home in June 2003, we spoke at length by phone, and I was thrilled to see him again when a conference brought him to Washington that summer. Tom enjoyed his company, to my great relief, and our get-togethers with Ruiz lifted any cloud of suspicion that may have been hanging over my battlefield friendship with the flight surgeon. Later we invited the whole family out for a visit: Bob; his wife, Phyllis; and their teenage children, Matthew and Chelsea. To me and Tom they were like long-lost relatives, not least because they had left the South and now were Chicago transplants.

I'd also been in touch with Colonel Forrester, who, before leaving Iraq, had handed over command of the 159th Brigade to Colonel William T. Harrison. Before Forrester's change-of-command ceremony, he e-mailed me an invitation: 0800 hours, 8 June 2003, Mosul Airfield's Northeast Ramp. It was tempting—exotic locales have a magnetic pull for me—but there was no way I was going back to Iraq, not just as I was starting to feel like my old self. I had been there, done that, gotten the T-shirt—if you count the plain, white Hanes undershirts I picked up for next to nothing at Camp Udairi's post exchange and ran through like Kleenex tissues.

I replied via e-mail to Forrester, asking about transportation to the ceremony. "Are you sending a bird for me?" I teased, knowing that the aircraft's range was less than four hundred miles. He returned fire with a two-letter response—"No"—and that was the end of that.

The colonel was typical of my former companions: after coming home from Iraq he was being assigned to a new installation. He was leaving Campbell to become the chief of staff at the Army Aviation Center in Fort Rucker, Alabama. Ruiz, for his part, had left Rucker for a new assignment at the U.S. Naval Station Great Lakes, just north of Chicago. Captain Jeff Beierlein, the Bravo Company commander who tipped me off to the Harley flag, wrote from Iraq to say he was destined for Fort Belvoir, Virginia.

Did I have that right? Forrester was moving to the place where Ruiz had been living but was leaving, Ruiz was moving near the place where I grew up, and Beierlein was moving to the vicinity of where I now resided. After trading messages with Beierlein, I never did catch up with him. Soon after he reached Belvoir, he returned for another tour of duty in Iraq. As I write, he's planning to leave the service of Uncle Sam and study for an MBA at Vanderbilt University in Nashville.

Figuring out who was who—and where—was like being at a masquerade teeming with revelers who were intent to play musical chairs until the wee hours of the morning. It was my first taste of trying to keep up with these flyboys stateside—if they stayed stateside, that is. Major Alex Covert—the burly, good-hearted brigade executive officer, the one with the pregnant spouse— left Iraq and returned to Campbell briefly. He next took his wife and namesake, Alex Covert, Jr., born in July 2003, to a new posting at the U.S. Embassy in Cairo. Now a lieutenant colonel, he's a security assistance officer for the Army's aviation programs in Egypt. Captain Goveo is wearing a new hat, too: after returning from the war, he studied psychological operations (PSYOP) at Fort Bragg, then jumped to Haiti to put his new training to work.

As I write, I await the arrival in Washington of Chief Warrant Officer 4 Ralph Ferrell, the short, agile, former research diver from Bangor, Maine, veteran of three wars, the flier whose own father had died in a helicopter crash in Vietnam. Ferrell's was my favorite quote of the whole war: "All I want to do when I get home is to crank the air conditioner all the way down and make snow angels on the carpet." He'll report to the Department of the Army to become the career manager for its multitude of Black Hawk pilots.

Earlier this year, while reading *USA Today*'s Life section, I spied the sunny Staff Sergeant William Tipton—"Tiptop" to me—and read that after leaving the Persian Gulf, he was reassigned to the Aberdeen Proving Ground in Maryland. Talking about the war, he told the paper, "It's all about the people I served with. You build a bond in a situation like that."

Tipton is the Detroit native who'd quipped, "Home is where I lay my helmet." He told *USA Today* that Iraq was his first taste of combat. "Everybody was scared," he admitted, "but as a platoon sergeant, I couldn't show that fear. It wouldn't do anyone any good, so I pushed it to the back of my mind and focused on getting others through safely."

The interview left me impressed with both Tipton's honesty and his sense of duty to the young soldiers with whom I'd shared a tent for several weeks.

The newspapers rarely kindled such warm memories in the months after my emotion-charged return from the Gulf. The U.S. Armed Forces' initial flush of success was punctuated by President Bush's landing on the USS *Lincoln,* which was adorned with a banner boasting "Mission Accomplished." That grand, highly orchestrated photo op soon was seen for the publicity stunt it was, as Americans collectively realized that the postwar mission had just begun, with the scattershot violence ripping up Iraq only one of the staggering challenges for coalition forces. An insurgency had caught fire, U.S. casualties were mounting, and the occupation over time—but seemingly overnight—seemed like a nightmare.

Perhaps Ted Koppel put it best, describing the transformation on the ground in Iraq in the introduction to the collected works of the late Michael Kelly, with whom Koppel had been embedded. Writing in *Things Worth Fighting For,* published by Penguin Press in 2004, Koppel said it was a strange war that took U.S. forces into Baghdad with brilliance and efficiency and subsequently metastasized into another war altogether.

The lamentable state of affairs reminded me of an axiom I'd picked up in a library book on the eve of joining the 101st Airborne: the textbook says that war never goes according to the textbook.

Periodically there were welcome developments, such as when the Screaming Eagles assisted Task Force 20, which included members of the Army's ultra-secret Delta Force, in taking out Saddam Hussein's sons, Uday and Qusay, in Mosul, on July 22, 2003. I happened to be lunching at the Pentagon with Bryan Whitman, the architect of the program to embed journalists, when he had to cut short the meal because his BlackBerry went into overdrive.

And who can forget December 14, 2003, when Paul Bremer enthused, "Ladies and gentlemen, we got him," after Saddam Hussein was plucked from a "spider hole" in Adwar, outside Tikrit, by coalition special forces and the Fourth Infantry Division?

My policeman brother, John, who was working third shift, telephoned me in the middle of the night with the news. "They got Saddam Hussein!"

he hollered, though my first groggy thought was, "John, this is too early in the morning for one of your police jokes." But John's heads-up allowed Tom and me to catch Bremer's televised press conference live from Baghdad before we each hustled to work to gather the reaction from Washington.

It was just after the Brothers Hussein were slain in the bloody gun battle that I met Bremer, a former ambassador who had been appointed the top U.S. official in Baghdad. He paid a visit to the National Press Club to appear at a "Newsmaker" luncheon at the time I chaired the club's speakers committee. He was short, taut, and, as an acquaintance from the State Department had told me earlier, had movie-star genes that shaved at least a decade off his age. He struck me as smart, suave, and brave for having accepted the task—though I had no means of assessing his work in Baghdad.

When we talked about religion—I'd read that Bremer was Catholic—he pulled from a pocket a miniature "pocket rosary" about the size of a quarter, which he carried with him at all times. Only several days later did I read that he was a marked man.

Bremer told the audience that Iraq was not a country in chaos, as sometimes portrayed. "There is not yet full democracy, but freedom is on the march," he stated. He went on to describe the establishment of a national governing council and municipal councils; the training of an Iraqi army, police force, and judiciary; the reopening of universities and hospitals; and streets bustling with all manner of commerce, from vegetable markets to satellite-dish shops.

He and others in the administration were keen to tout such advances; for a time the press drew sharp criticism for supposedly turning a blind eye to the good news in Iraq. But whatever the advances, and whatever the peace dividend Iraqis may have been enjoying, they were virtually drowned out by a drumbeat of bad news: the bombing of the United Nations headquarters, attacks on convoys, car bombings, kidnappings, assassinations, mutilations, beheadings. Each new revulsion seemed to be followed by a worse one, as the phrases "improvised explosive device" and "guerrilla war" and "Sunni Triangle" found their way from news stories into the nation's vocabulary.

As I prepared to return to Campbell in the spring of 2004, two new words were on everybody's lips: Abu Ghraib. I wondered what the soldiers would say about the Iraqi prison abuse case that was tarnishing the reputation of the United States around the world. I for one was astounded that the prison guards hadn't digested the same lecture the media received during our five-and-a-half-day, prewar "boot camp." During a session on the laws of warfare we were told, in effect, that the Geneva Conventions were to be followed in order for the United States to retain the moral high ground and, further, because it was hoped the accords would be respected if U.S. troops were taken captive.

But my wondering about Abu Ghraib was, oddly, a distraction from the hobgoblins that were staging periodic demonstrations in the distant recesses of my mind, telling me I had some nerve to go back. Didn't that make me the equivalent of a punk who'd dropped out of high school and later shown up for graduation? I'd been with the soldiers not quite two months, then bailed, while most of them had endured a full year's deployment.

On the outside, I feigned bravado, telling friends in Washington that I was going to Fort Campbell to see "my boys"—as if they were my posse. Sometimes it felt as though in the time it takes to snap a finger, I had a half-million brand-new friends, Army war fighters all. I could spot an officer in civvies from twenty feet away: high-and-tight haircut, trim waist, square shoulders, and muscular build. Once as a test of my radar I struck up a conversation on an Amtrak train with one such man in his thirties. He was seated across the aisle from me, buried in books on the Balkans. His name, I discovered, was Scott Fleeher; he was an Army major; he used to fly Apache helicopters; and he was headed to Washington to try to land a new assignment. After I rattled off a few of the highlights from my stay in Iraq, he remarked, "You've flown in combat more than I have." You could have scraped my jaw from the floor at that moment.

Around this time, though, I started to wonder how I would have felt if my husband had returned from a business trip with tales of hundreds of new, fun, and interesting acquaintances, the vast majority of them members of the opposite sex. I would have smelled a rat. Or two. Or four. Or four hundred.

The train was carrying me home from Atlantic City, where I'd covered the Miss America Pageant. After the winner was crowned, it struck me that being assigned to report on this rare assemblage of giraffe-legged women with looks that could kill, and bosoms to match, was God's way of saying, "Stop writing about G.I. Joes. Give women a little of your ink."

But on that day in May, as I was orbiting back into the universe called Fort Campbell, it would be all Army, all the time, regardless of arriving a lot later, and a little more rumpled, than intended.

First Lieutenant Walter G. Green, who was assigned to be my escort, met me outside Gate Four in the parking lot of U.S. Cavalry, the military store where I'd ruled out buying the gung-ho T-shirt that read "If you die first, we split your gear."

Immediately I recognized the boyish, twenty-five-year-old Green, who was lean and earnest, with translucent skin and light green eyes, and his background began to come into focus. He was the only American history major I'd met during the war. He had a II or a III after his name, though I couldn't remember which. He'd been in ROTC, but I couldn't place where.

He and pilot Gene Goetzke had flown me on the last mission I accompanied in Iraq, carrying infantrymen to Baghdad's city limits. Goetzke was the one who'd introduced me to the poem "High Flight," whose verses helped propel me home, as so many things midway through April 2003 seemed to do.

The lieutenant—"Call me Walt," he insisted—acted as if he was delighted to be at my disposal, calling me "Ma'am," offering to carry my bags, and treating me with kid gloves. Escort duty, it turned out, meant he was allowed to skip that morning's physical training at 0630 hours; it also would mean a reprieve from marching, with 12,000-plus other division soldiers, before Generals Petraeus and Turner and their boss, Lieutenant General John R. Vines, who commanded the XVIII Airborne Corps and Fort Bragg. The marching would take place in a ceremony known as the "pass in review," a tradition dating back to a time when the brass inspected the rank and file to evaluate the order in which units would enter battle.

Green was good company, but since I'm not one to stand on ceremony, I made sure the "Ma'am's" didn't last.

Our first stop was Sabre Army Heliport, so I could see the men and women from the flying companies in my old outfit, the Fourth Battalion of the 159th Aviation Brigade. At the entrance to Hangar Three I spotted dusty black boxes the size of steamer trunks, marked with the King of Spades from a deck of cards. The crates belonged to Bravo Company, the "Kingsmen," leading Green to observe that their stuff still was coming back in dribs and drabs from Iraq—no FedEx for these soldiers, apparently.

The hangar had eight helicopter bays where Black Hawks were being inspected and repaired. Men wearing flight suits and carrying power tools swarmed around the birds; some of the crew chiefs worked from elevated platforms, allowing top-to-bottom access to the aircraft. The helicopters were being "reset," Green said—taken apart piece by piece, examined, and refitted as needed with new components such as gear boxes and hydraulic pumps. The stress of the war—the long hours of flight, the extreme temperatures, and the unforgiving sand—had so fatigued the flying machines that, as one pilot put it, by the time the battalion left Iraq, "They were pretty much falling apart."

Some of the faces I recognized. Specialist Scott Kaeding, the crew chief who'd placed a one-dollar bet that he'd be out of Iraq by the previous August 2, stepped down from a platform to say hello and shake hands. The twenty-eight-year-old had lost a buck, but at this point was on the brink of retiring.

Next I spotted Jenkins, the young southerner who'd joked about a Humvee in Iraq stenciled with the identification number 69. The twenty-two-year-old crew chief didn't have a clue who I was; nor did he remember giving us reason to laugh by christening the vehicle the "Party Humvee." As I took notes, he seemed amazed that I'd remembered him as "Jon," not "John."

"How are you doing?" I inquired.

"Still alive," he told me. "Still getting paid."

"How long do you have left in the Army?"

"Two years, one month, and twenty-nine days."

Then I mentioned the rumor I'd heard that Fourth Bat might be going back to Iraq, possibly in 2005. "How do you feel about the prospect of going back?" I asked.

"That's my job" is all he would say.

Green and I left for the airfield, where in the distance we could see two helicopters hovering side by side at a low altitude. One carried a novice pilot who was practicing slinging a load; the other contained an instructor who I imagined was watching the trainee like a hawk. The battalion was rapidly "training up" its newcomers, who were typically in their early to mid-twenties, since so many experienced fliers, including several from my old unit, were checking out of the Army for civilian life.

Back in the hangar, as I followed Green to the battalion's flight company offices, I stopped for a few seconds to give a Black Hawk the once-over. Its dark, olive-drab nose featured the Screaming Eagle logo stenciled in black paint, just the way I remembered. Helicopters are a dime a dozen in the skies over the Washington area; even in my little cul-de-sac, a week doesn't go by without a helo thundering overhead, leading me to look through the leafy trees to see if I can make out the model—and travel back in time to the war. Still, I hadn't inspected one close up for more than a year. It felt something like running into an old flame, and being buoyed on the wings of memory to another time and place.

My old ride, I thought. I'd flown in it, slept in it, eaten in it, taken photographs in it, listened to the Dixie Chicks in it. Once I'd let one of its machine guns rip over the desert. Time and again, people had confided their life stories from within it, and based on the fragments of a diary I brought home, I'd put to paper a few tales of my own from it.

The flight company offices were located up a flight of stairs, off a long corridor bearing huge aerial maps of the United States and mementos such as photos of the Kingsmen in Vietnam. A long, intense parade of familiar faces came streaming my way as I visited these spare quarters. There were my battle-tested buddies: the captains and lieutenants and sergeants, the warrant officers, the specialists and privates. Some looked better than I remembered—more muscular or confident—but some were flabbier or paler than I recalled from our days in the desert, since if nothing else they'd lost their suntans. It startled me to see them in drab-olive camouflage now instead of beige "desert camo"; and their inexpensive desks, chairs, and office fixtures seemed like small wonders, since I'd known these soldiers in such primitive surroundings.

There was thirty-seven-year-old 1st Sergeant Lance Peeler, the Miami native who'd served in Special Forces, the soldier I'd turned to for self-defense lessons. There was my occasional tentmate Alicia Chivers, the captain, the woman who hailed from Montana and made it through West Point, the one who married a tall, fair-haired West Pointer from Idaho, himself a captain in the 101st, whose sweet, blond looks brought to mind a Hummel doll. And there was another alum of the U.S. Military Academy, Captain Mark Lynskey, who conjured up the impromptu sleeping arrangements after the first wild sandstorm in Kuwait.

"Do you remember that night?" he asked me. "You were on the floor between me and Major Shenk. We were spooning," he joked, to laughter.

I'd completely forgotten that, having spent the night ruing the day Matt Cox was born, blaming my journalist friend for my accidental plunge into a pool of water, and, more to the point, my shivering wet feet.

During such "How the heck are you?" reminiscing, the soldiers and I traded stories fast and furiously. Just like Jenkins, sometimes I had amnesia over who someone was or what had happened or why or when or where.

As I passed by the staff of the flight operations office, I was met with some blank faces, so someone called out a verbal prompt to trigger their memory of who I was. This person—it might have been Chivers, who'd been promoted to commander of Alpha Company—remarked: "You remember Katherine, the girl with the snake in her bag!"

The appellation struck me as something out of Homer's *Odyssey*, more mysterious and apt to inspire terror than another of my wartime nicknames, "Reporter Lady," a moniker as intimidating as a cone of soft-serve vanilla ice cream, and as likely to melt in the heat, which Lynskey informed me had climbed to fifty-two degrees Celsius—or almost 126 degrees Fahrenheit—after I'd bagged out.

As our minds reeled back to the camps we'd called home in Kuwait and Iraq, some soldiers injected a serious note into the otherwise jovial storytelling. "It meant a lot to me when you asked your editor to e-mail my father and to tell him that I was OK, and to make sure he knew about your paper's Web site," one told me.

"We knew you were coming," a pilot remarked. "And my wife made a point to tell me to thank you for your stories."

"There were some days you hung in there better than we did," a sergeant volunteered. "And that's saying something, since you're from the civilian sector."

Meantime there were mutterings about the former commander of the Fourth Battalion whom many loved to loathe: Lieutenant Colonel Sabb. I knew he'd gone on to study at the Air Force War College at Maxwell Air Force Base in Alabama; the word was that he'd been offered a teaching job there.

Our discussion of Sabb's temperament was like a long, intense game of Kick the Can. People had long memories, offering up Exhibits A, B, and C as if trying to persuade a judge to rule the evidence admissible in the court of public opinion. I was flabbergasted, since in the field people either regarded Sabb with a modicum of respect or toted an invisible ten-foot pole when he was in the vicinity. Of course I knew where Ruiz and a few confidantes stood, but now I was surprised to find nary a single Friend of Tony.

One enlisted man said that before leaving Iraq, Sabb had chewed out a captain who commanded a company until this subordinate was in tears. Sabb called him a piece of crap and a disgrace to the entire United States Army, then twisted the knife by vowing that he would "do everything in his power to see [the captain's] command fail."

A pilot said that once before he set out to fly with Sabb, someone took him aside and suggested, "Why don't you 'auger' the helicopter and take one for the team?" Translated: Crash the bird, plummet to your death, but liberate us from our commander.

A sergeant told me he refused to salute Sabb at the conclusion of command-and-staff meetings; instead, he slid his notebook off the table so he could bend over, collect the book, and skip the show of respect.

A warrant officer brought up Sabb's farewell to the troops. "It was like a bad B-grade movie," the officer said. "We were all, like, 'Go away.'"

"Cruel" was another sergeant's shorthand description of Sabb. "Difficult" was another assessment. "Never worked with anyone like him before" was the most generous view I picked up.

As I listened to the stories, I shook my head, deadpanning, "We'll all be in therapy for a long time over Lieutenant Colonel Sabb."

In retrospect, I understood that my present confidantes had been my allies. Sensing that the lieutenant colonel and I were engaged in a cold war, they'd watched my back, tipped me off to the latest news, and signaled when big missions were in the offing. "They thought you were a nice person," one of their wives said to me, "and they felt they had to take care of you."

One soldier told me he felt badly that I'd been assigned to Sabb's Fourth Battalion. I told him that by the time I'd gotten the commander's number, I had plenty of other allies in Fourth and was ambivalent about switching units. I said that I simply decided to give Sabb a wide berth, reasoning that "sometimes the devil you know is better than the devil you don't."

My friends were earnest, level-headed fliers who hadn't seemed to mind a civilian in a dirty ponytail running around and rattling off questions when she wasn't waving around a cigarette and asking why on earth the Army insisted on this or that.

Another wife from the 101st, meeting me at a book signing in Washington held for Rick Atkinson, who also wrote about the division's time in Iraq, blew me away with an offhand comment. "The soldiers must have *loved* having you around," she said. "You look like Marilyn Monroe."

"I can assure you," I told her, "that I did not look like Marilyn Monroe then." Trust me, I continued, there were days comedienne Phyllis Diller compared favorably to me. What I neglected to say is that one of my jokes—the one from Paul Eshom—was raunchier than anything Diller ever told. I repeated Eshom's joke "Why does it suck to be an egg?" across southern and central Iraq only to learn, after I was home in Virginia, that the joke was even dirtier than I had thought.

Q: Why does it suck to be an egg?

A: Because you only get laid once. You only get eaten once. When someone sits on your face, it's your mother. And when you come, you're in a box with eleven other guys.

My husband Tom, hearing this too many times, finally asked me if I knew what "box" meant in slang. I didn't. When he enlightened me, my hand sprang to my mouth; I'd assumed Eshom was referring to an egg carton.

But at Campbell, my comedic miscalculation just gave me and my old buddies another Beetle Bailey moment to guffaw over. There was lots of laughter during my few days' reunion back at Campbell. Surviving a war inspires a certain euphoria. Our basic differences—their being warriors, me a wannabe armed with a gel pen—dissolved under the glare of one fundamental truth: we'd returned from Iraq with the ultimate treasure—our lives. At times it felt as though we'd staged a jail break, evaded the long arm of the law, and reconnoitered in a lush forest draped in the morning mist, precisely at the spot where we'd buried our loot.

Not that everyone was delighted to see me. Amid the pats on the back there was at least one cold-eyed stare, and some others appeared to be indifferent. It seemed that people who loved me still loved me; the ones who hated me, hated me; and those who didn't care one way or the other hadn't budged an inch. I could live with that. The Army's soldiers were simply a microcosm of the larger world: some folks like journalists, some don't, and some don't care one way or the other.

To be sure, there was much I hadn't shared with these men and women whose memories rattled around my head and danced in my heart for many months afterward. They'd traveled many miles and endured much after I left them—and I was all ears.

I'd missed the move to Baghdad International Airport, where many fell ill with gastrointestinal troubles; the long, nervous convoy to Tall Afar; the occasional mortar attacks; and even an outbreak of leishmaniasis—an ailment I'd inserted into a story in part for the challenge of spelling the word correctly. And it actually happened! Those who caught what I'd dubbed the "sand fly's revenge" were shipped all the way to Walter Reed Army Medical Center for treatment, which happened to be just a twenty-minute cab ride from my Washington office. I wished they'd thought to call me; I would have visited them. In fact, they might have been there while I was at Walter Reed, profiling a soldier who'd lost both of his legs in Iraq.

I was home, too, while the 159th Brigade endured the on-again, off-again rumors that had the unit packing up and heading home, invariably followed by clarifications that had their hopes crash and burn.

From a crew chief: "First they said we'll be home in June; then June came and went. Then it was we'll be home in September; and September came and went. There were times I sat on my cot and said, 'When is this crap going to end?' Finally they said we'll be home by March 1, 2004. It was a relief to know. Our orders had us on a deployment for up to 364 days, so that was the longest time that we could be there."

Late in the afternoon Green drove me to see the Fourth Battalion's Command Sergeant Major, Don Gregg. He fit into the category of people who looked better than ever; he seemed calmer and cleaner, with a spiffier haircut. After we exchanged hugs, he told me there was someone new in his life.

We stepped outside his office and headed for the parking lot, where I bummed one of his familiar Marlboro Ultra Lights. Gregg stopped and leaned against a turquoise-colored sports car, a 1994 Chevy Camaro, which I learned was his. Grinning, he explained, "Still gotta have my toys."

Except for the snazzy car, the scene was pure déjà vu: the afternoon sun was sinking, my work was temporarily on hold, and Gregg and I were trying to make sense of it all. Overseas, we'd shared at least a dozen afternoons like this; and here, as there, conversation came easily. He didn't even flinch from Abu Ghraib. "Those prison guards were shitbags. They dishonored the uniform," he said. "But it wasn't torture. They didn't cut anyone's head off."

It was classic Gregg: blunt, colorful, and idiosyncratic. The plain-spoken command sergeant major characteristically lobbed verbal gems such as "shit storm" and "cosmic coincidence" and "It was like having your ass handed back to you."

Gregg was the one who had decided, during the war, that I had "balls" after the Iraqi missile careened dangerously toward our camp and was destroyed by a Patriot. At the time, his offhand comment was the equivalent of my being handed long-stemmed red roses bound together with a gossamer ribbon—and was one of the reasons he was among those I turned to if I needed an Army acronym deciphered or had to decide whether to go on the first air assault into Iraq.

To my surprise, he told me he'd hung on to the reading glasses I'd given him when I'd left Iskandariyah for home. I went through "readers" the way some people lose winter gloves, so it was unthinkable to me that he still had them.

But Gregg, on the surface at least, was nothing like me. He'd had three marriages, three divorces, and eleven addresses in the last seven years—which made me like him more, for keeping on keeping on, if nothing else. Now he was preparing to retire, and had mixed emotions about it. Like so many others I'd come to know, Gregg used the word "love" when talking about the Army and its soldiers.

We went back into his large, neat-as-a-pin office and with no prodding whatsoever he began telling me what happened within the Fourth Battalion after I'd left the field. He brightened as he told me of his homecoming on February 3, which fell on his fifty-first birthday, then said drily, "It had been a real long trip."

When I asked him to tell me about the highs and lows, he immediately identified getting out of my last encampment, Iskandariyah—"the most god-awful place you can imagine"—and making a safe passage to the unit's final home many miles to the north in Tall Afar. "We were able to drive there unmolested, which was a good thing, since there was still fighting going on."

The battalion, early on, enjoyed relatively calm days and nights, while other parts of Iraq simmered and boiled over. The aviation unit was working hand in glove with the so-called Rakkasans, the soldiers of the Third Brigade of the 101st, and ferried them on missions in an expansive section of northern Iraq that shared strategically important borders with Syria, Turkey, and Iran. Their area of operation, in fact, was named "AO Rakkasan" in a nod to the infantry.

According to Gregg, the quiet came to an abrupt end when insurgents killed two infantrymen during an attack on July 20, 2003, at a security checkpoint near Tall Afar, which is situated about eighteen miles outside of Iraq's third-largest city, Mosul.

"There were some rocket-propelled grenades and small-arms fire, and the two guys went to other checkpoints to warn them," he said.

And the dead? "A guy named Jordan and a guy named Garvey," he answered. "It was a little bit of a wake-up call, because for four months we were not molested," he continued. "Later there was some activity, but it was nothing like the Sunni Triangle."

In addition to supporting the Rakkasans of the Third Brigade, the Fourth Battalion flew missions on behalf of the entire 101st Airborne Division while contending with a diminishing pool of veteran pilots and shortages of aircraft maintenance parts. By the time they arrived home in 2004, battalion fliers had logged more than 10,000 hours of combat flying.

Gregg related some of the lighter moments of the deployment, such as a Fourth of July cookout when men kept an eye on the grills while wearing frilly, old-fashioned aprons. Air temperatures on the holiday rivaled the blast emanating from the red-hot charcoal. One perk was an Internet café. Another was a place they named "The Cantina," an air-conditioned room where refreshments were served and the soldiers could unwind. Some were given passes to enjoy R&R in a Kurdish area, Dihok, near Turkey; others got to make a short trip into Turkey; and the luckiest of all were given permission for a two-week leave to the States. In the last case, Gregg said, the priority went to those who had served in Afghanistan in advance of Iraq.

By the time I talked with Gregg, I'd heard plenty of complaints from the other soldiers about the withering heat, the uncertainty over the length of the deployment, and the déjà vu feel that some of the air missions took on. But what Gregg told me next made it clear that these were petty frustrations. Nothing compared to what went down as Thanksgiving neared.

The old soldier took a deep breath, remembering Saturday, November 15, 2003. "That was the darkest day," he said.

After sunset that evening two Black Hawks from the 159th Brigade collided in midair over a residential section of Mosul. One helicopter's rotor blades tore into the other's tail boom during the collision, sending both into dangerous spins before they slammed onto rooftops, roughly 250 yards apart, and burst into flames.

It was at that point the single deadliest incident of the war in Iraq for the U.S. Armed Forces. Seventeen soldiers, from thirteen different states, were dead. From Vermont to New Jersey to North Carolina to West Virginia to Kentucky to Mississippi to Illinois to Wisconsin to Texas to South and North Dakotas to Oregon to California, the country shuddered at news of the catastrophe.

Even President Bush, who seemed reluctant to address the mounting casualties, spoke to White House reporters about the crash after returning from Camp David. "It doesn't matter whether it's in a chopper crash or an IED [improvised explosive device], the loss of life is sad," he said.

According to Gregg, one of the helicopters was from his Fourth Battalion; the other was from the Ninth Battalion. Both were part of the 101st

Aviation Regiment under the command of the 159th Aviation Brigade. The birds, on separate missions, had flown without their exterior lights as a precautionary measure to avoid becoming the target of small-arms fire, a rocket-propelled grenade, or worse.

Both helicopters' pilots and crew were using night-vision goggles, according to Gregg, who didn't have to remind me of one of the lessons I picked up during the war: flying helicopters in combat is inherently hazardous, and the difficulty multiplies when flying with NVG.

The skies were dark when the aircraft collided about 6:30 p.m. local time. Initial reports were sketchy, especially at the outlying Tall Afar. "All we had is broken [radio] transmissions from the tower," Green, my escort, told me. "Nobody knew what went down."

Officials said the Fourth Battalion bird, transporting soldiers from Tall Afar, was in its final approach to Runway 15 at Mosul Airport. In two miles—just minutes—it would have made it to the ground. The Ninth Battalion aircraft, operating out of Mosul, was carrying artillerymen during a routine evening mission known as "Eyes over Mosul." That mission had airborne soldiers keeping their eyes fixed on the city for about three hours at a stretch; the idea was to have a helicopter loaded with troops in the vicinity if activity on the ground called for more firepower and support.

Initial news accounts indicated that the Fourth Battalion aircraft may have been hit by gunfire or a rocket-propelled grenade, leading to speculation that it made an evasive maneuver and careened into the other aircraft. But at Fort Rucker, where the Army Aviation Center is based, the commanding general, E. J. Sinclair, whom I'd met at Camp Udairi in Kuwait, discounted those reports. He and others familiar with the crash said that while there had been fighting on the ground, no evidence from the crash sites confirmed that either aircraft had been hit by hostile fire. "Bottom line, it was an aircraft accident," Sinclair said.

The birds dropped from the sky so hard that an eyewitness saw the Ninth Battalion's main rotor blade flex and shear off part of the roof of its cockpit. There was so much confusion initially that the first official account of the disaster listed twelve dead and nine injured.

Gregg raced from Tall Afar to the grisly scene, accompanied by Lieutenant Colonel Steve Burns, a forty-year-old who had taken Sabb's place as commander of the Fourth Battalion. Gregg told me that as soon as he and Burns laid eyes on the charred, twisted heap of metal—the only remnants of the Fourth Battalion aircraft—they lost hope that anyone inside had survived. "We pretty much knew when we saw the wreckage that no one was getting out of that one," Gregg said. "We were heartbroken. It was numbing. It stung."

One by one, he recited the names of the six who perished from his battalion, then exhaled deeply. They'd been dead only six months, too short a time for anyone to shake the overwhelming shock and sadness. "Everybody in the battalion knew them," Gregg said of the dead. "These were the guys they worked with and were friends with."

He asked me whether I'd ever heard of the Final Roll Call, a ritual enacted during a memorial to a fallen soldier. As roll is called, those soldiers present say, "Here," but when the names of the dead are sounded, there is only a gut-wrenching silence.

Gregg said the names of the departed were called out three times: first, by rank and surname; then by rank, first name, and surname; and finally by rank, first name, middle name, and surname. His description made my heart heavy. "It's the part of the service when people lose it," he volunteered. "That's when they come unglued. I saw full-bird colonels in tears that day. They feel responsible for every soldier."

Later, while watching a video from the service, I learned that Gregg himself had conducted the final roll call. It went like this:

Specialist Baker. Specialist Ryan Baker. Specialist Ryan Travis Baker.

Specialist Digiovanni. Specialist Jeremiah Digiovanni. Specialist Jeremiah Joseph Digiovanni.

Specialist Dusenbery. Specialist William Dusenbery. Specialist William David Dusenbery.

Sergeant Russell. Sergeant John Russell. Sergeant John Wayne Russell.

CW 2 Saboe. CW 2 Scott Saboe. Chief Warrant Officer 2 Scott Arlo Saboe.

Lieutenant Wolfe. Lieutenant Jeremy Wolfe. Second Lieutenant Jeremy Lee Wolfe.

The Final Roll Call suggested that all that these soldiers were, all the names that they carried, all the things that they had achieved, all the plans that they had made, all their yesterdays, todays, and tomorrows—had vanished.

As Lieutenant Green described it, I understood how the anguish that had met the initial reports of the crash—amid the uncertainty about what had happened and who had been killed—had been followed by new spasms of sadness. The dead soldiers' belongings remained at Tall Afar, frozen in place, exactly as they'd been left: empty green cots and perspiration-drenched pillows, shaving kits and dirty socks, prized compact discs, books, and magazines, cherished family photos, half-finished letters home. I recalled the sleeping quarters so well that I could practically taste the sweat.

"It was a job for the crew chiefs to sort through it," Green said. "All their stuff just left as it was. Someone found a letter tucked in a Bible, in an envelope marked, 'A Letter to My Son, if Something Ever Happens to Me.' "

As Green told it, the loss of these comrades prompted some soldiers to make it known that if something happened to them, they did not want to put their families through the ordeal of having to sort through their things. They expressed a desire that only a few things of theirs be sent back, like a watch or a wallet or their dog tags.

Krystal Carter, the young cook who regarded me like a mother, said living through the deaths of the soldiers was like nothing she'd been through. She was a twenty-year-old private when I first met her as Sha-Nay-Nay; she turned twenty-one on the day I left Iraq. Now promoted to the rank of specialist, my friend was all of twenty-two.

Carter told me about the memorial—six helmets, six pairs of desert boots, and six framed portraits in place of the six men who had disappeared as if into thin air. "You probably would have cried, Momma," she said. "They were there, and all of a sudden, they were gone."

For Burns, the Fourth Battalion's new commander, the deaths presented a dual challenge. He said he wanted nothing more than to give care and comfort to those who had lost friends, but on tap the very next day was a major air move involving eighteen aircraft—ten Black Hawks and eight Chinooks—transferring Rakkasans from the Third Brigade of the 101st to the Third Armored Cavalry Regiment. The combat mission went forward. Afterward, Burns wrote letters to the families of the six soldiers; and, recognizing that his surviving troops were grieving, urged them to share their memories, to keep the names of the dead alive, to never let them be forgotten, and to refuse to have their deaths be in vain. Talking about the memorial service, he said: "People put their hearts into it. Everybody was friends with these guys; we'd been living in an area the size of a football field together for six months at the end of an airstrip: just tents, a mess hall, and some shower points. Everybody had a personal stake in it. These people were wonderful soldiers, friends, persons, and fathers."

I saw from the video that Major Jerzy Rsazowski, the brigade's Polish-American chaplain who was my fast friend, opened the service with a prayer. Captain Kerry Greene then proceeded to conduct the memorial. Greene was the Southerner, the Bible-thumper whom I initially found too touchy-feely, the officer who urged me not to leave before the push into Iraq, the person who'd called me a "positive force." Greene had believed in me—something I came to appreciate only in retrospect.

As American flags whipped in brisk winds, mourners in desert-camouflage uniforms rose from ordinary white plastic patio chairs, the kind they sell during the summer months in front of grocery stores for $4.99, and sang "The Star-Spangled Banner." Later in the service came "Amazing Grace." Burns, the battalion boss, called the six men "best of the best."

"A dangerous mission continues with great sacrifices now made willingly every day by our nation's finest young souls, all ready to make the ultimate act of service, if necessary, to ensure the mission is achieved," he said. "The loss of these great men has hurt us all, but the pain will pass. We will remember the best of each of them and move forward, because that is what they would want us to do, and that is what our mission demands."

Gregg, telling me about the disaster, remarked, "Five people lived from the Ninth Battalion bird. I don't know how. I haven't figured that out yet. In one of those cosmic coincidences, one of them was a pilot named Gregg. A chief warrant officer 4. Spelled the same way. No relation."

When I returned home from Campbell, I examined old news stories of the crash. Immediately after the collision, Ruiz had e-mailed me, urging me to pray for the soldiers and their families and saying he'd tell me more later. But before I heard from him again, I read the names of the dead in the newspaper; none at the time rang a bell. Some had arrived in theater only after I left. As I studied their photographs, I suspected I'd crossed paths with Saboe, a pilot from Alpha Company who was distinctive not only for his height, but for his blond hair and mustache, which were the color of wheat.

Far be it for me to pretend to know what it felt like to descend into a black hole of grief, hurt, and tears in the aftermath of the loss of the seventeen soldiers. Mine was only a "keyhole" view of the 159th Aviation Brigade, limited to the time I was there, the major combat phase of the war. Even then I bore witness in only a small way to a military conflict that was grand in scale, taking in sailors, airmen, and marines I'd never met, just as events were constantly changing, like the brilliant pieces of cut glass mirrored in a kaleidoscope. I absorbed only what I was close enough to see and hear, or what soldiers who weren't allergic to journalists cared to pass on.

There's so much I'd like to know but don't, like what became of the young man who was having dinner while I was at the Horseshoe Steak House in Hopkinsville, Kentucky. I'd eavesdropped as he and his parents said their good-byes, conjuring up extreme outcomes for him, from a Bronze Star to an Arlington burial.

But that mystery aside, a few things I do know. I've seen the faded and tired yellow ribbons sagging from utility poles up and down Fort Campbell Boulevard, dampened by spring's rainfall, bleached by summer's sunshine, blown by autumn's winds, bruised by winter's tempests. By the time I returned in May 2004, the ribbons had faded to pearly white and, in the wake of the steady rain, might have been weeping for the sixty soldiers from

Fort Campbell and the 101st Airborne Division who'd lost their lives during the first year of Operation Iraqi Freedom.

I've sat across from officers from the 101st and watched them tear up, recalling the circumstances that took a friend's life and struggling to maintain a stiff upper lip. They never seemed to want to cry in front of me. One of these men confided over dinner that he never wants to go to another war; he told me he would be a happy man if he never heard a bugle intoning "Taps" again. The very day after I heard this somber admission, a Cabinet secretary who had recently traveled to Iraq had his spokesman tell me that the secretary had found troop morale to be "high." Given what my acquaintance had told me, I chose not to put that lie into my story.

I've spoken to one of the Screaming Eagles' new widows, a woman who described her late husband's virtues in the present tense, as if, eight months after his death, he would stroll in the door at half past five with a chipper, "Honey, I'm home." She told of the grief groups dotting Fort Campbell that gather bereaved spouses together, as they try to salve some of the wounds I am sure will never truly disappear; she said the groups seem to help the adults more than the kids. She told me that she found the six-month milestone hard, but now she was doing better, trying to remain strong for her two sons, and holding fast to the "blessing" that she'd had her warrior husband for eighteen and a half years.

I cried as she spoke, sensing her pain and knowing that if I lost my own Tom, I'd be devastated. How empty the house would be. How strange to see his image in photos of us from black-tie dinners and far-flung trips lining the walls and bookshelves. How the dog would look up at me mournfully and whimper, as if I had an answer.

When I told Ruiz about my feelings, he told me he thought I was still feeling survivor's guilt, but my friend the flight surgeon didn't tell me what cured it.

I know now that if you go to war, you roll the dice and gamble everything for a paycheck or for glory or for a cause greater than yourself.

You might make it home just fine, find a girl, grab some gusto in Manhattan, decide that's not enough and move on to Disneyworld, then pop the question. That's what happened to Jamey Trigg, the officer who helped me edit my photos in the desert way back when. The Christmas cookies I sent him after I'd returned home were meant as a peace offering; only after he came home did I apologize for having lost my temper with him.

Or, as happened, you could return stripped of a command; booted home in disgrace; shipped back to the States because you're pregnant; sent packing because you'd lost your mind; or hurt so gravely you'll never fly again.

Was the outcome ruled by God, or the fates? Was it predestined? Was it happenstance?

You might come home missing your legs from the knees down, like Private First Class Alan Lewis, a young infantryman from Milwaukee whom I'd written about as he began to mend at Walter Reed. After doing one story on Lewis, I went back for a follow-up piece when he took his early steps with his high-tech prostheses. Lewis wound up collecting his Purple Heart from the president, appearing on CBS's *Forty-Eight Hours,* and being "adopted" by some good-hearted Vietnam veterans from a Veterans of Foreign Wars post in Lake Geneva, Wisconsin. One reader responding to my stories tucked a $100 bill into a Bible for his mother; a suburban Milwaukee police chief wrote how chastened he felt reading about Lewis; he'd just been diagnosed with diabetes and thought his world had come to an end.

Or you might come home as Paul Eshom did.

From the Associated Press, November 20, 2003. Dateline, Mosul. "A soldier from Wyoming is being credited with saving two fellow servicemen from a crashed Black Hawk. Pilot Richard Gregg, a chief warrant officer, said Wednesday in an interview with the *Los Angeles Times* that he owed his life to Specialist Paul Eshom, of Pinedale, Wyoming."

After coming across the story, I tracked down Eshom, whom, until then, I'd remembered chiefly for the infamous egg joke. I'd liked the twenty-two-year-old crew chief as much for his sense of humor as his upbringing in some of the West's sacred spaces.

Eshom had no qualms about speaking to me about the crash—he's an extroverted guy, and we'd clicked earlier—but at times I sensed that the retelling was tough for him. He said he'd acted as crew chief and door gunner on the "Eyes over Mosul" missions with fliers from his Ninth Battalion many times, always uneventfully. On November 15 things went sour about fifteen minutes after take-off, when his Black Hawk was about three hundred feet above ground, traveling a leisurely forty-four miles an hour.

A call over the radio told the pilots and crew to check for trouble on the streets after reports of an explosion and small-arms fire. From the air, Eshom spied what looked like a Dumpster on the street that seemed to be the spot where the blast erupted. Next he saw U.S. soldiers break from their routine of combing the streets in single-file columns; instead the troops ran, split up, and took cover, suggesting to Eshom that they'd engaged the enemy.

"I thought, 'Whoa, whoa, that's the first time I've seen that.' It seemed like a firefight," he remembered.

He didn't hold the thought for long. Next: "Boom, all of a sudden there was a loud bang and the aircraft went tail high, nose low, at about eighty degrees. And that is a bad deal."

Eshom, who was manning the machine gun on the left side of the aircraft, feared the helicopter had been hit by a rocket-propelled grenade or a missile. He had no clue that another Black Hawk was the culprit. All he knew was that his helicopter began spinning right, which was an ominous indication, suggesting the loss of tail-rudder thrust. Aviators know that two things cause a helicopter to plummet from the sky in a hurry: one is the loss of power in both engines; the other is the disappearance of tail-rudder thrust, in which case, as Eshom put it, "you have no control over how the aircraft is going to land."

A single sentence—practically a crude prayer—flashed through Eshom's consciousness as the aircraft tumbled toward rooftops: "I do not want my parents to get this phone call." The helicopter came down with a bang, slamming hard into a roof. Eshom sensed that he was jostled but not badly hurt, suffering only bumps and bruises and a cut to his face where his night-vision goggles had dug in. Immediately he wondered, "Who's still alive?"

He got out of the bird in such a hurry that he hadn't thought to remove his harness, so the tether slammed him backward against the helicopter's exterior. He used the Gerber knife he kept at hand to free himself from the cord and hastened to check on Gregg, the pilot who'd been directly in front of him. He got no response whatsoever from the flier.

Eshom knew that Gregg, an experienced, thirty-nine-year-old flier who'd risen to become a chief warrant officer 4, had done the only thing he could reasonably do: pull back on the helicopter's cyclic stick, thereby altering the aircraft's pitch to avoid the prospect of careening nose-first into the roof.

Now Gregg was lying very still, and the copilot, Erik C. Kesterson, a twenty-nine-year-old chief warrant officer 1, was in worse shape. Kesterson had suffered such severe head injuries that it was clear he was dead.

Then Eshom heard someone crying, "Get me out of here! Get me out of this aircraft!" He recognized the voice as belonging to Sergeant Robert "Burke" Shelton, who'd been manning the machine gun on the side of the helicopter opposite Eshom's position. When the helicopter had spun treacherously to the right and then had hit the roof, Shelton, seated on the right side of the aircraft, did the equivalent of a body-slam against the interior wall.

As he rounded the cockpit, Eshom felt heat emanating from the aircraft; it had caught fire. Equally threatening was the gunfire coming from the ground below. For a split second he took stock of the situation—"We're taking fire. Should I take cover?"—but ignored that impulse, instead rushing over to the window to yank Shelton out.

Eshom's fellow crew chief was banged up from head to toe, with injuries to his head and back, a broken collarbone, cracked ribs, and a shattered leg.

Eshom recalls that as he dragged Shelton out, his colleague passed out, so searing was the pain.

Next Eshom returned to the cockpit, where he heard Gregg muttering softly. He tugged at the pilot's legs, trying to ascertain whether he had sensation in his limbs. It was just what the manual said: check for a spinal-cord injury before moving an injured soldier so as not to exacerbate a broken neck or back. Gregg, sensing that time was precious, would have none of it, insisting, "Just get me outta here, man!"

As the young crew chief began to pull the pilot out, U.S. soldiers appeared on the rooftop from the streets; some hurried to help Eshom extract Gregg, while others began to lay down suppressive fire to put an end to the shooting coming from below. Talking about the reinforcements, Eshom remembers his sense of wonder. "It was like they appeared out of thin air," he said. "All of a sudden, five dudes, standing on the roof."

By then another passenger, who'd survived with only a broken arm, had climbed out on his own. Another was seriously burned; he was helped out by the reinforcements from the ground. "Everybody," Eshom told me, "did everything they could to make it a better situation." Altogether, seven men aboard his aircraft died; and five, including Eshom and the two he helped carry to safety, survived.

When he retrieved his M-60D to help put down the enemy fire, the weapon wouldn't fire, as its barrel had been badly bent in the accident. Eshom and other soldiers used it as a battering ram to break open a door on the rooftop; the reinforcements had scrambled to the crash scene via an exterior staircase, which was not considered a safe evacuation route in light of the persistent gunfire.

Eshom received the Purple Heart for his injuries, a torn knee and sprained ankle and wrist. His name also was put forward for a Bronze Star; but nine months later, when he and I spoke, it hadn't arrived.

"I'm not an award hunter," he told me, insisting that it didn't matter, though I didn't agree.

Eshom was the kind of guy who knew his weapon, his aircraft, and its manuals; moreover he was so fit he hardly broke into a sweat during physical training. He'd always been physically active, having first strapped on skis when he was five years old, and it was just the beginning of a love affair with the rugged, majestic mountains of his boyhood, where he camped, hiked, hunted, and later, only weeks before the war in Iraq, proposed to his girlfriend with a plastic ring from a gumball machine.

Though the 101st generals knew him now, before the crash he wouldn't have been considered recruiting-poster material. The problem? It may have been his mouth. Once, during a mission in Iraq months earlier, he was fed up with being chewed out by a superior, so he replied to the officer over the radio, "I'm sorry, Sir, but your brain is operating at a lower frequency than the rest of us, causing your speech to come in broken and unreadable."

Another time this same superior, while filling sandbags, was struggling with the string used to seal the bags, giving Eshom another opening. "That's the 10 percent rule," he cracked, loud enough for those in the vicinity to hear. "You have to be 10 percent smarter than the equipment you're working with."

His back talk didn't go unnoticed; in fact, it caused him to be reassigned from the superior's helicopter to other aircraft. The transfer didn't faze Eshom, who was not unlike the craggy-faced wranglers he'd seen in his youth. They would sooner turn in their spurs than lick another man's boots.

The crash gave Eshom fifteen days leave stateside, which allowed him to return to his fiancée, Jamie Cunningham, a twenty-one-year-old who'd just finished Army service. She'd been a specialist working in supply for the Ninth Battalion; in fact, they'd served together in Iraq for half a year. But she'd received orders to return home after those six months, completing her time in the Army at the end of 2003.

They'd met in Clarksville, Tennessee, just outside Campbell, at a "battle of the bands" concert. Just in from a tour in Korea, Cunningham was alone, having a cigarette, so Eshom asked her for a match, never mind that he had a lighter in his pocket. Cunningham struck him as outgoing, free-spirited, and fun-loving. She was a small-town girl from Chelsea, Oklahoma, and he was a small-town guy, from Pinedale, Wyoming, population 1,200, smack in the middle of ranching country, a town without so much as a stop light.

His parents had divorced when he was two, but his father, who ran a Western art and framing shop, remarried a woman with a son just four months Eshom's junior. The stepbrothers, just one grade apart in school, were inseparable in their boyhood, and remained close. The Eshoms were regulars at Pinedale Bible Church—not that the family, in Paul's words, "threw a Bible in your face every time they saw you."

Eshom admitted to having "raised a little hell" now and again in a place known for big-game hunting and an annual three-day rodeo. Over time he yearned for a life beyond the region's snaggle-toothed mountains. He'd developed an interest in flying, and had been making model airplanes from the time he could fold paper, and advanced to rehearsing before flight simulators "from the time I knew how to turn on a computer."

After he talked to an Army recruiter, Eshom signed up for a six-year hitch under the delayed-entry program, allowing him to graduate from high school, in his class of sixty, before heading off in 2000 to basic training at Fort Jackson, South Carolina.

Eshom found the physical training a breeze; the bigger adjustment was living in close quarters with big-city kids, some of whom had never seen the inside of a tent. He'd felt completely in command of things in his small Western town, but he soon realized that Uncle Sam now controlled virtually his every waking hour. "In the Army, you are never in control," he said, "so you just simply hang on and go for the ride."

Drill sergeants, sleep deprivation, homesickness—none of the usual things rankled him, because he always saw the whimsical, ironic, absurd side of life, and he was quick with a quip. "I love to make people laugh—even if it involves making an ass out of myself," he told me. "I think life is too short not to smile, and if you go through life as a grumpy old man, it's not fun."

Jamie Cunningham sensed that life with this "goofy, laid-back guy" would never lack for laughter—or adventure. In January 2003, before deploying to the Persian Gulf, they'd scraped together enough leave time to visit his family out West. His family took a liking to her, and before their return to Campbell, Eshom drove his girlfriend to a favorite place, an overlook in the Wind River Range situated above a pine-fringed, peacock-blue glacial lake. The plastic ring he had in his pocket had set him back twenty-five cents. There, in the mountains, he proposed to her.

Not stopping to think, she said yes.

After Eshom returned from Iraq, they wed on March 26, 2004, in Nampa, Idaho, where Eshom's father and stepmother had moved. The couple chose "Hotel California" for the bridal march and had their wedding cake topped with a Barbie, a G.I. Joe, and a model of a Black Hawk.

A couple of months into their marriage, Jamie Eshom was pregnant. By then, her husband's Ninth Battalion was reassigned to the Army's Third Infantry Division out of Fort Stewart, Georgia.

Eshom shrugs off the word "hero," saying that when the helicopters collided, "what I did, I did it right" and insisting that any soldier would have done the same, ignoring the fact that manuals and simulators can't replicate a crash landing, nor can rehearsals and training predict how a soldier will behave in a do-or-die situation.

The crew chief spoke about the prospect that somebody was watching over him. "There's a good chance God had a hand in helping me that day," he said. "I had so many people praying for me, and maybe I survived so I could save the lives of those two other guys, or it may have been so I could do something thirty years down the road."

By the time his baby is born in February 2005 Eshom may be redeployed to Iraq, his heroics in Mosul no longer an exclamation point—just a semicolon in his Army service.

"I'm a little bit scared, but at the same time, this is where I belong, and what I have to do," Eshom said. "I hate to say that I'm glad I'm alive [after the crash], because I was willing—and still am willing—to pay that price for the freedom of my country. I'm a red-, white- and blue-blooded American.

"I'm a patriot."

Afterword

People curious about my stint with the Army as an embedded reporter at the onset of the war in Iraq in the winter and spring of 2003 seem to ask the same few questions: How was it? How did the war change you? What most surprised you?

As to how it went, my stock answer is the war was three things: challenging, frightening, and unexpectedly exhilarating.

As to how it changed me, I say I'm still figuring that out. I'm no longer afraid of stepping onto the impossibly tall escalators at the Rosslyn subway in Arlington, Virginia. They used to send me into a little panic, but after the war something changed. I must have told myself, "You survived a war. Get over this." I did. It was like a light switch had flipped off.

I think that I have more respect now for the chain of command in my own office—but you'd have to ask my editors to know for sure.

I suspect, too, that my experience with the Army gave me a more powerful sense of community. I'm more apt to jump in and offer help when a stranger takes a spill in the street, perhaps thanks to a brief course on combat first aid.

And I try to "soldier on" when confronted with an irritant or two or more. When, for example, I was reporting from the 2004 Democratic National Convention, I faced multiple deadlines during sixteen-hour days; meantime the convention managers had confined the event's boisterous protesters so close to the media tent that I wondered once, amid the racket, if what I was hearing was an evacuation order, since even before I left for Boston, the press had been assigned escape routes in the event that terror struck the FleetCenter. Once assured by a colleague that it was only the chants of demonstrators ringing in my ears, I went back to my keyboard, traveling in my mind's eye back to Iraq and thanking the stars above for a morning shower, toilet, desk, land-line phone, and something to eat besides an MRE. At least I'm not coated in desert sand, I told myself.

Evacuations, though, fray my nerves. Not long ago, on June 9, 2004, a couple of hours before the remains of the late President Ronald Reagan were carried to the steps of the U.S. Capitol to lay in state under the Rotunda, the working press, along with lawmakers, visiting foreign ambassadors, spouses, staffers, and members of the ceremonial military units were abruptly ordered to leave the building. A private plane had invaded restricted airspace during what was, like the national political convention, deemed a National Special Security Event. The plane's transponder, which signals its tail number, altitude, and air speed, had been turned off, leading authorities to fear it had been hijacked.

As I fled the Capitol I saw high-heeled Jimmy Choos flying off women's feet like projectiles. I was glad I had chosen sensible shoes that day. Still, not knowing why we were being ordered to leave, or where the safest place to go was, or why the capital region kept getting targeted—after the 9-11 attack, the anthrax-tainted letters, the discovery of ricin on Capitol Hill—I found myself brushing tears from the corners of my eyes. In Iraq, at least, I had battle buddies.

Running toward Union Station, I caught a man in uniform alongside me wearing what I thought was an Air Assault badge. "Are you Airborne?" I shouted.

"No," he replied. "I'm with the Air Force 'Singing Sergeants.' "

I kept on running. And missed my buddies.

The errant plane, we found out afterward, belonged to Governor Ernie Fletcher of Kentucky, who was traveling in for the late president's funeral.

As to what most surprised me, it was the tender moments and acts of kindness that I'd never seen in war films or read in books or heard from veterans during interviews. In the popular media I'd seen guns blazing and bombs dropping; beyond-exhausted troops carrying on; bloodied, mangled soldiers wincing in pain; and corpses dragged through dusty streets in faraway lands—and less often, the camaraderie that keeps the others going.

Until the war, I never saw a friend give a friend a package of Gummi Bears, or share a letter from home, or ask after the welfare of another after the twenty-first missile alert required a twenty-first trip to the foxhole.

People also ask me something else: Would I go back to Iraq?

That's a tough question to answer.

The Democratic political convention I recently covered required a laser-like focus; there was just too much going on at the convention and in the larger presidential contest to think about much else. Only after the convention, as I read "The Week in Iraq" in the *Washington Post,* did I discover what I'd missed: a bombing killed seventy people in Baqubah; roadside bombings and rocket attacks killed at least a dozen more civilians in Baghdad, Bagubah, Mosul, Ramadi, and Fallujah; the death toll for U.S. soldiers and Marines since March 20, 2003, reached 910.

Would I go back?

Would I do it again, when I feel like I've expended one or two of a cat's proverbial nine lives?

Could I justify chasing after career glory, knowing only afterward how much the separation pained the people I love most? Those at home, thanks to the preponderance of media accounts, seem to see chiefly the worst of war; they never see the Gummi Bears, literally and figuratively.

Could I do it again? It's a crystal-ball question, bringing to mind the old saying "If you want to see God laugh, make plans."

"Never," I tell my inquisitors, "say never."

Vale

Sixty soldiers from the 101st Airborne Division and Fort Campbell lost their lives in Operation Iraqi Freedom during the division's initial, yearlong deployment, which ended in February 2004. Source: Public Affairs Office, 101st Airborne.

23 March 2003
Captain Christopher Scott Seifert, 27, of Easton, Pennsylvania, 1st Brigade Combat Team, died as a result of a grenade attack at Camp Pennsylvania in Kuwait that would leave two dead and fourteen wounded. Sergeant Hasan Akbar, 32, faces the death penalty in the case.

25 March 2003
Major Gregory Stone, 40, of Boise, Idaho, died from wounds received in the grenade attack at Camp Pennsylvania. The Air Force officer was attached to the 19th Air Support Operations Squadron from Fort Campbell, but assigned to the 124th Air Support Operations Squadron, Idaho Air National Guard.

31 March 2003
Specialist Brandon J. Rowe, 20, of Roscoe, Illinois, died as a result of enemy artillery fire near Ayyub, Iraq. He was assigned to the 502nd Infantry Regiment.

13 April 2003
Specialist Gil Mercado, 25, of Paterson, New Jersey, died as a result of a self-inflicted gunshot wound near Baghdad. He was assigned to the 187th Infantry Regiment.

14 April 2003
Specialist Thomas A. Foley III, 23, of Dresden, Tennessee, died as a result of noncombat wounds when a grenade accidentally detonated near Baghdad. He was assigned to the 244th Air Defense Artillery Regiment.

Private 1st Class John E. Brown, 21, of Troy, Alabama, died as a result of noncombat wounds when a grenade accidentally detonated near Baghdad. He was assigned to the 244th Air Defense Artillery Regiment.

24 April 2003
Sergeant Troy D. Jenkins, 25, of Repton, Alabama, died at Landstuhl Regional Medical Center in Germany. He was wounded 19 April 2003 near Baghdad when a young Iraqi girl handed him unexploded ordnance—a cluster bomb—and it detonated. He was assigned to the 187th Infantry Regiment.

14 May 2003
Specialist David T. Nutt, 32, of Blackshear, Georgia, died as a result of a traffic accident near Mosul. He was driving a five-ton truck when an Iraqi citizen driving a car approached him head-on. Nutt swerved to avoid a collision, causing his vehicle to overturn. He was assigned to the 101st Corps Support Group.

5 June 2003
Private 1st Class Branden F. Oberleitner, 20, of Worthington, Ohio, died near Fallujah when his unit came under attack while on a dismounted patrol. He was assigned to the 502nd Infantry Regiment.

7 July 2003
Staff Sergeant Barry Sanford, Sr., 46, of Aurora, Colorado, died of a noncombat gunshot wound near Balad. He was assigned to the 101st Corps Support Group.

8 July 2003
Private Robert L. McKinley, 23, of Kokomo, Indiana, died in Homberg, Germany. He suffered heat stroke in Mosul, Iraq, in mid-June. He was assigned to the 327th Infantry Regiment.

20 July 2003
Sergeant Jason D. Jordan, 24, of Elba, Alabama, died of wounds from an attack near Tall Afar. He was assigned to the 187th Infantry Regiment.

Sergeant Justin W. Garvey, 23, of Townsend, Massachusetts, died of wounds from an attack near Tall Afar. He was assigned to the 187th Infantry Regiment.

23 July 2003
Specialist Brett T. Christian, 27, of Cleveland, Ohio, died when an explosive device struck two military vehicles traveling on Highway 1 outside of Mosul. He was assigned to the 502nd Infantry Regiment.

24 July 2003
Private 1st Class Raheen T. Heighter, 22, of Bay Shore, New York, died in an ambush near Qayarrah, Iraq. He was assigned to the 320th Field Artillery Regiment.

Sergeant Evan A. Ashcraft, 24, of West Hills, California, died in an ambush near Qayarrah, Iraq. He was assigned to the 327th Infantry Regiment.

Staff Sergeant Hector R. Perez, 40, of Corpus Christi, Texas, died in an ambush near Qayarrah, Iraq. He was assigned to the 327th Infantry Regiment.

5 August 2003
Specialist Farao K. Letufuga, 20, a native of Pago Pago, American Samoa, died after falling from a building while performing guard duty in Mosul. He was assigned to the 327th Infantry Regiment.

6 August 2003
Sergeant Leonard D. Simmons, 33, of New Bern, North Carolina, died after suffering a seizure while performing duties near Mosul. He was assigned to the 502nd Infantry Regiment.

12 August 2003
Private 1st Class Daniel R. Parker, 18, of Lake Elsinore, California, died after he was thrown from a military vehicle when its driver swerved to avoid hitting a vehicle driven by an Iraqi citizen. He was assigned to the 44th Field Artillery Regiment.

12 September 2003
Master Sergeant Kevin N. Morehead, 33, of Little Rock, Arkansas, died while conducting a raid near Ar Ramadi, Iraq. He was assigned to the 5th Special Forces Group (Airborne), which is stationed at Fort Campbell.

Sergeant 1st Class William M. Bennett, 35, of Seymour, Tennessee, died while conducting a raid near Ar Ramadi, Iraq. He was assigned to the 5th Special Forces Group (Airborne), which is stationed at Fort Campbell.

15 September 2003
Specialist Alyssa R. Peterson, 27, of Flagstaff, Arizona, died in Tall Afar from a weapons discharge not related to combat. She was assigned to the 311th Military Intelligence Battalion.

22 September 2003
Specialist Paul J. Sturino, 21, of Rice Lake, Wisconsin, died in Hatra, Iraq, after a noncombat gunshot wound. He was assigned to the 320th Field Artillery Regiment.

16 October 2003
Lieutenant Colonel Kim S. Orlando, 43, of Nashville, Tennessee, died after attempting to negotiate with armed men congregating after curfew near a mosque in Karbala. The Iraqis opened fire, killing three soldiers and wounding seven. Orlando was commander of the 716th Military Police Battalion.

Staff Sergeant Joseph P. Bellavia, 28, of Wakefield, Massachusetts, died after attempting to negotiate with armed men congregating after curfew near a mosque in Karbala. Bellavia was assigned to the 716th Military Police Battalion.

Corporal Sean R. Grilley, 24, of San Bernardino, California, died after attempting to negotiate with armed men congregating after curfew near a mosque in Karbala. He was assigned to the 716th Military Police Battalion.

24 October 2003
Sergeant Michael S. Hancock, 29, of Yreka, California, died in an exchange of gunfire while performing guard duty in Mosul. His position was approached by five to ten armed Iraqis who opened fire. He was assigned to the 320th Field Artillery Regiment.

2 November 2003
First Lieutenant Joshua C. Hurley, 24, of Clifton Forge, Virginia, died in Mosul when an improvised explosive device (IED) exploded near the Humvee in which he was traveling. He was assigned to the 326th Engineer Battalion.

Specialist Maurice J. Johnson, 21, of Levittown, Pennsylvania, died in Mosul when an improvised explosive device (IED) exploded near the Humvee in which he was traveling. He was assigned to the 501st Signal Battalion.

7 November 2003

Captain Benedict J. Smith, 29, of Monroe City, Missouri, died when a helicopter ferrying passengers went down on the east side of the Tigris River near Tikrit. He was assigned to the 101st Aviation Regiment.

Chief Warrant Officer 3 Kyran E. Kennedy, 43, of Boston, Massachusetts, died when a helicopter ferrying passengers went down on the east side of the Tigris River near Tikrit. He was assigned to the 101st Aviation Regiment.

Staff Sergeant Paul M. Neff II, 30, of Fort Mill, South Carolina, died when a helicopter ferrying passengers went down on the east side of the Tigris River near Tikrit. He was assigned to the 101st Aviation Regiment.

Sergeant Scott C. Rose, 30, of Fayetteville, North Carolina, died when a helicopter ferrying passengers went down on the east side of the Tigris River near Tikrit. He was assigned to the 101st Aviation Regiment.

Staff Sergeant Morgan D. Kennon, 23, of Memphis, Tennessee, was guarding a bank in Mosul when his position came under attack by a rocket-propelled grenade. He was assigned to the 327th Infantry Regiment.

15 November 2003

These soldiers from the 101st Aviation Regiment died when two Black Hawks collided in Mosul:

Sergeant Michael D. Acklin II, 25, of Louisville, Kentucky, who was assigned to the 320th Field Artillery Regiment.

Specialist Ryan T. Baker, 24, of Brown Mills, New Jersey, who was assigned to the 101st Aviation Regiment.

Sergeant 1st Class Kelly Bolor, 37, of Whittier, California, who was attached to the 101st Corps Support Group and Division Support Command, but assigned to 137th Quartermaster Company, U.S. Army Reserve, based in South El Monte, California.

Specialist Jeremiah J. Digiovanni, 21, of Tylertown, Mississippi, who was assigned to the 101st Aviation Regiment.

Specialist William D. Dusenbery, 30, of Fairview Heights, Illinois, who was assigned to the 101st Aviation Regiment.

Specialist Richard W. Hafer, 21, of Cross Lanes, West Virginia, who was assigned to the 320th Field Artillery Regiment.

Sergeant Warren S. Hansen, 36, of Clintonville, Wisconsin, who was assigned to the 101st Aviation Regiment.

Private 1st Class Sheldon R. Hawk Eagle, 21, of Grand Forks, North Dakota, who was assigned to the 320th Field Artillery Regiment.

Specialist Damian L. Heidelberg, 21, of Shubuta, Mississippi, who was assigned to the 187th Infantry Regiment.

Chief Warrant Officer 1 Erik C. Kesterson, 29, of Independence, Oregon, who was assigned to the 101st Aviation Regiment.

Captain Pierre E. Piche, 29, of Starksboro, Vermont, who was assigned to the 626th Forward Support Battalion, Division Support Command.

Sergeant John Wayne Russell, 26, of Portland, Texas, who was assigned to the 101st Aviation Regiment.

Chief Warrant Officer 2 Scott A. Saboe, 33, of Willow Lake, South Dakota, who was assigned to the 101st Aviation Regiment.

Specialist John R. Sullivan, 26, of Countryside, Illinois, who was assigned to the 626th Forward Support Battalion, Division Support Command.

Specialist Eugene A. Uhl III, 21, of Amherst, Wisconsin, who was assigned to the 320th Field Artillery Regiment.

Private 1st Class Joey D. Whitener, 19, of Nebo, North Carolina, who was assigned to the 320th Field Artillery Regiment.

Second Lieutenant Jeremy L. Wolfe, 27, of Menomonie, Wisconsin, who was assigned to the 101st Aviation Regiment.

23 November 2003
Command Sergeant Major Jerry L. Wilson, 45, of Thomson, Georgia, died when hostile forces attacked the vehicle in which he was riding in Mosul. He was the command sergeant major for the 2nd Brigade, 502nd Infantry Regiment.

Specialist Rel A. Ravago IV, 21, of Glendale, California, died when hostile forces attacked the vehicle in which he was riding in Mosul. He was assigned to the 502nd Infantry Regiment.

28 November 2003
Sergeant Ariel Rico, 25, of El Paso, Texas, died of injuries sustained during an enemy mortar attack in Mosul. He was assigned to the 320th Field Artillery Regiment.

7 December 2003
Private 1st Class Ray J. Hutchinson, 20, of League City, Texas, died of injuries he received after his vehicle was hit by an improvised explosive device (IED) near Mosul. He was assigned to the 502nd Infantry Regiment.

8 December 2003
Private 1st Class Jason G. Wright, 19, of Luzerne, Michigan, died after his vehicle came under fire while he was performing security duties at a gas station in Mosul. He was assigned to the 502nd Infantry Regiment.

10 December 2003
Private 1st Class Jerrick M. Petty, 25, of Idaho Falls, Idaho, died after he was shot while performing guard duty in Mosul. He was assigned to the 502nd Infantry Regiment.

Staff Sergeant Richard A. Burdick, 24, of National City, California, died after his vehicle was hit by an improvised explosive device (IED) in Mosul. He was assigned to the 502nd Infantry Regiment.

23 January 2004
Chief Warrant Officer 2 Michael T. Blaise, 29, of Macon, Missouri, died after his OH-58D Kiowa Warrior helicopter crashed while returning from a combat mission near Mosul. He was assigned to the 17th Cavalry Regiment.

Acknowledgments

I wish to thank the many friends who gave me advice, encouragement, strength, and succor when I returned from a war and believed I had a book. I'll begin with the "A Team": Anne Bernays, Jeff Brown, H. G. (Buzz) Bissinger III, and Michael Ruby, each gifted writers and editors who listened, urged me to go forward, and gave me important guidance. The team is rounded out by Sarah Flynn, who helped draw the story out of me, and in the process became like a sister; Laura Steele, editorial assistant and cherished associate; and Army Colonel Don Sando of Fort Benning, Georgia, whose infectious determination pushed me onward.

I am also grateful to friends and colleagues who helped me keep the faith as I journeyed to completion: James Baughman, Betty Winston Bayé, Deborah Block, Michael Carlisle, Melinda Cooke, Matthew J. Cox, Jim Dawson, Marilou Donahue, Michael Doyle, Kristi Ellis, Lois Fiore, Joe Galloway, Craig Gilbert, Carol Guensburg, Audrey E. Hoffer, Jenny Hosny, Salah H. Hosny, Brenda Ingersoll, Rosiland Jordan, Steve Koff, Tammy Lytle, Doris Margolis, Joe Marquette, Bill McCarren, Dave Moniz, Jeff Nelson, Mike Nichols, Marian Pehowski, Joanna Ramey, Dick Ryan, John Shaw, Mark Shields, and Chris Tuttle.

At the University Press of Kansas, I thank Editor-in-Chief Michael J. Briggs for unwavering support—and intelligent, straightforward, and kind direction—from Day One, and Susan Schott, assistant director of the press and its marketing manager, who is the personification of élan.

At the *Milwaukee Journal Sentinel*, I thank Martin Kaiser, editor in chief, and his wife, Claudia Booth; George Stanley, managing editor; and Carl Schwartz, senior editor for national and international news. They believed in this effort and backed it. A note of appreciation to Marilyn Krause, senior editor for administration, and Jim Spangler, vice president of human resources and labor relations for Journal Sentinel, Inc. Thanks also to the many editors, researchers, and other staffers who made the stories I filed from the

Persian Gulf look better as they boosted my morale. I remain touched by my colleagues' letters and packages, particularly a box of goodies from Schwartz's wife, journalist Barbara Dembski. These colleagues deserve a bow.

I thank Colonel William H. Forrester for enduring my many questions about "helos" and other things military. I send my appreciation both to Captain Sean Connolly for sharing his writings about the 159th Brigade in Kuwait and Iraq and to his wife, Carol, for welcoming me into the world of an Army wife, just as the inimitable Phyllis Ruiz has. I thank Sergeant Nelda Scenie for being fact-checker extraordinaire when the Fourth Battalion soldiered on in northern Iraq; she filled in the many blanks when my notebooks failed. My appreciation goes also to the many others in the United States Armed Forces, including Brigadier General E. J. Sinclair, who shared information, photographs, and memories.

At the U.S. Army Center of Military History, I thank William M. Hammond for sharing a historian's perspective as well as literary counsel.

I thank my siblings for the love and encouragement they have given me. Thomas J. Skiba, Stephen G. Skiba, Nancy L. Mangan, and John P. Skiba are, time and again, the wind beneath my wings. Likewise, I extend appreciation to the Vanden Brooks, the second family I entered through marriage, for their acceptance, intellect, laughter, and enduring love.

I am grateful to the many military families who sent me poignant e-mail messages both before and after my deployment. Their correspondence was an unexpected gift that I shall never forget. My experience gave me but a wee taste of the incalculable hardships they endure when their loved ones venture into harm's way; the courage and sacrifices of the families of service members are inestimable.

I thank the United States Department of Defense for its short course on combat survival and for giving me a place with the 101st Airborne Division. A special note of thanks to Lieutenant Colonel Hugh (Trey) Cate III, who was public affairs chief for the division, and his successor, Lieutenant Colonel Edward S. Loomis.

I thank the Army's aviators, especially for their indomitable spirit. I admire their bravery, sacrifice, dedication to duty, work ethic, intelligence, gutsiness, and zest for life. They reminded me of the power of chasing a dream and, by their example, urged me to soar.

Finally, from the bottom of my heart, I thank my husband, Tom, this book's sine qua non. To let your wife traipse off to war and afterward disappear into a book required more love, patience, sacrifice, and tolerance than either of us anticipated. Tom was my first reader, adding invaluable insight as well as his trademark wit and grace, and remains the unsung hero of my war, and of this work.

Index